Do it Now. George Merriam, one of the founders of Merriam-Webster, kept that motto posted above his rolltop desk. It was this slogan that motivated George and his younger brother, Charles, as they carried forward the work of Noah Webster, the United States' first great lexicographer, after his death in 1843. George and Charles Merriam recognized the significance of Webster's great dictionary and worked to continue his tradition of excellence. Their efforts made "Merriam-Webster" the most important name in American dictionaries.

Today, Merriam-Webster maintains an ongoing commitment to innovation and scholarship. Our dictionaries and other reference products are prepared by a distinguished staff of scholars who rely on a file of more than 14,500,000 citations documenting actual word usage to ensure that every Merriam-Webster publication meets the highest standards of quality and reliability. Other publishers may use the name *Webster*, but only Merriam-Webster products are backed by 150 years of accumulated knowledge and experience. The name *Merriam-Webster* is your assurance that you are purchasing the most authoritative, accurate, and well-designed language reference products in the world.

Merriam-Webster's
Guide to
Punctuation
and
Style

Merriam-Webster, Incorporated
Springfield, Massachusetts

A GENUINE MERRIAM-WEBSTER

The name *Webster* alone is no guarantee of excellence. It is used by a number of publishers and may serve mainly to mislead an unwary buyer.

Merriam-Webster™ is the name you should look for when you consider the purchase of dictionaries and other fine reference books. It carries the reputation of a company that has been publishing since 1831 and is your assurance of quality and authority.

ISBN 0-87779-912-1

Printed and bound in the United States of America

23456QP/B98979695

Contents

Preface

Merriam-Webster's Guide to Punctuation and Style is designed to be a practical handbook on the conventions of written English. These conventions include such day-to-day matters as punctuating sentences, capitalizing names and terms, using italics and quotation marks, spelling compound words and the plural and possessive forms of words, and deciding when to use abbreviations and numerals. This book also offers information and advice on grammar and composition, specific word usage, and the documentation of sources in notes and bibliographies. For each topic, it describes the rules and practices developed by writers and editors to help them prepare copy that is clear, consistent, and attractive. Where the rules have exceptions and variations, these are also presented.

In many cases, the conventions discussed in this book represent choices rather than a single rule, since over the years writers and editors have developed differing sets of rules to guide them. Two writers may favor two different ways to use numerals and words for numbers or to form possessives of proper names ending in *s*. Neither is necessarily wrong; each may simply be following a different style.

There are, of course, limits on the range of acceptable uses, and most writers try to be consistent in the choices they make. This book is designed to help you make those acceptable and consistent choices.

Merriam-Webster's Guide to Punctuation and Style is based on a continuous study of the ways that Americans use their language, and it draws on Merriam-Webster's extensive citation files of more than 14 million examples of English words used in context, gathered from a broad selection of books, newspapers, magazines, and other publications. Based as it is on real-life source material, this book offers readers information about both the consensus and the variety in standard American writing.

The consensus is recorded with simple descriptive statements, such as "A period ends a sentence or a sentence fragment that is neither interrogative nor exclamatory."

Sometimes these statements have to be qualified, as in "The abbreviations A.D. and B.C. usually appear in typeset matter as punctuated, unspaced small capitals. . . ." The term *usually* is used to indicate that a minority of writers and editors follow a practice different from the one described. Hence, the writer who prefers AD or A.D. or AD knows that he or she is departing from the prevalent practice but that such departures are not unprecedented in standard writing.

The word *sometimes* is used in describing practices that are clearly not prevalent, as in "Commas are sometimes used to separate main clauses that are not joined by conjunctions." Here the reader is told that this use of the comma is likely to be found only if the main clauses are short and obviously parallel, and that clauses not joined by conjunctions are usually separated with a semicolon.

The qualifiers *often* and *frequently* are used without suggesting anything about the prevalence of the practice being described except that it is not universally followed. For instance, the statement "A comma is often used to set off the word *Incorporated* or the abbreviation *Inc.* from the rest of a corporate name; however, many companies elect to omit this comma from their names" is not meant to indicate whether *most* companies favor using a comma in this position, since both practices are well-established within standard style.

Finally, when a practice raises questions that demand an explanation that goes beyond the use of a simple qualifier, a brief note is added to explain variations, exceptions, and fine points.

Merriam-Webster's Guide to Punctuation and Style is adapted from *Merriam-Webster's Standard American Style Manual* and various other Merriam-Webster publications and, as such, is based on work done by the writers and editors of those books. This adaptation was carried out by Jocelyn White Franklin with the assistance of Mark A. Stevens. The index was prepared by Maria A. Sansalone with assistance from Eileen M. Haraty, and was typed by Georgette B. Boucher and Florence A. Fowler. Proofreading was done by Susan L. Brady, Deanna Chiasson, Jill J. Cooney, Jennifer S. Goss, Amy K. Harris, and Adrienne M. Scholz.

Chapter 1

Punctuation

Punctuation marks are used to help clarify the structure and meaning of sentences. They separate groups of words for meaning and emphasis; they convey an idea of the variations in pitch, volume, pauses, and intonation of the spoken language; and they help avoid ambiguity. In many cases, the choice of which mark of punctuation to use will be clear and unambiguous. In other cases, the structure of a sentence may allow for several patterns of punctuation. In cases like these, varying notions of correctness have grown up, and two writers might, with equal correctness, punctuate the same sentence quite differently. In this chapter, wherever more than one pattern of punctuation may be used, each is explained. If there are reasons to prefer one over another, the reasons are presented; however, punctuation frequently requires the exercise of individual judgment and taste.

Ampersand

The ampersand (&) represents the word *and*. The ampersand is usually used in correspondence only within proper names and abbreviations.

1. The ampersand is used in the names of companies but not in the names of agencies that are part of the federal government.

    American Telephone & Telegraph Co.
    Dow Jones & Company, Inc.
    Occupational Safety and Health Administration
    Securities and Exchange Commission

In writing corporate names, writers often try to reproduce the form of the name preferred by the company (taken from an annual report or company letterhead). However, this information may not be available and, even if it is available, can lead to apparent inconsistencies if several corporate names are used. If this is the case, choose one styling, preferably the one with the ampersand, and use it in all corporate names as a substitute for *and*.

2. When ampersands are used with abbreviations in general correspondence, spaces are often left

around the ampersand. Writing that makes extensive use of abbreviations, such as technical writing, more commonly omits the spacing.

> Such loans may be available at your bank or S & L.
> The R&D budget looks adequate for the next fiscal year.

3. When an ampersand is used between the last two elements in a series, the comma is omitted.

> the law firm of Shilliday, Fraser & French

Apostrophe

1. The apostrophe is used to indicate the possessive case of nouns and indefinite pronouns. For details regarding this use, see the section beginning on page 106.

2. Apostrophes are sometimes used to form plurals of letters, numerals, abbreviations, symbols, and words referred to as words. For details regarding this use, see the section beginning on page 99.

3. Apostrophes mark omissions in contractions made of two or more words that are pronounced as one word.

> didn't
> you're
> o'clock

4. The apostrophe is used to indicate that letters have been intentionally omitted from the spelling of a word in order to reproduce a perceived pronunciation or to give a highly informal flavor to a piece of writing.

"Get 'em while they're hot."
The club's sign will read "Dancin' till three."

Sometimes words are so consistently spelled with an apostrophe that the spelling with the apostrophe becomes an accepted variant.

rock 'n' roll [for *rock and roll*]
fo'c'sle [for *forecastle*]
bos'n [for *boatswain*]

5. Apostrophes mark the omission of digits in numerals.

class of '95
politics in the '90s

Writers who use the apostrophe when writing the plurals of words expressed in numerals usually avoid the use of the apostrophe illustrated in the second example above. Either they omit the apostrophe that stands for the missing figures, or they spell the word out.

90's *or* nineties *but not* '90's

6. Apostrophes are used to produce the inflected forms of verbs that are made of numerals or individually pronounced letters. Hyphens are sometimes used for this purpose also.

86'ed our proposal
OK'ing the manuscripts

7. An apostrophe is often used to add an *-er* ending to an abbreviation, especially if some confusion might result from its absence. Hyphens are sometimes used for this purpose also. If no confusion is likely, the apostrophe is usually omitted.

4-H'er	IBMer
AA'er	RVer

8. The use of apostrophes to form abbreviations (such as *ass'n* for *association* or *sec'y* for *secretary*) is avoided in most formal writing.

Brackets

1. Brackets enclose editorial comments, corrections, clarifications, or other material inserted into a text, especially into quoted matter.

> This was the first time since it became law that the Twenty-first Amendment [outlining procedures for the replacement of a dead or incapacitated President or Vice President] had been invoked.
>
> He wrote, "I am just as cheerful as when you was [sic] here."

2. Brackets enclose insertions that supply missing letters.

> "If you can't persuade the P[resident], I'm sure no one can."

3. Brackets enclose insertions that take the place of words or phrases that were used in the original version of a quoted passage.

> The report, entitled "A Decade of Progress," begins with a short message from President Stevens in which she notes that "the loving portraits and revealing accounts of [this report] are not intended to constitute a complete history of the decade. . . . Rather [they] impart the flavor of the events, developments, and achievements of this vibrant period."

4. Brackets enclose insertions that slightly alter the form of a word used in an original text.

The magazine reported that thousands of the country's children were "go[ing] to bed hungry every night."

5. Brackets are used to indicate that the capitalization or typeface of the original passage has been altered in some way.

As we point out later, "The length of a quotation usually determines whether it is run into the text or set as a block quotation. . . . [L]ength can be assessed in terms of number of words, the number of typewritten or typeset lines, or the number of sentences in the passage."

They agreed with and were encouraged by her next point: "In the past, many secretaries have been placed in positions of responsibility *without being delegated enough authority to carry out the responsibility.*" [Italics added.]

The use of brackets to indicate altered capitalization is optional in most situations. It is required only in cases where meticulous handling of original source material is crucial (particularly legal contexts).

6. Brackets function as parentheses within parentheses.

The company was incinerating high concentrations of pollutants (such as polychlorinated biphenyls [PCBs]) in a power boiler.

7. Brackets are used in combination with parentheses to indicate units contained within larger units in mathematical copy. They are also used in chemical formulas.

$$x + 5[(x + y)(2x - y)]$$
$$Ag[Pt(NO_2)_4]$$

8. No punctuation mark (other than a period after an abbreviation) precedes bracketed material within a sentence. If punctuation is required, the mark is placed after the closing bracket.

> The report stated, "If we fail to find additional sources of supply [of oil and gas], our long-term growth will be limited."

9. When brackets enclose a complete sentence, the required punctuation should be placed within the brackets.

> [A paw print photographed last month in the Quabbin area has finally verified the cougar's continued existence in the Northeast.]

10. No space is left between brackets and the material they enclose or between brackets and any mark of punctuation immediately following.

Colon

The colon is a mark of introduction. It indicates that what follows it—whether a clause, a phrase, or even a single word—is tightly linked with some element that precedes it. For information on capitalizing the first word following a colon, see paragraphs 7 and 8 on page 66.

With Phrases and Clauses

1. A colon introduces a clause or phrase that explains, illustrates, amplifies, or restates what has gone before.

> The sentence was poorly constructed: it lacked both unity and coherence.

The organization combines a tradition of excellence with a dedication to human service: educating the young, caring for the elderly, assisting in community-development programs.

Computer disks provide high-density storage capacity: hundreds of megabytes of information.

Time was running out: a decision had to be made.

2. A colon directs attention to an appositive.

The question is this: Where will we get the money?

He had only one pleasure: eating.

3. A colon is used to introduce a series. The introductory statement often includes a phrase such as *the following* or *as follows.*

The conference was attended by representatives of five nations: England, France, Belgium, Spain, and Portugal.

Anyone planning to participate should be prepared to do the following: hike five miles with a backpack, sleep on the ground without a tent, and paddle a canoe through rough water.

Opinion varies regarding whether a colon should interrupt the grammatical continuity of a clause (for example, by coming between a verb and its objects). Although many writers avoid this practice and use a full independent clause before the colon, the interrupting colon is common. It is especially likely to be used before a lengthy and complex list, where the colon serves to set the list apart from the normal flow of running text. With shorter or less complex lists, the colon is usually not used.

Our programs to increase profitability include: continued modernization of our manufacturing facilities; consolidation of distribution terminals; discontinuation of unprofitable retail outlets; and reorganization of our personnel structure, along with across-the-board staff reductions.

Our programs to increase profitability include plant modernization, improved distribution and retailing procedures, and staff reductions.

Our programs to increase profitability include the following: continued modernization of our manufacturing facilities; consolidation of distribution terminals; discontinuation of unprofitable retail outlets; and reorganization of our personnel structure, along with across-the-board staff reductions.

4. A colon is used like a dash to introduce a summary statement following a series.

Physics, biology, sociology, anthropology: she discusses them all.

With Quotations

5. A colon introduces lengthy quoted material that is set off from the rest of a text by indentation but not by quotation marks.

He took the title for his biography of Thoreau from a passage in *Walden:*
I long ago lost a hound, a bay horse, and a turtle-dove, and am still on their trail. ... I have met one or two who had heard the hound, and the tramp of the horse, and even seen the dove disappear behind a cloud, and they seemed as anxious to recover them as if they had lost them themselves.
However, the title *A Hound, a Bay Horse, and a Turtle-Dove* probably puzzled some readers.

6. A colon may be used before a quotation in running text, especially when (1) the quotation is lengthy, (2) the quotation is a formal statement or is being given special emphasis, or (3) the quotation is an appositive.

Said Murdoch: "The key to the success of this project is good planning. We need to know precisely all of the steps that we will need to go through, what kind of staff we will require to accomplish each step, what the entire project will cost, and when we can expect completion."

The inscription reads: "Here lies one whose name was writ in water."

In response, he had this to say: "No one knows better than I do that changes will have to be made soon."

Other Uses

7. A colon separates elements in page references, bibliographical and biblical citations, and fixed formulas used to express time and ratios.

> *Journal of the American Medical Association* 48:356
> Stendhal, *Love* (New York: Penguin, 1975)
> John 4:10
> 8:30 a.m.
> a ratio of 3:5

8. A colon separates titles and subtitles (as of books).

> *The Tragic Dynasty: A History of the Romanovs*

9. A spaced colon is used to join terms that are being contrasted or compared.

> The budget shows an unfavorable difference in research : advertising dollars.

10. A colon punctuates the salutation in formal correspondence.

> Dear Mrs. Wright:
> Dear Laurence:
> Dear Product Manager:

Ladies and Gentlemen:
To whom it may concern:

11. A colon punctuates memorandum and government correspondence headings and subject lines
in general business letters.

TO: VIA:
SUBJECT: REFERENCE:

12. A colon separates writer/dictator/typist initials in
the identification lines of business letters.

WAL:jml
WAL:WEB:jml

13. A colon separates carbon-copy or blind carbon-
copy abbreviations from the initials or names of
copy recipients in business letters.

cc:RSP   bcc:MWK
   JES   FCM

With Other Marks of Punctuation

14. A colon is placed outside quotation marks and parentheses.

There's only one thing wrong with "Harold's Indis-
cretion": it's not funny.
I quote from the first edition of *Springtime in Savan-
nah* (published in 1952):

Spacing

15. No space precedes or follows a colon when it is
used between numerals.

9:30 a.m.
a ratio of 2:4

16. No space precedes or follows a colon in a business-letter identification line or in a carbon-copy notation that indicates a recipient designated by initials. One space follows a colon in a carbon-copy notation that indicates a recipient designated by a full name.

> FCM:hg
> cc:FCM
> cc: Mr. Johnson

Comma

The comma is the most frequently used punctuation mark in English. Its most common uses are to separate items in a series and to set off or distinguish grammatical elements within sentences. This section explains the most common aspects of the comma.

Between Main Clauses

1. A comma separates main clauses joined by a coordinating conjunction: *and, but, or, nor, for,* and sometimes *so* and *yet.* (For use of commas with clauses joined by correlative conjunctions, see paragraph 24 on page 20.)

> She knew very little about the new system, and he volunteered nothing.
> We will not respond to any more questions on that topic this afternoon, nor will we respond to similar questions at any time in the future.
> His face showed disappointment, for he knew that he had failed.
> The acoustics in this hall are good, so every note is clear.
> We have requested this information many times before, yet we have never gotten a satisfactory reply.

2. When one or both of the clauses are short or closely related in meaning, the comma is often omitted.

> The sun was shining and the birds were singing.
> Six thousand years ago, the top of the volcano blew off in a series of powerful eruptions and the sides collapsed into the middle.

In punctuating sentences such as these, writers have to use their own judgment. There are no clear-cut rules to follow; however, factors such as the rhythm, parallelism, or logic of the sentence often influence how clearly or smoothly it will read with or without the comma.

3. Commas are sometimes used to separate main clauses that are not joined by conjunctions. This is especially likely if the clauses are short and obviously parallel.

> One day you are a successful corporate lawyer, the next day you are out of work.
> The city has suffered terribly in the interim. Bombs have destroyed most of the buildings, disease has ravaged the population.

Using a comma to join clauses that are neither short nor obviously parallel is usually called *comma fault* or *comma splice* and should be avoided. In general, clauses not joined by conjunctions are separated by semicolons.

4. If a sentence is composed of three or more clauses, the clauses may be separated by either commas or semicolons. Clauses that are short and free of commas can be separated by commas even if they are not joined by a conjunction. If the clauses are long or punctuated, they are separated with semicolons; the last two clauses may

be separated by a comma, but usually only if they are joined by a conjunction. (For more examples of clauses separated with commas and semicolons, see paragraph 5 on page 59.)

> Small fish fed among the marsh weed, ducks paddled along the surface, a muskrat ate greens along the bank.
> The policy is a complex one to explain; defending it against its critics is not easy, nor is it clear the defense is always necessary.

With Compound Predicates

5. Commas are not normally used to separate the parts of a compound predicate.

> The firefighter tried to enter the burning building but was turned back by the thick smoke.

However, many writers do use commas to separate the parts of a compound predicate if the predicate is especially long and complicated, if one part of the predicate is being stressed, or if the absence of a comma could cause a momentary misreading of the sentence.

> The board helps to develop the financing, new product planning, and marketing strategies for new corporate divisions, and issues periodic reports on expenditures, revenues, and personnel appointments.
> This is an unworkable plan, and has been from the start.
> I try to explain to him what I want him to do, and get nowhere.

With Subordinate Clauses and Phrases

6. Adverbial clauses and phrases that precede a main clause are usually set off with commas.

As cars age, they depreciate.

Having made that decision, we turned our attention to other matters.

From the top of this rugged and isolated plateau, I could see the road stretching out for miles across the desert.

In addition, staff members respond to queries, take new orders, and initiate billing.

7. If a sentence begins with an adverbial clause or phrase and can be easily read without a comma following it, the comma may be omitted. In most cases where the comma is omitted, the phrase will be short—four words or less. However, the comma can be omitted even after a longer phrase if the sentence can be easily read or seems more forceful that way.

In January the company will introduce a new line of entirely redesigned products.

On the map the town appeared as a small dot in the midst of vast emptiness.

If the project cannot be done profitably perhaps it should not be done at all.

8. Adverbial clauses and phrases that introduce a main clause other than the first main clause are usually set off with commas. However, if the adverbial clause or phrase follows a conjunction, two commas are usually used: one before the conjunction and one following the clause or phrase. In some cases three commas are used: one before the conjunction and two more to enclose the clause or phrase. Some writers use only one comma to separate the main clauses.

His parents were against the match, and had the couple not eloped, their plans for marriage would have come to nothing.

> They have redecorated the entire store, but, to the delight of their customers, the store retains much of its original flavor.
>
> We haven't left Springfield yet, but when we get to Boston we'll call you.

9. A comma is not used after an introductory phrase if the phrase immediately precedes the main verb.

> In the road lay a dead rabbit.

10. A subordinate clause or phrase that follows a main clause or falls within a main clause is usually not set off by commas if it is *restrictive*—that is, if its removal from the sentence would alter the meaning of the main clause. If the meaning of the main clause would not be altered by removing the subordinate clause or phrase, the clause or phrase is considered *nonrestrictive* and usually is set off by commas.

> We will be delighted if she decides to stay. [*restrictive*]
>
> Anyone who wants his or her copy of the book autographed by the author should get in line. [*restrictive*]
>
> Her new book, which was based on a true story, was well received. [*nonrestrictive*]
>
> That was a good meal, although I didn't particularly like the broccoli in cream sauce. [*nonrestrictive*]

11. Commas are used to set off an adverbial clause or phrase that falls between the subject and the verb.

> The weather in the capital, fluctuating from very hot to downright chilly, necessitates a variety of clothing.

12. Commas set off modifying phrases that do not immediately precede the word or phrase they modify.

The negotiators, tired and discouraged, headed back to the hotel.

We could see the importance, both long-term and short-term, of her proposal.

The two children, equally happy with their lunches, set off for school.

13. Absolute phrases (phrases that stand alone and don't affect the grammar of the rest of the sentence) are set off with commas, whether they fall at the beginning, middle, or end of the sentence.

Our business being concluded, we adjourned for refreshments.

We headed southward, the wind freshening behind us, to meet the rest of the fleet in the morning.

I'm afraid of his reaction, his temper being what it is.

With Appositives

14. Commas are used to set off a word, phrase, or clause that is in apposition to (that is, equivalent to) a preceding noun and that is nonrestrictive.

My husband, Larry, is in charge of ticket sales for the fair.

George Washington, first president of the United States, has been the subject of countless biographies.

A nonrestrictive appositive phrase or clause sometimes precedes the noun it refers to. It is set off by commas in this position also.

A cherished landmark in the city, the Hotel Sandburg has managed once again to escape the wrecking ball.

15. Restrictive appositives are not set off by commas.

My daughter Andrea had the lead in the school play.

Note that if Andrea were the parent's *only* daughter, her name would be set off by commas.

With Introductory and Interrupting Elements

16. Commas set off transitional words and phrases.

> Indeed, close coordination between departments can minimize confusion during this period of expansion.
>
> We are eager to begin construction; however, the necessary materials have not yet arrived.
>
> The most recent report, on the other hand, makes clear why the management avoids such agreements.

When these words are not used to make a transition, no comma is necessary.

> The materials had indeed arrived.

17. Commas set off parenthetical elements, such as authorial asides and supplementary information, that are closely related to the rest of the sentence.

> All of us, to tell the truth, were completely amazed by his suggestion.
>
> The headmaster, now in his sixth year at the school, was responsible for the changes in the curriculum.

When the parenthetical element is digressive or otherwise not closely related to the rest of the sentence, it is often set off by dashes or parentheses. For examples, see paragraph 3 on page 30 and paragraph 1 on page 42.

18. Commas are used to set off words or phrases that introduce examples or explanations.

> He expects to visit three countries, namely, France, Spain, and Germany.

I would like to develop a good, workable plan, i.e.,
one that would outline our goals and set a time-
table for accomplishing them.

Words and phrases such as *i.e.*, *e.g.*, *namely*, *for example*, and *that is* are often preceded by a dash,
open parenthesis, or semicolon, depending on
the magnitude of the break in continuity created
by the examples or explanations. However, regardless of the punctuation that precedes the
word or phrase, a comma always follows it. For
examples of dashes, parentheses, and semicolons
with these words and phrases, see paragraph 6 on
page 31, paragraph 2 on page 43, and paragraph
6 on page 60.

19. Commas are used to set off words in direct address.

We would like to discuss your account, Mrs. Reid.
The answer, my friends, lies within us.

20. Commas set off mild interjections or exclamations such as *ah* or *oh*.

Ah, weekends—they don't come often enough.
Oh, what a beautiful baby.

With Contrasting Expressions

21. A comma is used to set off contrasting expressions within a sentence.

This project will take six months, not six weeks.

22. Style varies regarding use of the comma to set off
two or more contrasting phrases used to describe
a single word that follows immediately. Some
writers put a comma after the first modifier but
not between the final modifier and the word
modified. Other writers, who treat the contrast-

ing phrase as a nonrestrictive modifier, put a comma both before and after the phrase.

> The harsh, although eminently realistic critique is not going to make you popular.
> *or*
> The harsh, although eminently realistic, critique is not going to make you popular.
> This street takes you away from, not toward the capitol building.
> *or*
> This street takes you away from, not toward, the capitol building.

23. Adjectives and adverbs that modify the same word or phrase and that are joined by *but* or some other coordinating conjunction are not separated by a comma.

> the harsh but eminently realistic critique
> a multicolored but subdued carpet
> errors caused by working carelessly or too quickly

24. A comma does not usually separate elements that are contrasted through the use of a pair of correlative conjunctions (such as *either ... or, neither ... nor,* and *not only ... but also*).

> The cost is either $69.95 or $79.95.
> Neither my brother nor I noticed the error.
> He was given the post not only because of his diplomatic connections but also because of his great tact and charm.

Correlative conjunctions are sometimes used to join main clauses. If the clauses are short, a comma is not added. If the clauses are long, a comma usually separates them.

> Either you do it my way or we don't do it at all.
> Not only did she have to see three salesmen and a visiting reporter during the course of the day, but

she also had to prepare for the next day's meeting with the president.

25. Long parallel contrasting and comparing clauses are separated by commas; short parallel phrases are not.

> The more I hear about this new computer, the greater is my desire to obtain one for my office.
>
> "The sooner the better," I said.

With Items in a Series

26. Words, phrases, and clauses joined in a series are separated by commas. If main clauses are joined in a series, they may be separated by either semicolons or commas. (For more on the use of commas and semicolons to separate main clauses, see paragraphs 1, 3, and 4 on pages 12–13 and paragraph 5 on page 59.)

> Men, women, and children crowded aboard the train.
>
> Her job required her to pack quickly, to travel often, and to have no personal life.
>
> He responded patiently while reporters shouted questions, flashbulbs popped, and the crowd pushed closer.

Practice varies regarding the use of the comma between the last two items in a series if those items are also joined by a conjunction. Sometimes, as in the following example, omitting the final comma (often called the *serial comma*) can result in ambiguity. Some writers feel that in most sentences the use of the conjunction makes the comma superfluous, and they favor using the comma only when a misreading could result from omitting it. Others feel that it is easier to include the final comma routinely rather than try to consider each sentence separately to decide whether a misreading is possible without the comma. Most reference books, including this one, and most other book-length works of nonfiction use the serial comma. In most other kinds of writing, however, practice is nearly evenly divided on the use or omission of this comma.

> We are looking for a house with a big yard, a view of the harbor, and beach and docking privileges. [*with serial comma*]
>
> *or*
>
> We are looking for a house with a big yard, a view of the harbor and beach and docking privileges. [*without serial comma*]

27. A comma is not used to separate items in a series that are joined with conjunctions.

> I don't understand what this policy covers or doesn't cover or only partially covers.
>
> I have talked to the president and the vice president and three other executives.

28. When the elements in a series are long or complex or consist of clauses that themselves contain commas, the elements are usually separated by semicolons, not commas. For more on this use of the semicolon, see paragraphs 7 and 8 on page 60.

With Coordinate Modifiers

29. A comma is used to separate two or more adjectives, adverbs, or phrases that modify the same word or phrase. (For the use of commas with contrasting modifiers, see paragraphs 22 and 23 above.)

> She spoke in a calm, reflective manner.

> We watched the skier move smoothly, gracefully through the turns.

30. A comma is not used between two adjectives when the first modifies the combination of the second adjective plus the word or phrase it modifies.

> a good used car
> a small glass figurine

31. A comma is not used to separate an adverb from the adjective or adverb that it modifies.

> a truly distinctive manner
> running very quickly down the street

In Quotations and Questions

32. A comma separates a direct quotation from a phrase identifying its source or speaker. If the quotation is a question or an exclamation and the identifying phrase follows the quotation, the comma is replaced by a question mark or an exclamation point.

> Mary said, "I am leaving soon."
> "I am leaving soon," Mary said.
> Mary asked, "When are you going?"
> "When are you going?" Mary asked.
> "I am staying," Mary said, "even if it means missing the reception."
> "Don't forget the slides!" Mary shouted.

In some cases, a colon can replace a comma preceding a quotation. For more on this use of the colon, see paragraph 6 on page 9.

33. Commas are not used to set off a quotation that is an integral part of the sentence in which it appears.

>Throughout the session his only responses were "No comment" and "I don't think so."
>
>Just because he said he was "about to leave this minute" doesn't mean he actually left.

34. Practice varies regarding the use of commas to set off shorter sentences that fall within longer sentences and that do not constitute actual dialogue. These shorter sentences may be mottoes or maxims, unspoken or imaginary dialogue, or sentences referred to as sentences; and they may or may not be enclosed in quotation marks. (For more on the use of quotation marks with sentences like these, see paragraph 6 on page 52.) The shorter sentence usually functions as a subject, object, or complement within the larger sentence and does not require a comma. Where quotation marks are not used, a comma may be inserted simply to mark the beginning of the shorter sentence clearly.

>"The computer is down" was the response she dreaded.
>
>He spoke with a candor that seemed to insist, This actually happened to me and in just this way.
>
>The first rule is, When in doubt, spell it out.

When the shorter sentence functions as an appositive in the larger sentence, it is set off with a comma or commas when nonrestrictive and not when restrictive. (For more on restrictive modifiers and appositives, see paragraphs 10, 14, and 15 on pages 16–17.)

>He was fond of the slogan "Every man a king, but no man wears a crown."
>
>We had the association's motto, "We make waves," printed on our T-shirts.

35. A comma introduces a direct question, regardless of whether it is enclosed in quotation marks or if its first word is capitalized.

> I wondered, what is going on here?
> The question is, How do we get out of this situation?

36. The comma is omitted before quotations that are very short exclamations or representations of sounds.

> He jumped up suddenly and cried "I've got it!"

37. A comma is not used to set off indirect discourse or indirect questions introduced by a conjunction (such as *that* or *what*).

> Mary said that she was leaving.
> I wondered what was going on there.
> The clerk told me that the book I had ordered had just come in.

With Omitted Words

38. A comma indicates the omission of a word or phrase, especially in parallel constructions where the omitted word or phrase appears earlier in the sentence.

> Common stocks are preferred by some investors; bonds, by others.

39. A comma often replaces the conjunction *that*.

> The road was so steep and winding, we thought for sure we would go over the edge.
> The problem is, we don't know how to fix it.

With Addresses, Dates, and Numbers

40. A comma is used to set off the individual elements of an address except for zip codes; no punctuation appears between a state name and the zip code that follows it. If prepositions are used between the elements of the address, commas are not needed.

> Mrs. Bryant may be reached at 52 Kiowa Circle, Mesa, Arizona.
>
> Mr. Briscoe was born in Liverpool, England.
>
> Write to the Bureau of the Census, Washington, DC 20233.
>
> The White House is at 1600 Pennsylvania Avenue in Washington, D.C.

Some writers omit the comma that follows the name of a state (or province, country, etc.) when no other element of an address follows it, which usually occurs when a city name and state name are being used in combination to modify a noun that follows. However, retaining this comma is still the more common practice.

> We visited their Enid, Oklahoma plant.
> *but more commonly*
> We visited their Enid, Oklahoma, plant.

41. Commas are used to set off the year from the day of the month. (See also paragraph 50 below.)

> On October 26, 1947, the newly hired employees began work on the project.

When only the month and the year are given, the first comma is usually omitted.

> In December 1903, the Wright brothers finally succeeded in keeping an airplane aloft for a few seconds.

42. A comma groups numerals into units of three in order to separate thousands, millions, and so on; however, this comma is generally not used in page numbers, street numbers, or numbers

within dates. (For more on the use of the comma
with numbers, see paragraphs 1–3 on pages 156–
57.)

> a population of 350,000
> page 1419
> 4509 South Pleasant Street
> the year 1986

With Names, Degrees, and Titles

43. A comma punctuates an inverted name.

> Sagan, Deborah J.

44. A comma is often used between a surname and
Junior, Senior, or their abbreviations. (For more
on the use of *Jr.* and *Sr.*, see paragraph 44 on
page 148.)

> Morton A. Williams, Jr.
> Douglas Fairbanks, Senior

45. A comma is often used to set off the word *Incorporated* or the abbreviation *Inc.* from the rest of a
corporate name; however, many companies elect
to omit this comma from their names.

> Leedy Manufacturing Company, Incorporated
> Tektronics, Inc.
> Merz-Fortunata Inc.

46. A comma separates a surname from a following
academic, honorary, military, or religious degree
or title.

> Amelia P. Artandi, D.V.M.
> Robert Menard, M.A., Ph.D.
> John L. Farber, Esq.
> Admiral Herman Washington, USN
> Sister Mary Catherine, S.C.

In Correspondence

47. The comma follows the salutation in informal correspondence and often follows the complimentary close in both informal and formal correspondence. In formal correspondence, a colon follows the salutation. (For examples of this use of the colon, see paragraph 10 on page 10.)

> Dear Rachel,
> Affectionately,
> Very truly yours,

Other Uses

48. The comma is used to avoid ambiguity when the juxtaposition of two words or expressions could cause confusion.

> Whatever will be, will be.
> To John, Marshall Inc. was a special environment.
> I repaired the lamp that my brother had broken, and replaced the bulb.

49. A comma often follows a direct object or a predicate nominative or predicate adjective when they precede the subject and verb in the sentence. If the meaning of the sentence is clear without this comma, it is often omitted.

> That we would soon have to raise prices, no one disputed.
> A disaster it certainly was.

With Other Marks of Punctuation

50. Commas are used in conjunction with brackets, ellipsis points, parentheses, and quotation marks. Commas are not used in conjunction with colons, dashes, exclamation points, question marks, or semicolons. If one of these latter marks falls at

the same point in a sentence at which a comma would fall, the comma is dropped and the other mark is retained. For more on the use of commas with other marks of punctuation, see the sections for each of those marks of punctuation.

Dash

The dash can function like a comma, a colon, or a pair of parentheses. Like commas and parentheses, dashes set off parenthetic material such as examples, supplemental facts, or appositional, explanatory, or descriptive phrases. Like colons, dashes introduce clauses that explain or expand upon some element of the material that precedes them. The dash is sometimes considered to be a less formal equivalent of the colon and parenthesis, and it does frequently take their place in advertising and other informal contexts. However, dashes may be found in all kinds of writing, including the most formal, and the choice of which mark to use is usually a matter of personal preference.

The dash exists in a number of different lengths. The most common dash is the *em dash*, which is approximately the width of a capital M in typeset material. In typed and keyboarded material, it is represented by two hyphens. Word-processing programs often have special characters for em and en dashes. The en dash and the two- and three-em dashes have more limited uses, which are explained in paragraphs 13–15 on pages 33–34.

Abrupt Change or Suspension

1. The dash marks an abrupt change or break in the structure of a sentence.

The students seemed happy enough with the new plan, but the alumni—there was the problem.

2. A dash is used to indicate interrupted speech or a speaker's confusion or hesitation.

"The next point I'd like to bring up—" the speaker started to say.
"Yes," he went on, "yes—that is—I guess I agree."

Parenthetic and Amplifying Elements

3. Dashes are used in place of other punctuation (such as commas or parentheses) to emphasize parenthetic or amplifying material or to make such material stand out more clearly from the rest of the sentence.

Mail your subscription—now!
In 1976, they asked for—and received—substantial grants from the federal government.
The privately owned consulting firm—formerly known as Aborjaily & Associates—is now offering many new services.

When dashes are used to set off parenthetic elements, they often indicate that the material is more digressive than elements set off with commas but less digressive than elements set off by parentheses. For examples, see paragraph 17 on page 18 and paragraph 1 on page 42.

4. Dashes are used to set off or to introduce defining and enumerating phrases.

The fund sought to acquire controlling positions— a minimum of 25% of outstanding voting securities—in other companies.
The essay dealt with our problems with waste— cans, bottles, discarded tires, and other trash.

5. A dash is often used in place of a colon or semi-colon to link clauses, especially when the clause that follows the dash explains, summarizes, or expands upon the clause that precedes it.

> The test results were surprisingly good—none of the tested models displayed serious problems.

6. A dash or a pair of dashes often sets off parenthetic or amplifying material introduced by such phrases as *for example, namely, that is, e.g.,* and *i.e.*

> After some discussion the motion was tabled—that is, it was removed indefinitely from the board's consideration.
>
> Sports develop two valuable traits—namely, self-control and the ability to make quick decisions.
>
> Not all "prime" windows—i.e., the ones installed when a house is built—are equal in quality.

Commas, parentheses, and semicolons are often used for the same purpose. For examples, see paragraph 18 on page 18, paragraph 2 on page 43, and paragraph 6 on page 60.

7. A dash introduces a summary statement that follows a series of words or phrases.

> Unemployment, strikes, inflation, stock prices, mortgage rates—all are part of the economy.
>
> Once into bankruptcy, the company would have to pay cash for its supplies, defer maintenance, and lay off workers—moves that could threaten its long-term profitability.

8. A dash often precedes the name of an author or source at the end of a quoted passage. This method of attribution is most often used when the quoted material—such as quotations set as epigraphs or extracts—is not part of the main text. The attribution may appear immediately

after the quotation, or it may appear on the next line.

> "A comprehensive, authoritative, and beautifully written biography."—*National Review*
>
> Winter tames man, woman, and beast.
> —William Shakespeare

With Other Marks of Punctuation

9. If a dash appears at a point in a sentence where a comma could also appear, the dash is retained and the comma is dropped.

> If we don't succeed—and the critics say we won't—then the whole project is in jeopardy.
>
> Our lawyer has read the transcript—all 1,200 pages of it—and he has decided that an appeal would not be useful.
>
> Some of the other departments, however—particularly Accounting, Sales, and Credit Collection—have expanded their computer operations.

10. If the second of a pair of dashes would come at a point in a sentence where a period or semicolon should also appear, the period or semicolon is retained and the dash is dropped. (Writers will often avoid this construction by recasting the sentence.)

> His conduct has always been exemplary—near-perfect attendance, excellent productivity, a good attitude; nevertheless, his termination cannot be avoided.

11. Dashes are used with exclamation points and question marks. When a pair of dashes sets off material calling for either of these marks of punctuation, the exclamation point or the question mark is placed inside the second dash.

His hobby was getting on people's nerves—especially mine!—and he was extremely good at it.

When the committee meets next week—are you going to be there?—I will present all of the final figures.

12. Dashes and parentheses are used in combination to indicate parenthetic material appearing within parenthetic material. Dashes within parentheses and parentheses within dashes are used with about equal frequency.

We were looking for a narrator (or narrators—sometimes a script calls for more than one) who could handle a variety of assignments.

On our trip south we crossed a number of major rivers—the Hudson, the Delaware, and the Patapsco (which flows through Baltimore)—without paying a single toll.

If the inner parenthetic element begins with a dash and its closing dash would fall in the same position as the closing parenthesis, the closing dash is omitted, as in the first example above. If the inner element begins with a parenthesis and its closing parenthesis would coincide with the closing dash, both are retained, as in the second example above.

En Dash

13. En dashes generally appear only in typeset material; in typed or keyboarded material the simple hyphen is usually used. The en dash is shorter than the em dash but slightly longer than the hyphen. It is most frequently used (1) as a replacement for a hyphen following a prefix that is added to an open compound, (2) as an equivalent to "(up) to and including" when used between numbers, dates, or other notations to indicate

range, (3) as a replacement for the word *to* between capitalized names, and (4) to indicate linkages, such as boundaries, treaties, or oppositions.

> pre–Civil War architecture
> 1988–89
> pages 128–34
> 8:30 a.m.–4:30 p.m.
> the New York–Connecticut area
> Washington–Moscow diplomacy

Long Dashes

14. A two-em dash is used to indicate missing letters in a word and, less frequently, to indicate a missing word.

> Mr. P—— of Baltimore

15. A three-em dash indicates that a word has been left out or that an unknown word or figure is to be supplied. (For the use of this dash in bibliography listings, see page 310.)

> The study was carried out in ———, a fast-growing Sunbelt city.

Spacing

16. Practice varies as to spacing around the dash. Some publications insert a space before and after a dash, but most do not. Either practice is acceptable.

Ellipsis Points

Ellipsis points is the name most often given to periods when they are used, usually in groups of three, to signal an omission from quoted material or to indicate a pause or trailing off of speech. Other names for periods used in this way include *ellipses, points of ellipsis,* and *suspension points.* Ellipsis points are often used in conjunction with other marks of punctuation, including periods used to mark the ends of sentences. When ellipsis points are used in this way with a terminal period, the omission is sometimes thought of as being marked by four periods. Most of the conventions described in this section are illustrated with quoted material enclosed in quotation marks. However, the conventions are equally applicable to quoted material set as extracts. In the following examples, ellipsis points indicate omission of material. In most cases, the full text from which these omissions have been made is some portion of this paragraph.

1. Ellipsis points indicate the omission of one or more words within a quoted sentence.

> One book said, "Other names ... include *ellipses, points of ellipsis,* and *suspension points.*"

2. Ellipsis points are usually not used to indicate the omission of words that precede the quoted portion. However, practice varies on this point, and in some formal contexts, especially those in which the quotation is introduced by a colon, ellipsis points are used.

> The book maintained that "the omission is sometimes thought of as being marked by four periods."
> The book maintained: "... the omission is sometimes thought of as being marked by four periods."

3. Punctuation used in the original that falls on either side of the ellipsis points is often omitted;

however, it may be retained, especially if this helps clarify the sentence.

> According to the book, "*Ellipsis points* is the name most often given to periods when they are used . . . to signal an omission from quoted material or to indicate a pause or trailing off of speech."
>
> According to the book, "When ellipsis points are used in this way . . . , the omission is sometimes thought of as being marked by four periods."
>
> According to the book, "*Ellipsis points* is the name most often given to periods when they are used, usually in groups of three, . . . to indicate a pause or trailing off of speech."

4. If an omission includes an entire sentence within a passage, the last part of a sentence within a passage, or the first part of a sentence other than the first quoted sentence, the end punctuation preceding or following the omission is retained and is followed by three periods.

> That book says, "Other names for periods used in this way include *ellipses, points of ellipsis,* and *suspension points.* . . . When ellipsis points are used in this way with a terminal period, the omission is sometimes thought of as being marked by four periods."
>
> That book says, "*Ellipsis points* is the name given to periods when they are used, usually in groups of three, to signal an omission from quoted material. . . . Other names for periods used in this way include *ellipses, points of ellipsis,* and *suspension points.*"
>
> That book says, "Ellipsis points are often used in conjunction with other marks of punctuation, including periods used to mark ends of sentences. . . . The omission is sometimes thought of as being marked by four periods."

The capitalization of the word *The* in the third example is acceptable, even though that word did not begin a sentence in the original version. When the opening words of a quotation act as a sentence within the quotation, the first word is capitalized.

5. If the last words of a quoted sentence are omitted and if the original sentence ends with a period, that period is retained and three ellipsis points follow. However, if the original sentence ends with punctuation other than a period, the end punctuation often follows the ellipsis points, especially if it helps clarify the quotation.

> Their book said, "Ellipsis points are often used in conjunction with other marks of punctuation. . . ."
> He always ends his harangues with some variation on the question, "What could you have been thinking when you . . . ?"

Many writers and editors, especially when writing informally, choose to ignore the distinctions in paragraphs 4 and 5 and instead indicate all omissions by three periods, dropping all terminal periods that may precede or follow an omission.

6. Ellipsis points are used to indicate that a quoted sentence has been intentionally left unfinished. In situations such as this, the terminal period is not included.

> Read the statement beginning "*Ellipsis points* is the name most often given . . ." and then proceed to the numbered paragraphs.

7. A line of ellipsis points indicates that one or more lines of poetry have been omitted from a text. (For more on the treatment of poetry and extracts, see the section on pages 54–56.)

Whitman's attitude on the subject is revealed in these lines from "When I Heard the Learned Astronomer":

When I heard the learned astronomer,
. . . .
How soon unaccountable I became tired and sick,
Til rising and gliding out I wandered off by myself,
In the mystical moist night-air, and from time to time,
Looked up in perfect silence at the stars.

8. Ellipsis points are used to indicate faltering speech, especially if the faltering involves a long pause between words or a sentence that trails off or is intentionally left unfinished. In these kinds of sentences most writers treat the ellipsis points as terminal punctuation, thus removing the need for any other punctuation; however, some writers use other punctuation in conjunction with ellipsis points.

The speaker seemed uncertain how to answer the question. "Well, that's true . . . but even so . . . I think we can do better."

"Despite these uncertainties, we believe we can do it, but . . ."

"I mean . . ." he said, "like . . . How?"

9. Ellipsis points are sometimes used as a stylistic device to catch a reader's attention.

They think that nothing can go wrong . . . but it does.

10. Each ellipsis point is separated from other ellipsis points, adjacent punctuation (except for quotation marks), and surrounding text by a space. If a terminal period is used with ellipsis points, it precedes them with no space before it and one space after it.

Exclamation Point

The exclamation point is used to mark a forceful comment. Heavy use can weaken its effect, so it should be used sparingly.

1. An exclamation point can punctuate a sentence, phrase, or interjection.

> This is the fourth time in a row he's been late!
>
> No one that I talked to—not even the accounting department!—seemed to know how the figures were calculated.
>
> Oh! you startled me.

2. The exclamation point replaces the question mark when an ironic or emphatic tone is more important than the actual question.

> Aren't you finished yet!
>
> Do you realize what you've done!
>
> Why me!

3. Occasionally the exclamation point is used with a question mark to indicate a very forceful question.

> How much did you say?!
>
> You did what!?

4. The exclamation point is enclosed within brackets, dashes, parentheses, and quotation marks when it punctuates the enclosed material rather than the sentence as a whole. It should be placed outside them when it punctuates the entire sentence.

> All of this proves—at long last!—that we were right from the start.

Somehow the dog got the gate open (for the third time!) and ran into the street.

He sprang to his feet and shouted "Point of order!"

The correct word is "lax," not "lacks"!

5. Exclamatory phrases that occur within a sentence are set off by dashes or parentheses.

And now our competition—get this!—wants to start sharing secrets.

The board accepted most of the recommendations, but ours (alas!) was not even considered.

6. If an exclamation point falls at a place in a sentence where a comma or a terminal period could also go, the comma or period is dropped and the exclamation point is retained.

"Absolutely not!" he snapped.

She has written about 60 pages so far—and with no help!

If the exclamation point is part of a title, as of a play, book, or movie, it may be followed by a comma. If the title falls at the end of a sentence, the terminal period is usually dropped.

Marshall and Susan went to see *Oklahoma!*, and they enjoyed it very much.

His favorite management book is still *Up the Organization!*

Hyphen

1. Hyphens are used to link elements in compound words. For more on the styling of compound words, see the section beginning on page 112.

2. A hyphen marks an end-of-line division of a word when part of the word is to be carried down to the next line.

> We visited several car showrooms, looked at the latest models (it wasn't a pleasant experience; prices are still high), and asked all the questions we could think of.

3. A hyphen divides letters or syllables to give the effect of stuttering, sobbing, or halting speech.

> S-s-sammy
> ah-ah-ah
> y-y-yes

4. Hyphens indicate a word spelled out letter by letter.

> p-r-o-b-a-t-i-o-n

5. A hyphen indicates that a word element is a prefix, suffix, or medial element. (For more on using a hyphen with a prefix, see paragraph 61 on page 129.)

> anti-
> -ship
> -o-

6. A hyphen is generally used in typed or keyboarded material as an equivalent to the phrase "(up) to and including" between numbers and dates. (In typeset material this hyphen is replaced by an en dash. For more on the use of the en dash, see paragraph 13 on page 33.)

7. Hyphens are sometimes used to produce inflected forms of verbs that are made of individually pronounced letters or to add an -er ending to an abbreviation; however, apostrophes are more

commonly used for these purposes. (For more on these uses of the apostrophe, see paragraphs 6 and 7 on page 4.)

> DH-ing for the White Sox
> a dedicated UFO-er

Parentheses

Parentheses enclose material that is inserted into a main statement but is not intended to be an essential part of the statement. For some of the cases described below, especially those listed under the heading "Parenthetic Elements," commas and dashes are frequently used instead of parentheses. (For examples, see paragraph 17 on page 18 and paragraph 3 on page 30.) In general, commas tend to be used when the inserted material is closely related, logically or grammatically, to the main clause; parentheses are more often used when the inserted material is only incidental.

Parenthetic Elements

1. Parentheses enclose phrases and clauses that provide examples, explanations, or supplementary facts or numerical data.

> Nominations for the association's principal officers (president, vice president, treasurer, and secretary) were heard and approved.
> Three old destroyers (all now out of commission) will be scrapped.
> Their first baseman was hitting well that season (.297, 84 RBIs), and their left fielder was doing well also (21 HRs, 78 RBIs).

2. Parentheses enclose phrases and clauses introduced by expressions such as *namely, that is, e.g.,* and *i.e.* Commas, dashes, and semicolons are also used to perform this function. (For examples, see paragraph 18 on page 18, paragraph 6 on page 31, and paragraph 6 on page 60.)

> In writing to the manufacturer, be as specific as possible (i.e., list the missing or defective parts, describe the nature of the malfunction, and provide the name and address of the store where the unit was purchased).

3. Parentheses enclose definitions or translations in the main part of a sentence.

> The company announced plans to sell off its housewares (small-appliances) business.
> The hotel is located near the famous Paseo del Rio (river walk).

4. Parentheses enclose abbreviations that follow their spelled-out forms, or spelled-out forms that follow abbreviations.

> She cited a ruling by the Federal Communications Commission (FCC).
> They will study the disposal of PVC (polyvinyl chloride).

5. Parentheses often enclose cross-references.

> Telephone ordering service is also provided (refer to the list of stores at the end of this catalog).
> The diagram (Fig. 3) illustrates the action of the pump.

6. Parentheses enclose Arabic numerals that confirm a spelled-out number in a general text or in a legal document.

> Delivery will be made in thirty (30) days.

> The fee is Four Thousand Dollars ($4,000.00), payable to UNCO, Inc.

7. Parentheses enclose the name of a city or state that is inserted into a proper name for identification.

> the Norristown (Pa.) State Hospital
> the *Tulsa* (Okla.) *Tribune*

8. Some writers use parentheses to enclose personal asides.

> It was largely as a result of this conference that the committee was formed (its subsequent growth in influence is another story).

9. Parentheses are used to enclose quotations that illustrate or support a statement made in the main text.

> After he had had a few brushes with the police, his stepfather had him sent to jail as an incorrigible ("It will do him good").

Other Uses

10. Parentheses enclose unpunctuated numbers or letters separating and heading individual elements or items in a series within a sentence.

> We must set forth (1) our long-term goals, (2) our immediate objectives, and (3) the means at our disposal.

11. Parentheses indicate alternative terms.

> Please sign and return the enclosed form(s).

12. Parentheses may be used in combination with numbers for several other purposes, such as setting off area codes in telephone numbers and indicating losses in accounting.

(413) 555-7899

Operating Profits (in millions)	
Cosmetics	26.2
Food products	47.7
Food services	54.3
Transportation	(17.7)
Sporting goods	(11.2)
Total	99.3

With Other Marks of Punctuation

13. If a parenthetic expression is an independent sentence, its first word is capitalized and a period is placed *inside* the last parenthesis. A parenthetic expression that occurs within a sentence—even if it could stand alone as a separate sentence—does not end with a period. It may, however, end with an exclamation point, a question mark, a period after an abbreviation, or a set of quotation marks. A parenthetic expression within a sentence does not require capitalization unless it is a quoted sentence.

The discussion was held in the boardroom. (The results are still confidential.)

Although several trade organizations worked actively against the legislation (there were at least three paid lobbyists working on Capitol Hill at any one time), the bill passed easily.

After waiting in line for an hour (why do we do these things?), we finally left.

The conference was held in Vancouver (that's in B.C.).

He was totally confused ("What can we do?") and refused to see anyone.

14. If a parenthetic expression within a sentence is composed of two independent clauses, capitalization is avoided and semicolons are usually used instead of periods. Independent sentences enclosed in parentheses employ normal patterns of capitalization and punctuation.

> We visited several showrooms, looked at the prices (it wasn't a pleasant experience; prices in this area have not gone down), and asked all the questions we could think of.
>
> We visited several showrooms and looked at the prices. (It wasn't a pleasant experience. Prices in this area have not gone down.) If salespeople were available, we asked all of the questions we could think of.

15. No punctuation mark (other than a period after an abbreviation) is placed before parenthetic material within a sentence; if a break is required, the punctuation is placed after the final parenthesis.

> I'll get back to you tomorrow (Friday), when I have more details.

16. Parentheses sometimes appear within parentheses, although the usual practice is to replace the inner pair of parentheses with a pair of brackets. (For an example of brackets within parentheses, see paragraph 6 on page 6.)

> Checks must be drawn in U.S. dollars. (PLEASE NOTE: In accordance with U.S. Department of Treasury regulations, we cannot accept checks drawn on Canadian banks for amounts less than four U.S. dollars ($4.00). The same regulation applies to Canadian money orders.)

17. Dashes and parentheses are often used together to set off parenthetic material within a larger parenthetic element. For details and examples, see paragraph 12 on page 33.

Period

1. A period ends a sentence or a sentence fragment that is neither interrogative nor exclamatory.

   > Write the letter.
   > They wrote the required letters.
   > Total chaos. Nothing works.

2. A period punctuates some abbreviations. (For more on the punctuation of abbreviations, see the section beginning on page 133.)

fig.	Jr.
N.W.	e.g.
Assn.	Co.
U.S.	Ph.D.
Dr.	ibid.
No.	Corp.

3. Periods are used with an individual's initials. If all of the person's initials are used instead of the name, however, the unspaced initials may be written without periods.

   > F. Scott Fitzgerald
   > J.F.K. *or* JFK

4. A period follows Roman and Arabic numerals and also letters when they are used without parentheses in outlines and vertical lists.

   > I. Objectives
   >   A. Economy
   >   1. Low initial cost
   >   2. Low maintenance cost
   >   B. Ease of operation

Required skills are:
1. Shorthand
2. Typing
3. Transcription

5. A period is placed within quotation marks even when it does not punctuate the quoted material.

> The founder was known to his employees as "the old man."
>
> "I said I wanted to fire him," Henry went on, "but she said, 'I don't think you have the contractual privilege to do that.'"

6. When brackets or parentheses enclose a sentence that is independent of surrounding sentences, the period is placed inside the closing parenthesis or bracket. However, when brackets or parentheses enclose a sentence that is part of a surrounding sentence, the period for the enclosed sentence is omitted.

> On Friday the government ordered a 24-hour curfew and told all journalists and photographers to leave the area. [Authorities later confiscated the film of those who did not comply.]
>
> I took a good look at her (she was standing quite close to me at the time).

7. One space follows a period that comes after an initial in a name. If a name is composed entirely of initials, no space is required; however, the usual style for such names is to omit the periods.

> Mr. H. C. Matthews
> L.B.J. *or* LBJ

8. No space follows an internal period within a punctuated abbreviation.

f.o.b.	Ph.D.
i.e.	A.D.
M.L.S.	p.m.

Question Mark

1. The question mark terminates a direct question.

> What went wrong?
> "When do they arrive?" she asked.

The intent of the writer, not the word order of the sentence, determines whether or not the sentence is a question. Polite requests that are worded as questions, for instance, usually take periods, because they are not really questions. Similarly, a sentence that is intended as a question but whose word order is that of a statement is punctuated with a question mark.

> Will you please sit down.
> He did that?

2. The question mark terminates an interrogative element that is part of a sentence. An indirect question is not followed by a question mark.

> How did she do it? was the question on everybody's mind.
> She wondered, will it work?
> She wondered whether it would work.

3. The question mark punctuates each element of a series of questions that share a single beginning and are neither numbered nor lettered. When the series is numbered or lettered, only one question mark is used, and it is placed at the end of the series.

Can you give us a reasonable forecast? back up your predictions? compare them with last year's earnings?

Can you (1) give us a reasonable forecast, (2) back up your predictions, (3) compare them with last year's earnings?

4. The question mark indicates uncertainty about a fact.

Geoffrey Chaucer, English poet (1340?–1400)

5. The question mark is placed inside a closing bracket, dash, parenthesis, or pair of quotation marks when it punctuates only the material enclosed by that mark and not the sentence as a whole. It is placed outside that mark when it punctuates the entire sentence.

What did Andrew mean when he called the project "a fiasco from the start"?

I took a vacation in 1989 (was it really that long ago?), but I haven't had time for one since.

He asked, "Do you realize the extent of the problem [the housing shortage]?"

Quotation Marks, Double

The following paragraphs describe the use of quotation marks to enclose quoted matter in regular text, to enclose translations of words, or to enclose single letters within sentences. For the use of quotation marks or italics to enclose titles of poems, paintings, or other works, see paragraphs 77 and 82 on pages 90 and 91.

Basic Uses

1. Quotation marks enclose direct quotations but not indirect quotations.

> She said, "I am leaving for Frankfurt Monday."
> "I am leaving Monday," she said, "and I'm not coming back until the 1st."
> "I am leaving," she said. "This meeting could go on forever."
> She said that she was leaving.

2. Quotation marks enclose fragments of quoted matter when they are reproduced exactly as originally stated.

> The agreement makes it clear that he "will be paid only upon receipt of an acceptable manuscript."
> As late as 1754, documents refer to him as "yeoman" and "husbandman."

3. Quotation marks enclose words or phrases borrowed from others, words used in a special way, or words of marked informality when they are introduced into formal writing.

> That kind of corporation is referred to as "closed" or "privately held."
> Be sure to send a copy of your résumé, or as some folks would say, your "biodata summary."
> They were afraid the patient had "stroked out"— had had a cerebrovascular accident.

4. Quotation marks are sometimes used to enclose words referred to as words. Italic type or underlining is also frequently used for this purpose. (For more on this use of italics, see paragraph 4 on page 96.)

> He went through the manuscript and changed every "he" to "she."

5. Quotation marks enclose short exclamations or representations of sounds. Representations of sounds are also frequently set in italic type or underlined. (For more on this use of italics, see paragraph 6 on page 97.)

> "Ssshh!" she hissed.
> They never say anything crude like "shaddap."

6. Quotation marks enclose short sentences that fall within longer sentences, especially when the shorter sentence is meant to suggest spoken dialogue. Kinds of sentences that may be treated in this way include mottoes and maxims, unspoken or imaginary dialogue, and sentences referred to as sentences.

> Throughout the camp, the spirit was "We can do."
> She never could get used to their "That's the way it goes" attitude.
> In effect, the voters were saying "You blew it, and you don't get another chance."
> Their reaction could only be described as "Kill the messenger."

Some writers omit the quotation marks in sentences whose structure is clear without them. However, in general, quotation marks set the shorter sentence off more distinctly and convey more of the feel of spoken dialogue. (For more on the use of commas in sentences like these, see paragraphs 32–34 on pages 23–24.)

> The first rule is, When in doubt, spell it out.
> They weren't happy with the impression she left: "Don't expect favors, because I don't have to give them."

7. Quotation marks are not used to enclose paraphrases.

> Build a better mousetrap, Emerson says, and the world will beat a path to your door.

8. Direct questions are usually not enclosed in quotation marks unless they represent quoted dialogue.

> As we listened to him, we couldn't help wondering, Where's the plan?
> The question is, What went wrong?
> She asked, "What went wrong?"

As in the sentences presented in paragraph 6 above, style varies regarding the use of quotation marks with direct questions, and writers will often include the quotation marks.

> As we listened to him, we couldn't help wondering, "Where's the plan?"

9. Quotation marks are used to enclose translations of foreign or borrowed terms.

> The term *sesquipedalian* comes from the Latin word *sesquipedalis*, meaning "a foot and a half long."
> While in Texas, he encountered the armadillo ("little armored one").

10. Quotation marks are sometimes used to enclose single letters within a sentence.

> The letter "m" is wider than the letter "i."
> Put an "x" in the right spot.
> The metal rod was shaped into a "V."

However, practice varies on this point. Letters referred to as letters are commonly set in italic type or underlined. (For more on this use of italics, see paragraphs 4 and 5 on page 96.) Letters often appear undifferentiated from the surrounding text where no confusion would result.

> How many *e*'s are in her name?
> a V-shaped blade
> He was happy to get a B in the course.

With Other Marks of Punctuation

11. When quotation marks follow a word in a sentence that is also followed by a period or comma, the period or comma is placed within the quotation marks.

> He said, "I am leaving."
> The packages are labeled "Handle with Care."
> The cameras were described as "waterproof," but "moisture-resistant" would have been a better description.

12. When quotation marks follow a word in a sentence that is also followed by a colon or semicolon, the colon or semicolon is placed outside the quotation marks.

> There was only one thing to do when he said, "I may not run": promise him a larger campaign contribution.
> She spoke of her "little cottage in the country"; she might better have called it a mansion.

13. The dash, question mark, and exclamation point are placed inside quotation marks when they punctuate the quoted matter only. They are placed outside the quotation marks when they punctuate the whole sentence.

> He asked, "When did they leave?"
> What is the meaning of "the open door"?
> Save us from his "mercy"!
> "I can't see how—" he started to say.
> He thought he knew where he was going—he remembered her saying, "Take two lefts, then stay to the right"—but the streets didn't look familiar.

With Extracts

14. Quotation marks are not used with longer passages of prose or poetry that are indented as separate paragraphs, called *extracts* or *block quotations*. Extracts, as opposed to run-in quotations, are usually longer than a sentence or run to at least four lines, but individual situations of clarity and emphasis may alter these limits. Extracts are set off from the normal text by (1) indenting the passage and (2) setting it in smaller type. Extracts are usually preceded by a sentence ending with a colon, and they begin with a capitalized first word. For information on using ellipsis points to show omissions within extracts, see the section beginning on page 34.

> The chapter begins with a general description of interoffice memorandums:
>> The interoffice memorandum or memo is a means of informal communication within a firm or organization. Its special arrangement replaces the salutation, complimentary close, and written signature of the letter with identifying headings.

If the extract continues the flow of an incomplete sentence, no punctuation is required and a lowercase letter can introduce the extract.

> They describe the interoffice memorandum as
>> a means of informal communication within a firm or organization. Its special arrangement replaces the salutation, complimentary close, and written signature of the letter with identifying headings.

If the sentence preceding the extract does not refer directly to it, the sentence ends with a period.

> As of the end of April she believed that the product had been introduced well and that it stood a good chance of success.
>> Unit sales are strong, revenues are better than forecast, shipments are being made on schedule, and inventory levels are stable.

When poetic lines are set as extracts, the lines are divided exactly as in the original; a spaced slash separates lines of run-in poetry.

> The experience was one that reminded them of the wisdom of Pope's observation:
> A little learning is a dang'rous thing;
> Drink deep, or taste not the Pierian spring:
> There shallow draughts intoxicate the brain,
> And drinking largely sobers us again.

> When Gerard Manley Hopkins wrote that "Nothing is so beautiful as spring— / When weeds, in wheels, shoot long and lovely and lush," he probably had my yard in mind.

15. When an extract itself includes quoted material, double quotation marks enclose the material.

> The authors of the book recommend the following procedures for handling reports:
> The presiding officer will call for the appropriate report from an officer, a board member, a standing committee, or a special committee by saying, "Will the chairperson of the Ways and Means Committee please present the committee's report?" After the report is presented, a motion is heard to accept the report.

16. Quotation marks are not used with an epigraph set off like an extract.

> The whole of science is nothing more than a refinement of everyday thinking.
> —Albert Einstein

Quotation Marks, Single

1. Single quotation marks enclose a quotation within a quotation. When both single and double quotation marks occur at the end of a sentence, the period typically falls within *both* sets of marks.

The witness said, "I distinctly heard him say, 'Don't be late,' and then I heard the door close."

The witness said, "I distinctly heard him say, 'Don't be late.' "

2. Single quotation marks are occasionally used in place of double quotation marks. This is far more common in British usage.

The witness said, 'I distinctly heard him say, "Don't be late," and then I heard the door close.'

3. On rare occasions, writers face the question of how to punctuate a quotation within a quotation within a quotation. Standard practice would be to enclose the innermost quotation in double marks; however, this can be confusing, and rewriting the sentence can often remove the need for it.

The witness said, "I distinctly heard him say, 'Don't you say "Shut up" to me.' "

The witness said that she distinctly heard him say, "Don't you say 'Shut up' to me."

Semicolon

The semicolon is used in ways similar to those in which periods and commas are used. Like a period, the semicolon marks the end of a complete clause, but it also signals that the clause that follows it is closely related to the one that precedes it. The semicolon is also used to distinguish major divisions from the minor pauses that are represented by commas.

Between Clauses

1. A semicolon separates independent clauses that are joined together in one sentence without a coordinating conjunction.

The river rose and overflowed its banks; roads became flooded and impassable; freshly plowed fields disappeared from sight.

Cream the shortening and sugar; add the eggs and beat well.

2. Ordinarily a comma separates main clauses joined with a coordinating conjunction. However, if the sentence might be confusing with a comma in this position, a semicolon is used in its place. Potentially confusing sentences include those with other commas in them or with particularly long clauses.

We fear that this situation may, in fact, occur; but we don't know when.

In a society that seeks to promote social goals, government will play a powerful role; and taxation, once simply a means of raising money, becomes, in addition, a way of furthering those goals.

3. A semicolon joins two statements when the grammatical construction of the second clause is elliptical and depends on that of the first.

The veal dishes were very good; the desserts, too.

In many cases the conference sessions, which were designed to allow for full discussions of topics, were much too long and tedious; the breaks between them, much too short.

4. A semicolon joins two clauses when the second begins with a conjunctive adverb, such as *accordingly, however, indeed,* and *thus.* Phrases such as *in that case, as a result,* and *on the other hand* can also act as conjunctive adverbs. (For more on conjunctive adverbs, see the section beginning on page 195.)

Most people are covered by insurance of one kind
or another; indeed, many people don't even see
their medical bills.

It won't be easy to sort out the facts; however, a decision must be made.

The case could take years to work its way through
the court system; as a result, many plantiffs will accept out-of-court settlements.

Practice varies regarding the treatment of clauses
introduced by *so* and *yet*. Although many writers continue to treat *so* and *yet* as adverbs, it has
become standard to treat these words as coordinating conjunctions that join clauses. In this
treatment, a comma precedes *so* and *yet* and
no punctuation follows them. (For examples, see
paragraph 1 on page 12.)

5. When three or more clauses are separated by
semicolons, and a coordinating conjunction precedes the final clause, the final semicolon is often
replaced with a comma. (For the use of commas
to separate three or more clauses without conjunctions, see paragraph 4 on page 13.)

They don't understand; they grow bored; and they
stop learning.

The report recounted events leading up to this inci-
dent; it included observations of eyewitnesses, but
it drew no conclusions.

The choice of whether or not to use a conjunction, and whether to use a semicolon or a comma
with the conjunction, are matters of personal
preference. In general, the semicolon makes the
transition to the final clause more abrupt, which
often serves to place more emphasis on that
clause. The comma and conjunction ease the
transition and make the sentence seem less
choppy.

With Introductory Expressions

6. A semicolon is sometimes used before expressions (such as *for example, for instance, that is, namely, e.g.,* or *i.e.*) that introduce expansions or series. Commas, dashes, and parentheses are also used in sentences like these. (For examples, see paragraph 18 on page 18, paragraph 6 on page 31, and paragraph 2 on page 43.)

> On one point only did everyone agree; namely, too much money had been spent already.
>
> We were fairly successful on that project; that is, we made our deadlines and met our budget.
>
> Most had traveled great distances to participate; for example, three had come from Australia, one from Japan, and two from China.

In a Series

7. A semicolon is used in place of a comma to separate phrases in a series when the phrases themselves contain commas. A comma may replace the semicolon before the last item in a series if the last item is introduced with a conjunction.

> The visitor to Barndale can choose from three sources of overnight accommodation: The Rose and Anchor, which houses Barndale's oldest pub; The Crawford, an American-style luxury hotel; and Ellen's Bed and Breakfast on Peabody Lane.
>
> We studied mathematics in the morning; English, French, and Spanish right after lunch, and science in the late afternoon.

8. When the individual items in an enumeration or series are long or are sentences themselves, they are usually separated by semicolons.

> Among the committee's recommendations were the following: more hospital beds in urban areas

where there are waiting lines for elective surgery; smaller staff size in half-empty rural hospitals; review procedures for all major purchases.

9. A semicolon separates items in a list in cases where a comma alone would not clearly separate the items or references.

The votes against were: Precinct 1, 338; Precinct 2, 627; Precinct 3, 514.
(Friedlander 1957; Ballas 1962)

With Other Marks of Punctuation

10. A semicolon is placed outside quotation marks and parentheses.

They referred to each other as "Mother" and "Father"; they were the archetypal happily married elderly couple.

She accepted the situation with every appearance of equanimity (but with some inward qualms); however, all of that changed the next day.

Slash

The slash is known by many names, including *virgule*, *diagonal*, *solidus*, *oblique*, and *slant*. Most commonly, the slash is used to represent a word that is not written out or to separate or set off certain adjacent elements of text.

In Place of Missing Words

1. A slash represents the words *per* or *to* when used with units of measure or when used to indicate the terms of a ratio.

40,000 tons/year
9 ft./sec.

price/earnings ratio
a 50/50 split

2. A slash separates alternatives. In this context, the slash usually represents the words *or* or *and/or*.

alumni/ae
his/her
oral/written tests

3. A slash replaces the word *and* in some compound terms.

molybdenum/vanadium steel
in the May/June issue
1993/94
an innovative classroom/laboratory

4. A slash is used, although less commonly, to replace a number of prepositions, such as *at, versus, with,* and *for.*

U.C./Berkeley	parent/child issues
table/mirror	Vice President/Editorial

With Abbreviations

5. A slash punctuates some abbreviations.

c/o	V/STOL
A/R	d/b/a
I/O	P/E

In some cases the slash may stand for a word that is not represented in the abbreviation (e.g., *in* in *W/O,* the abbreviation for *water in oil*).

To Separate Elements

6. The slash may be used in a number of different ways to separate groups of numbers, such as ele-

ments in a date and numerators and denominators in fractions.

7. The slash serves as a divider between lines of poetry that are run in with the text around them. This method of quoting poetry is usually limited to passages of no more than three or four lines. Longer passages are usually set off from the text as extract quotations.

> When Samuel Taylor Coleridge wrote in "Christabel" that "'Tis a month before the month of May,/And the Spring comes slowly up this way," he could have been describing New England.

Spacing

8. In general, no space is used between the slash and the words, letters, or figures separated by it; however, some writers do prefer to place spaces around a slash used to separate lines of poetry.

Chapter 2

Capitals, Italics, and Quotation Marks

Words and phrases are capitalized, italicized or underlined (underlining in typed or handwritten material is equivalent to italics in keyboarded or typeset material), or enclosed in quotation marks in order to indicate that they have a special significance in particular contexts. This chapter is divided into four sections that describe these contexts. The first section explains the use of capitalized words to begin sentences and phrases. The second explains the use of capitals, italics, and quotation marks to indicate that a word or phrase is a proper noun, pronoun, or adjective. The third and fourth sections explain other uses of capital letters and italics. For other uses of quotation marks, see the section beginning on page 50.

Beginnings

1. The first word of a sentence or sentence fragment is capitalized.

The meeting was postponed.
No! I can't do it.
Total chaos. Nothing works.

2. The first word of a sentence contained within parentheses is capitalized. However, a parenthetical sentence occurring inside another sentence is not capitalized unless it is a complete quoted sentence.

> The discussion was held in the boardroom. (The results are still confidential.)
>
> Although we liked the restaurant (the seafood was especially good), we could not afford to go there often.
>
> After waiting in line for an hour (why do we do these things?), we finally left.
>
> He was totally demoralized ("There is just nothing we can do") and was contemplating resignation.

3. The first word of a direct quotation is capitalized. However, if the quotation is interrupted in midsentence, the second part does not begin with a capital.

> The President said, "We have rejected this report entirely."
>
> "We have rejected this report entirely," the President said, "and we will not comment on it further."

4. When a quotation, whether a sentence fragment or a complete sentence, is syntactically dependent on the sentence in which it occurs, the quotation does not begin with a capital.

> The President made it clear that "there is no room for compromise."

5. The first word of a sentence within a sentence is usually capitalized. Examples of sentences within

sentences include mottoes and rules, unspoken or imaginary dialogue, sentences referred to as sentences, and direct questions. (For an explanation of the use of commas and quotation marks with sentences such as these, see paragraphs 34 and 35 on pages 24–25 and paragraphs 6 and 8 on pages 52–53.)

> You know the saying "Honesty is the best policy."
> The first rule is, When in doubt, spell it out.
> The clear message coming back from the audience was "We don't care."
> My question is, When can we go?

6. The first word of a line of poetry is usually capitalized.

> The best lack all conviction, while the worst
> Are full of passionate intensity.
> —W. B. Yeats

7. The first word following a colon may be either lowercased or capitalized if it introduces a complete sentence. While the former is the usual style, the latter is also common, especially when the sentence introduced by the colon is lengthy and distinctly separate from the preceding clause.

> The advantage of this particular system is clear: it's inexpensive.
> The situation is critical: This company cannot hope to recoup the fourth-quarter losses that were sustained in five operating divisions.

8. If a colon introduces a series of sentences, the first word of each sentence is capitalized.

> Consider the following steps that we have taken: A subcommittee has been formed to evaluate our past performance and to report its findings to the full organization. New sources of revenue are

being explored, and relevant organizations are being contacted. And several candidates have been interviewed for the new post of executive director.

9. The first words of run-in enumerations that form complete sentences are capitalized, as are the first words of vertical lists and enumerations. Numbered phrases *within* a sentence, however, are lowercased.

> Do the following at the end of the day: 1. Turn off your computer. 2. Clear your desktop of papers. 3. Cover office machines. 4. Straighten the contents of cabinets and bookcases.
>
> This is the agenda:
> Call to order
> Roll call
> Minutes of the previous meeting
> Treasurer's report
>
> On the agenda will be (1) call to order, (2) roll call, (3) minutes of the previous meeting, (4) treasurer's report . . .

10. In minutes and legislation, the introductory words *Whereas* and *Resolved* are capitalized (and *Resolved* is also italicized). The word *That* or an alternative word or expression which immediately follows *Whereas* or *Resolved* has its first letter capitalized.

> Whereas, Substantial benefits . . .
> *Resolved,* That . . .

11. The first word in an outline heading is capitalized.

> I. Editorial tasks
> II. Production responsibilities
>   A. Cost estimates
>   B. Bids

12. The first word of the salutation of a letter and the first word of a complimentary close are capitalized.

Dear Mary,   Sincerely yours,
Ladies and Gentlemen: Very truly yours,

13. The first word and each subsequent major word following a SUBJECT or TO heading (as in a memorandum) are capitalized.

SUBJECT: Pension Plans
TO: All Department Heads and Editors

Proper Nouns, Pronouns, and Adjectives

The following paragraphs describe the ways in which a broad range of proper nouns, pronouns, and adjectives are styled—with capitals, italics, quotation marks, or some combination of these devices. In almost all cases, proper nouns, pronouns, and adjectives are capitalized. In many cases, proper nouns are italicized (or underlined in typed or handwritten material) or enclosed in quotation marks in addition to being capitalized. No clear distinctions can be drawn between the kinds of words that are capitalized and italicized, capitalized and enclosed in quotation marks, or simply capitalized.

Abbreviations

1. Abbreviated forms of proper nouns and adjectives are capitalized, just as the spelled-out forms would be. (For more on the capitalization of abbreviations, see the section on page 134.)

Dec. [for *December*]

Col. [for *Colonel*]
Wed. [for *Wednesday*]
Brit. [for *British*]

Abstractions and Personifications

2. Abstract terms, such as names of concepts or qualities, are usually not capitalized unless the concept or quality is being presented as if it were a person. If the term is simply being used in conjunction with other words that allude to human characteristics or qualities, it is usually not capitalized. (For more on the capitalization of abstract terms, see paragraph 2 on page 94.)

> a time when Peace walked among us
> as Autumn paints each leaf in fiery colors
> an economy gripped by inflation
> hoping that fate would lend a hand

3. Fictitious names used as personifications are capitalized.

> Uncle Sam
> Ma Bell
> Jack Frost

Academic Degrees

4. The names of academic degrees are capitalized when they follow a person's name. The names of specific academic degrees not following a person's name may be capitalized or not capitalized, according to individual preference. General terms referring to degrees, such as *doctorate*, *master's degree*, or *bachelor's*, are not capitalized. Abbreviations for academic degrees are always capitalized.

> E. Terence Ford, Doctor of Divinity

earned her Doctor of Laws degree
   or   earned her doctor of laws degree
working for a bachelor's degree
Susan Wycliff, M.S.W.
received her Ph.D.

Animals and Plants

5. The common names of animals and plants are not capitalized unless they contain a proper noun as a separate element, in which case the proper noun is capitalized and elements preceding (but not following) the proper noun are usually but not always capitalized. If the common name contains a word that was once a proper noun but is no longer thought of as such, the word is usually not capitalized. When in doubt, consult a dictionary. (For the capitalization of scientific names, see paragraphs 66–72 on pages 87–89.)

cocker spaniel	Great Dane
lily of the valley	black-eyed Susan
Bengal tiger	ponderosa pine
Rhode Island red	holstein

In references to specific breeds, as distinguished from the animals that belong to the breed, all elements of the name are capitalized.

Gordon Setter
Rhode Island Red
Holstein

Awards, Honors, and Prizes

6. Names of awards, honors, and prizes are capitalized. Descriptive words and phrases that are not actually part of the award's name are lowercased. (For capitalizing the names of military decorations, see paragraph 44 on page 81.)

Academy Award	Nobel Prize winner
Emmy	Nobel Prize in medicine
Rhodes Scholarship	Nobel Peace Prize
Rhodes scholar	

Derivatives of Proper Names

7. Derivatives of proper names are capitalized when they are used in their primary sense. However, if the derived term has taken on a specialized meaning, it is usually not capitalized.

Roman architecture	manila envelope
Victorian customs	pasteurized milk
an Americanism	french fries

Geographical and Topographical References

8. Terms that identify divisions of the earth's surface and distinct areas, regions, places, or districts are capitalized, as are derivative nouns and adjectives.

the Great Plains	the Southwest
the Mariana Trench	Chicago, Illinois
the Riviera	the Middle Eastern situation

9. Popular names of localities are capitalized.

the Big Apple	the Twin Cities
the Village	Hell's Kitchen
the Loop	the Valley

10. Compass points are capitalized when they refer to a geographical region or when they are part of a street name. They are lowercased when they refer to a simple direction.

back East	east of the Mississippi
out West	traveling north on I-91
West Oak Street	

11. Nouns and adjectives that are derived from compass points and that designate or refer to a specific geographical region are usually capitalized.

> a Southern accent
> Northerners
> a Western crop
> part of the Eastern establishment

12. Words designating global, national, regional, or local political divisions are capitalized when they are essential elements of specific names. However, they are usually lowercased when they precede a proper name or when they are not part of a specific name.

> the British Empire   New York City
> the fall of the empire   the city of New York
> Washington State   Ward 1
> the state of Washington   fires in three wards

In legal documents, these words are often capitalized regardless of position.

> the State of Washington
> the City of New York

13. Common geographical terms (such as *lake, mountain, river, valley*) are capitalized if they are part of a specific proper name.

> Crater Lake   Hudson Bay
> Lake Como   Ohio Valley
> Rocky Mountains   Great Barrier Reef
> the Columbia River   Strait of Gibraltar

14. Common geographical terms preceding names are usually capitalized.

> Lakes Mead and Powell
> Mounts Whitney and Shasta

When *the* precedes the common term, the term is lowercased.

> the river Thames

15. Common geographical terms that are not used as part of a proper name are not capitalized. These include plural terms that follow two or more proper names and terms that are used descriptively or alone.

> the Himalaya and Andes mountains
> the Missouri and Platte rivers
> the Atlantic coast of Labrador
> the Caribbean islands
> the river valley

16. The names of streets, monuments, parks, landmarks, well-known buildings, and other public places are capitalized. However, common terms that are part of these names (such as *avenue, park,* or *bridge*) are lowercased when they occur after multiple names or are used alone (but see paragraph 17 below).

> Fifth Avenue   Rock Creek Park
> Fifth and Park avenues   walking to the park
> the Pyramids   Golden Gate Bridge
> the Capitol   on the bridge

17. Well-known informal or shortened forms of place-names are capitalized.

> the Avenue [for *Fifth Avenue*]
> the Street [for *Wall Street*]
> the Exchange [for the *New York Stock Exchange*]

Governmental, Judicial, and Political Bodies

18. Full names of legislative, deliberative, executive, and administrative bodies are capitalized, as are

easily recognizable short forms of these names. However, nonspecific noun and adjective references to them are usually lowercased.

> United States Congress
> Congress
> the House
> congressional hearings
> the Federal Bureau of Investigation
> a federal agency

When words such as *department, committee,* or *agency* are used in place of the full name of a specific body, they are most often capitalized when the department or agency is referring to itself in print; in most other cases, these words are lowercased.

> The Connecticut Department of Transportation is pleased to offer this new booklet on traffic safety. The Department hopes that it will be of use to all drivers.
>
> We received a new booklet from the Connecticut Department of Transportation. This is the second pamphlet the department has issued this month.

19. The full and short names of the U.S. Supreme Court are capitalized.

> The Supreme Court of the United States
> the United States Supreme Court
> the Supreme Court
> the Court

20. Official and full names of higher courts and names of international courts are capitalized. Short forms of official higher-court names are often capitalized in legal documents but lowercased in general writing.

The International Court of Arbitration
the United States Court of Appeals for the Second
  Circuit
the Virginia Supreme Court
the Court of Queen's Bench
a ruling by the court of appeals
the state supreme court

21. Names of city and county courts are usually lowercased.

the Lawton municipal court
the Owensville night court
small-claims court
the county court
juvenile court

22. The designation *court,* when it applies to a specific
judge or presiding officer, is capitalized.

It is the opinion of this Court that . . .
The Court found that . . .

23. The terms *federal* and *national* are capitalized only
when they are essential elements of a name or
title.

Federal Trade Commission
federal court
National Security Council
national security

24. The word *administration* is capitalized by some
writers when it refers to the administration of a
specific U.S. president, but is more commonly
lowercased. If the word does not refer to a specific presidency, it is not capitalized except when
it is a part of the official name of a government
agency.

the Truman administration
  or   the Truman Administration
the administration   *or*   the Administration
the Farmers Home Loan Administration
The running of the White House varies considerably from one administration to another.

25. Names of political organizations and their adherents are capitalized, but the word *party* may or may not be capitalized, depending on the writer's preference.

the Democratic National Committee
the Republican platform
Tories
Nazis
the Democratic party   *or*   the Democratic Party

26. Names of political groups other than parties are usually lowercased, as are their derivative forms.

the right wing
the liberals
  but usually
the Left
the Right

27. Terms describing political and economic philosophies and their derivative forms are usually capitalized only if they are derived from proper names.

authoritarianism   civil libertarian
democracy   Marxist
nationalism   fascism   *or*   Fascism

Historical Periods and Events

28. The names of conferences, councils, expositions, and specific sporting, historical, and cultural events are capitalized.

the Yalta Conference
the Minnesota State Fair
the World Series
the Series
the San Francisco Earthquake
the Boston Tea Party
the Philadelphia Folk Festival

29. The names of some historical and cultural periods and movements are capitalized. When in doubt, consult a dictionary or encyclopedia.

the Augustan Age   the Great Depression
Prohibition   fin de siècle
the Renaissance   the space age
the Enlightenment   the cold war
the Stone Age   *or*   the Cold War

30. Numerical designations of historical time periods are capitalized only when they are part of a proper name; otherwise they are lowercased.

the Roaring Twenties
the Third Reich
the seventeenth century
the eighties

31. Full names of treaties, laws, and acts are capitalized.

Treaty of Versailles
The Clean Air Act of 1990

32. The full names of wars are capitalized. However, words such as *war, revolution, battle,* and *campaign* are capitalized only when they are part of a proper name. Descriptive terms such as *assault, siege,* and *engagement* are usually lowercased even when used in conjunction with the name of the place where the action occurred.

> the French and Indian War
> the Battle of the Bulge
> the Peninsular Campaign
> the American and French revolutions
> the second battle of Manassas
> the siege of Yorktown
> the winter campaign
> through most of the war

Hyphenated Compounds

33. Elements of hyphenated compounds are generally capitalized only if they are proper nouns or adjectives.

> Arab-Israeli negotiations
> East-West trade agreements
> French-speaking peoples
> Thirty-second Street
> an eighteenth-century poet

34. Word elements (such as prefixes and combining forms) may or may not be capitalized when joined to a proper noun or adjective. Common prefixes (such as *pre-* or *anti-*) are usually not capitalized in such cases. Geographical and ethnic combining forms (such as *Anglo-* or *Sino-*) are capitalized; *pan-* is usually capitalized when attached to a proper noun or adjective.

> the anti-Yeltsin faction
> pre-Civil War politics
> African-Americans
> Greco-Roman architecture
> Sino-Japanese relations
> Pan-Slavic nationalism

Legal Material

35. The names of both plaintiff and defendant in legal case titles are italicized (or underlined in typewritten material). The *v.* (for *versus*) may be roman or italic. Cases that do not involve two opposing parties have titles such as *In re Watson* or *In the matter of John Watson,* which are also italicized. When the person involved rather than the case itself is being discussed, the reference is not italicized.

> *Jones* v. *Massachusetts*
> *In re Jones*
> *Smith et al. v. Jones*
> She covered the Jones trial for the newspaper.

In running text, a case name involving two opposing parties may be shortened.

> The judge based his ruling on a precedent set in the *Jones* decision.

Medical Terms

36. Proper names that are elements in terms designating diseases, symptoms, syndromes, and tests are capitalized. Common nouns are lowercased.

> Parkinson's disease
> Down's Syndrome
> German measles
> Rorschach test
> mumps
> herpes simplex

37. Scientific names of disease-causing organisms follow the rules discussed in paragraph 66 on page 87. The names of diseases or conditions derived from scientific names of organisms are lowercased and not italicized.

> a neurotoxin produced by *Clostridium botulinum*
> nearly died of botulism

38. Generic names of drugs are lowercased; trade names should be capitalized.

> a prescription for chlorpromazine
> had been taking Thorazine

Military Terms

39. The full titles of branches of the armed forces are capitalized, as are easily recognized short forms.

> U.S. Marine Corps   the Marines
> the Marine Corps   the Corps

40. The terms *air force, army, coast guard, marine(s),* and *navy* are lowercased unless they form part of an official name or refer back to a specific branch of the armed forces previously named. They are also lowercased when they are used collectively or in the plural.

> the combined air forces of the NATO nations
> the navies of the world
> the American army

41. The adjectives *naval* and *marine* are lowercased unless they are part of a proper name.

> naval battle
> marine barracks
> Naval Reserves

42. The full titles of units and organizations of the armed forces are capitalized. Elements of full titles are often lowercased when they stand alone.

> U.S. Army Corps of Engineers
> the Reserves
> a reserve commission
> First Battalion
> the battalion

43. Military ranks are capitalized when they precede the names of their holders, and when they take the place of a person's name (as in direct address). Otherwise they are lowercased.

> General Colin Powell
> I can't get this rifle any cleaner, Sergeant.
> The major arrived precisely on time.

44. The specific names of decorations, citations, and medals are capitalized.

> Medal of Honor
> Navy Cross
> Purple Heart
> Distinguished Service Medal

Numerical Designations

45. A noun introducing a reference number is usually capitalized.

> Order 704   Form 2E
> Flight 409   Policy 118-4-Y

46. Nouns used with numbers or letters to designate major reference headings (as in a literary work) are capitalized. However, nouns designating minor reference headings are typically lowercased.

> Book II   page 101
> Volume V   line 8
> Division 4   paragraph 6.1
> Chapter 2   item 16
> Table 3   question 21

Organizations

47. Names of firms, corporations, schools, and organizations and terms derived from those names to

designate their members are capitalized. However, common nouns used descriptively or occurring after the names of two or more organizations
are lowercased.

> University of Michigan
> Washington Huskies
> played as a Pirate last year
> Kiwanians
> American and United airlines

The word *the* at the beginning of such names is
capitalized only when the full legal name is used.

48. Words such as *agency, department, division, group,*
or *office* that designate corporate and organiza-
tional units are capitalized only when they are
used with a specific name.

> while working for the Criminal Division in the De-
> partment of Justice
> a notice to all department heads

Style varies regarding the capitalization of these
words when they are used in place of the full
name of a specific body; see paragraph 18 on
page 73.

49. Nicknames, epithets, or other alternative terms
for organizations are capitalized.

> referred to IBM as Big Blue
> the Big Three automakers
> trading stocks on the Big Board

People

50. The names and initials of persons are capitalized.
If a name is hyphenated, both elements are capitalized. Particles forming the initial elements of
surnames (such as *de, della, der, du, la, ten, ter, van,*

and *von*) may or may not be capitalized, depending on the practice of the family or individual. However, the particle is always capitalized at the beginning of a sentence.

> E. I. du Pont de Nemours
> James Van Allen
> Sir Arthur Thomas Quiller-Couch
> Wernher von Braun
> the paintings of de Kooning
> De Kooning's paintings are . . .

51. The name of a person or thing can be added to or replaced entirely by a nickname or epithet (a characterizing word or phrase). Nicknames and epithets are capitalized.

> Calamity Jane   Ol' Blue Eyes
> Buffalo Bill   Attila the Hun
> Magic Johnson   Meadowlark Lemon

52. Nicknames and epithets are frequently used in conjunction with both the first and last name of a person. If it is placed between the first and last name, it will often be enclosed in quotation marks or parentheses. However, if the nickname is in general use, the quotation marks or parentheses are often omitted. If the nickname precedes the first name, it is sometimes enclosed in quotation marks but more often not.

> Earl ("Fatha") Hines
> Joanne "Big Mama" Carner
> Dennis (Oil Can) Boyd
> Mother Maybelle Carter
> Kissin' Jim Folsom

53. Words of family relationship preceding or used in place of a person's name are capitalized. However, these words are lowercased if they are part of a noun phrase that is being used in place of a name.

> Cousin Mercy
> Grandfather Barnes
> I know when Mother's birthday is.
> I know when my mother's birthday is.

54. Words designating languages, nationalities, peoples, races, religious groups, and tribes are capitalized. Descriptive terms used to refer to groups of people are variously capitalized or lowercased. Designations based on color are usually lowercased.

> Latino
> Caucasians
> Canadians
> African-American
> Muslims
> Ibo
> Bushman (nomadic hunter of southern Africa)
> bushman (inhabitant of the Australian bush)
> black, brown, and white people

55. Corporate, professional, and governmental titles are capitalized when they immediately precede a person's name, unless the name is being used as an appositive.

> President Roosevelt
> Queen Elizabeth
> Doctor Malatesta
> Professor Kaiser
> Senator Sam Nunn
> Pastor Linda Jones
> the new pastor, Linda Jones
> Chrysler's former president, Lee Iacocca

56. When corporate or governmental titles are used as part of a descriptive phrase to identify a person rather than as a person's official title, the title is lowercased.

> Senator Bill Bradley of New Jersey
> *but*
> Bill Bradley, senator from New Jersey

Style varies when governmental titles are used in descriptive phrases that precede a name.

> New Jersey senator Bill Bradley
> *or* New Jersey Senator Bill Bradley

57. Specific governmental titles may be capitalized when they are used in place of particular individuals' names. In minutes and official records of proceedings, corporate titles are capitalized when they are used in place of individuals' names.

> The Secretary of State gave a news conference.
> The Judge will respond to questions in her chambers.
> The Treasurer then stated his misgivings about the project.

58. Some writers always capitalize the word *president* when it refers to the U.S. presidency. However, the more common practice is to capitalize the word *president* only when it refers to a specific individual.

> It is the duty of the president [President] to submit a budget to Congress.

59. Titles are capitalized when they are used in direct address.

> Tell me the truth, Doctor.
> Where are we headed, Captain?

Religious Terms

60. Words designating the Deity are capitalized.

> Allah   Yahweh
> Jehovah   the Creator
> God Almighty   the Holy Spirit

61. Personal pronouns referring to the Deity are usually capitalized. Relative pronouns (such as *who*, *whom*, and *whose*) usually are not.

> God in His mercy
> believing that it was God who created the universe

62. Traditional designations of apostles, prophets, and saints are capitalized.

> our Lady
> the Prophet
> the Lawgiver

63. Names of religions, denominations, creeds and confessions, and religious orders are capitalized, as are adjectives derived from these names. The word *church* is capitalized only when it is used as part of the name of a specific body or edifice or, in some publications, when it refers to organized Christianity in general.

> Judaism
> the Southern Baptist Convention
> Apostles' Creed
> the Poor Clares
> the Society of Jesus
> Islamic
> Hunt Memorial Church
> the Baptist church on the corner

64. Names of the Bible or its books, parts, versions, or editions of it and other sacred books are capitalized but not italicized. Adjectives derived from the names of sacred books are variously capitalized and lowercased. When in doubt, consult a dictionary.

Gospel of Saint Mark   Talmud
Old Testament   Talmudic
Authorized Version   Koran
biblical   Koranic

65. The names of prayers and well-known passages of the Bible are capitalized.

the Ave Maria
the Lord's Prayer
the Our Father
the Ten Commandments
the Sermon on the Mount
the Beatitudes

Scientific Terms

66. Genus names in biological binomial nomenclature are capitalized; species names are lowercased, even when derived from a proper name. Both genus and species names are italicized.

Both the wolf and the domestic dog are included in the genus *Canis*.
The California condor *(Gymnogyps californianus)* is facing extinction.

The names of races, varieties, or subspecies, when used, are lowercased. Like genus and species names, they are italicized.

Hyla versicolor chrysoscelis
Otis asio naevius

67. The New Latin names of classes, families, and all groups above the genus level in zoology and botany are capitalized but not italicized. Their derivative adjectives and nouns in English are neither capitalized nor italicized.

Gastropoda	gastropod
Thallophyta	thallophyte

68. The names, both scientific and informal, of planets and their satellites, asteroids, stars, constellations, groups of stars, and other specific celestial objects are capitalized. However, the words *sun*, *earth*, and *moon* are usually lowercased unless they occur with other astronomical names. A generic term that follows the name of a celestial object is usually lowercased.

the Milky Way	Big Dipper
Pleiades	the Moon and Mars
Sirius	Barnard's star

69. Names of meteorological phenomena are lowercased.

aurora borealis
northern lights
parhelic circle

70. Terms that identify geological eras, periods, epochs, and strata are capitalized. The generic terms that follow them are lowercased. The words *upper*, *middle*, and *lower* are capitalized when they are used to designate an epoch or series within a period; in most other cases, they are lowercased. The word *age* is capitalized in names such as *Age of Reptiles* or *Age of Fishes*.

Mesozoic era
Upper Cretaceous
Quaternary period
Middle Ordovician

Oligocene epoch
Lower Silurian

71. Proper names forming essential elements of scientific laws, theorems, and principles are capitalized. However, the common nouns *law, theorem, theory*, and the like are lowercased.

Boyle's law
the Pythagorean theorem
Planck's constant
Einstein's theory of relativity

In terms referring to popular or fanciful theories or observations, descriptive words are usually capitalized as well.

Murphy's Law
the Peter Principle

72. The names of chemical elements and compounds are lowercased.

hydrogen fluoride
ferric ammonium citrate

73. The names of computer services and databases are usually trademarks and should always be capitalized. Some names of computer languages are written with an initial capital letter, some with all letters capitalized. Some are commonly written both ways. When in doubt, consult a dictionary.

CompuServe	PL/1
Atek	APL
BASIC	PASCAL *or* Pascal
TeleTransfer	COBOL *or* Cobol

Time Periods and Zones

74. The names of the days of the week, months of the year, and holidays and holy days are capitalized.

Tuesday	Thanksgiving
June	Easter
Independence Day	Yom Kippur

75. The names of time zones are capitalized when abbreviated but usually lowercased when written out, except for words that are themselves proper names.

CST	mountain time
central standard time	Pacific standard time

76. Names of the seasons are lowercased if they simply declare the time of year; however, they are capitalized if they are personified.

> My new book is scheduled to appear this spring.
> the sweet breath of Spring

Titles

77. Words in titles of books, long poems, magazines, newspapers, plays, movies, novellas that are separately published, and works of art such as paintings and sculpture are capitalized except for internal articles, conjunctions, prepositions, and the *to* of infinitives. (Some writers also capitalize prepositions of five or more letters such as *about* or *toward*.) The entire title is italicized. Regarding the Bible and other sacred works, see paragraph 64 on page 86.

> *The Lives of a Cell*
> *Of Mice and Men*
> *National Geographic*
> *Christian Science Monitor*
> Shakespeare's *Othello*
> the movie *Wait until Dark*
> Géricault's *The Raft of the Medusa*

78. An initial article that is part of a title is often omitted if it would be awkward in context. However, when it is included it is capitalized and italicized or underlined. For books that are referred to by an abbreviation, the initial article is neither capitalized nor italicized.

> *The Oxford English Dictionary*
> the 20-volume *Oxford English Dictionary*
> the *OED*

79. Practice varies widely regarding the capitalization and italicization or underlining of initial articles and city names in the titles of newspapers. The most common practice is to italicize the city name but not to capitalize or italicize the initial article.

> the *New York Times*
> the *Wall Street Journal*

80. Many publications, especially newspapers, do not use italics for titles. They either simply capitalize the words of the title or capitalize the words and enclose them in quotation marks.

> the Heard on the Street column in the Wall Street Journal
> our review of "The Volcano Lover" in last week's issue

81. The first word following a colon in a title is capitalized.

> *Jane Austen: A Literary Life*

82. The titles of short poems, short stories, essays, lectures, dissertations, chapters of books, articles in periodicals, radio and television programs, and novellas that are published in a collection are capitalized and enclosed in quotation marks. The capitalization of articles, conjunctions, and prepositions is the same as it is for italicized titles, as explained in paragraph 77 above.

> Robert Frost's "Dust of Snow"
> Cynthia Ozick's "Rosa"
> John Barth's "The Literature of Exhaustion"
> The talk, "Labor's Power: A View for the Nineties," will be given Friday.
> the third chapter of *Treasure Island*, entitled "The Black Spot"
> Her article, "Computer Art on a Micro," was in *Popular Computing*.
> listening to "All Things Considered"
> watching "The Tonight Show"

83. Common titles of book sections (such as *preface, introduction,* or *index*) are capitalized but not enclosed in quotation marks when they refer to a section of the same book in which the reference is made. If they refer to another book, they are usually lowercased.

> See the Appendix for further information.
> In the introduction to her book, the author explains her goals.

84. Practice varies regarding the capitalization of the word *chapter* when it is used with a cardinal number to identify a specific chapter in a book. Most writers capitalize the word, but some do not.

> See Chapter 3 for more details.
> is discussed further in Chapter Four
> *but*
> in the third chapter

85. The titles of long musical compositions are generally capitalized and italicized; the titles of songs and other short compositions are capitalized and enclosed in quotation marks. The titles of compositions identified only by the nature of the musical form in which they were written are capitalized only, regardless of their length.

> Verdi's *Don Carlos*
> Beethoven's "Für Elise"
> "America the Beautiful"
> Symphony No. 8 in F Major

Trademarks

86. Registered trademarks, service marks, collective marks, and brand names are capitalized.

Band-Aid	Velcro
College Board	Diet Pepsi
Kellogg's All-Bran	Kleenex
Jacuzzi	Lay's potato chips

Transportation

87. The names of individual ships, submarines, airplanes, satellites, and space vehicles are capitalized and italicized. The designations *U.S.S.*, *S.S.*, *M.V.*, and *H.M.S.* are not italicized.

Apollo 11	*Enola Gay*
Spirit of St. Louis	M.V. *West Star*

Other Uses of Capitals

1. Full capitalization of a word is sometimes used for emphasis or to indicate that a speaker is talking very loudly. Both of these uses of capitals are usually avoided in formal writing. Italicizing words for emphasis is more common (for examples, see paragraph 7 on page 97).

Results are not the only criteria for judging performance. HOW we achieve results is important also.

All applications must be submitted IN WRITING before January 31.

The waiter rushed by yelling "HOT PLATE! HOT PLATE!"

2. A word is sometimes capitalized to indicate that it is being used as a philosophical concept or that it stands for an important concept in a discussion.

Many people seek Truth, but few find it.

the three M's of advertising: Message, Media, and Management

3. Full capitals or a mixture of capitals and lower-case letters or sometimes even small capitals are used to reproduce the text of signs, labels, or inscriptions.

a poster reading SPECIAL THRILLS COMING SOON

a Do Not Disturb sign

a barn with CHEW MAIL POUCH on the side

4. A letter used to indicate a shape is capitalized.

an A-frame house

a J-bar

V-shaped

Other Uses of Italics

For each of the uses listed below, italic type is used in keyboarded or typeset material (or where it is otherwise available); in typed or handwritten material, underlining is used.

1. Foreign words and phrases that have not been fully adopted into the English language are italicized. The decision whether or not to italicize a word will vary according to context and the audience for which the writing is intended. In general, however, any word that appears in the main A–Z vocabulary section of *Merriam-Webster's Collegiate Dictionary, Tenth Edition* does not need to be italicized.

> These accomplishments will serve as a monument, *aere perennius,* to the group's skill and dedication.
>
> "The cooking here is *wunderbar,*" he said.
>
> After the concert, the crowd headed en masse for the parking lot.
>
> The committee meets on an ad hoc basis.

A complete sentence (such as a motto) can also be italicized. However, passages that consist of more than one sentence, or even a single sentence if it is particularly long, are usually treated as quotations; that is, they are set in roman type and enclosed in quotation marks.

2. Unfamiliar words or words that have a specialized meaning are set in italics, especially when they are accompanied by a short definition. Once these words have been introduced and defined, they do not need to be italicized in subsequent references.

> *Vitiligo* is a condition in which skin pigment cells stop making pigment.
>
> Another method is the *direct-to-consumer* transaction, in which the publisher markets directly to the individual by mail or door-to-door.

3. Latin abbreviations are usually not italicized, although the traditional practice has been to italicize them, and some writers still do so.

et al.   i.e.

cf.   viz.

e.g.

4. Italic type is used to indicate words referred to as words, letters referred to as letters, or numerals referred to as numerals. However, if the word referred to as a word was actually spoken, it is often enclosed in quotation marks. If the letter is being used to refer to its sound and not its printed form, slashes or brackets can be used instead of italics. And if there is no chance of confusion, numerals referred to as numerals are often not italicized. (For plurals of words, letters, and numerals referred to as such, see paragraphs 17–19 and 23–25 on pages 104–6.)

> The panel could not decide whether *data* was a singular or plural noun.
>
> *Only* can be an adverb, as in the case of "I *only* tried to help."
>
> We heard his warning, but we weren't sure what "other repercussions" meant in that context.
>
> You should dot your *i*'s and cross your *t*'s.
>
> He was still having trouble with the /p/ sound.
>
> The first *2* and the last *1* are barely legible.

A letter used to indicate a shape is capitalized but not set in italics (for examples, see paragraph 4 on page 94).

5. Individual letters are sometimes set in italic type to provide additional typographical contrast. This use of italics is common when letters are used in enumerations within sentences or when they are used to identify elements in an illustration.

> providing information about *(a)* typing, *(b)* transcribing, *(c)* formatting, and *(d)* graphics
>
> located at point *A* on the diagram

6. Italics are used to indicate a word created to suggest a sound.

> We sat listening to the *chat-chat-chat* of the sonar.

7. Italics are used to emphasize or draw attention to a word or words in a sentence.

> Students must notify the dean's office *in writing* of all courses added to or dropped from their original list.

> She had become *the* hero, the one everyone else looked up to.

Italics serve to draw attention to words in large part because they are used so infrequently. The overuse of italics may cause them to lose their effectiveness.

Chapter 3

Plurals, Possessives, and Compounds

This chapter describes the ways in which plurals, possessives, and compounds are most commonly formed. For some of the questions treated here, various solutions have been developed over the years but no single solution has come to be universally accepted. In these cases, the range of available solutions is described and you must use your own judgment to choose among them.

In regard to plurals, consulting a good dictionary will solve many of the problems that are discussed in this chapter. The best dictionary to consult is an unabridged dictionary, such as *Webster's Third New International Dictionary*. The next best is a good college dictionary, such as *Merriam-Webster's Collegiate Dictionary, Tenth Edition*. Any dictionary that is much smaller than the *Collegiate* will often be more frustrating in what it fails to show than helpful in what it shows.

In giving examples of plurals, possessives, and compounds, this chapter uses both *or* and *also* to separate variant forms of the same word. The word *or* is used when both forms of the word are used with approximately equal frequency in standard writing; the first form is probably slightly more common than the second. The word *also* is used when the first form of the word is much more common than the second.

Plurals

The plurals of most English words are formed by adding *-s* to the singular. If the noun ends in *-s, -x, -z, -ch,* or *-sh,* so that an extra syllable must be added in order to pronounce the plural, *-es* is added to the singular. If the noun ends in a *-y* preceded by a consonant, the *-y* is changed to *-i-* and *-es* is added.

However, many English nouns do not follow this general pattern. Most good dictionaries give thorough coverage to irregular and variant plurals, so they are often the best place to start to answer questions about the plural form of a specific word. The paragraphs that follow describe how plurals are formed for a number of categories of words whose plural forms are most apt to raise questions. The symbol → is used here to link the singular and plural forms.

Abbreviations

1. The plurals of abbreviations are commonly formed by adding *-s* or an apostrophe plus *-s;* however, there are some significant exceptions. (For more on forming plurals of abbreviations, see paragraphs 1–5 on pages 135–36.)

    COLA → COLAs   Ph.D. → Ph.D.'s
    f.o.b. → f.o.b.'s   bldg. → bldgs.
    CPU → CPUs   p. → pp.

Animals

2. The names of many fishes, birds, and mammals have both a plural formed with a suffix and one

that is identical with the singular. Some have only one or the other.

> flounder → flounder   *or*   flounders
> quail → quail   *or*   quails
> mink → mink   *or*   minks
> caribou → caribou   *or*   caribous
> rat → rats
> monkey → monkeys
> moose → moose

3. Many of the animals that have both plural forms are ones that are hunted, fished, or trapped; those who hunt, fish for, and trap them are most likely to use the unchanged form. The -*s* form is often used to emphasize diversity of kinds.

> caught four trout
> *but*
> trouts of the Rocky Mountains
> a place where fish gather
> *but*
> the fishes of the Pacific Ocean

Compounds and Phrases

4. Most compounds made up of two nouns— whether they appear as one word, two words, or a hyphenated word—form their plurals by pluralizing the final element only.

> matchbox → matchboxes
> judge advocate → judge advocates
> city-state → city-states
> crow's-foot → crow's-feet

5. The plural form of a compound consisting of an -*er* noun and an adverb is made by pluralizing the noun element only.

> hanger-on → hangers-on

onlooker → onlookers
looker-on → lookers-on
passerby → passersby

6. Nouns made up of words that are not nouns form their plurals on the last element.

also-ran → also-rans
put-down → put-downs
changeover → changeovers
ne'er-do-well → ne'er-do-wells
set-to → set-tos
blowup → blowups

7. Plurals of compounds that are phrases consisting of two nouns separated by a preposition are regularly formed by pluralizing the first noun.

aide-de-camp → aides-de-camp
attorney-at-law → attorneys-at-law
power of attorney → powers of attorney
base on balls → bases on balls
man-of-war → men-of-war
coup d'état → coups d'état

8. Compounds that are phrases consisting of two nouns separated by a preposition and a modifier form their plurals in various ways.

flash in the pan → flashes in the pan
jack-in-the-box → jack-in-the-boxes *or* jacks-in-the-box
jack-of-all-trades → jacks-of-all-trades
stick-in-the-mud → stick-in-the-muds

9. Compounds consisting of a noun followed by an adjective are usually pluralized by adding -s or -es to the noun.

cousin-german → cousins-german

heir apparent → heirs apparent
knight-errant → knights-errant

If the adjective in such a compound tends to be construed as a noun, the compound may have more than one plural form.

attorney general → attorneys general *or* attorney generals
sergeant major → sergeants major *or* sergeant majors
poet laureate → poets laureate *or* poet laureates

Foreign Words and Phrases

10. Many nouns of foreign origin retain the foreign plural. However, most of them also have a regular English plural.

alumnus → alumni
beau → beaux *or* beaus
crisis → crises
index → indexes *or* indices
phenomenon → phenomena *or* phenomenons
schema → schemata *also* schemas
series → series
tempo → tempi *or* tempos

A foreign plural may not be used for all senses of a word, or may be more commonly used for some senses than for others.

antenna (on an insect) → antennae
antenna (on a radio) → antennas

11. Phrases of foreign origin may have a foreign plural, an English plural, or both.

carte blanche → cartes blanches
hors d'oeuvre → hors d'oeuvres
beau monde → beau mondes *or* beaux mondes

Words Ending in -*ful*

12. A plural -*fuls* can be used for any noun ending in -*ful*, but some of these nouns also have an alternative plural with -*s*- preceding the suffix.

> eyeful → eyefuls
> bucketful → bucketfuls *or* bucketsful
> cupful → cupfuls *also* cupsful

Irregular Plurals

13. A small group of English nouns form their plurals by changing one or more of their vowels.

> foot → feet
> goose → geese
> louse → lice
> man → men
>
> mouse → mice
> woman → women
> tooth → teeth

14. A few nouns have -*en* or -*ren* plurals.

> ox → oxen
> child → children
> brother → brethren

15. Some nouns ending in -*f*, -*fe*, and -*ff* have plurals that end in -*ves*. Some of these also have regularly formed plurals.

> elf → elves
> knife → knives
> life → lives
> beef → beefs *or* beeves
> staff → staffs *or* staves
> wharf → wharves *also* wharfs

Italic Elements

16. Italicized words, phrases, abbreviations, and letters may be pluralized with either an italic or, more commonly, a roman *s*. If the plural is

formed with an apostrophe and an -s, the -s is almost always roman.

> fifteen *Newsweek*s on the shelf
> answered with a series of *uh-huh*s
> a row of *x*'s

Letters

17. The plurals of letters are usually formed by adding an apostrophe and an -s, although capital letters are sometimes pluralized by adding an -s alone.

> p's and q's
> V's of geese flying overhead
> dot your *i*'s
> straight As

Numbers

18. Numerals are pluralized by adding an -s or, less commonly, an apostrophe and an -s.

> two par 5s   *or*   two par 5's
> 1970s   *or*   1970's
> in the 80s   *or*   in the 80's
> the mid-$20,000s   *or*   the mid-$20,000's

19. Spelled-out numbers are usually pluralized without an apostrophe.

> in twos and threes
> scored two sixes

Words Ending in -o

20. Most words ending in -o are pluralized by adding an -s. However, some words ending in -o preceded by a consonant take -es plurals, and some may take either *-s* or *-es*. When in doubt, consult a dictionary.

alto → altos
echo → echoes *also* echos
motto → mottoes *also* mottos

Proper Nouns

21. The plurals of proper nouns are usually formed with *-s* or *-es*.

Bruce → Bruces
Hastings → Hastingses
Velázquez → Velázquezes

22. Proper nouns ending in *-y* usually retain the *-y* and add *-s*.

February → Februarys
Marys → Marys
Mercury → Mercurys
but
Ptolemy → Ptolemies
Sicily → The Two Sicilies
The Rockies

Words that were originally proper nouns and that end in *-y* are usually pluralized by changing *-y* to *-i* and adding *-es*, but a few retain the *-y*.

bobby → bobbies
Jerry → Jerries
johnny → johnnies
Tommy → Tommies
Bloody Mary → Bloody Marys

Quoted Elements

23. Practice varies regarding the plural form of words in quotation marks. Some writers form the plural by adding an -*s* or an apostrophe plus -*s* within the quotation marks. Others add an -*s* outside the quotation marks. Both arrangements look awkward, and writers generally try to avoid this construction.

> too many "probably's" in the statement
> one "you" among millions of "you"s
> a response characterized by its "yes, but"s

Symbols

24. Symbols are not usually pluralized except when being referred to as characters in themselves, without regard to meaning. The plural is formed by adding an -*s* or an apostrophe plus -*s*.

> used &'s instead of *and*'s
> his π's are hard to read
> printed three *s

Words Used as Words

25. Words used as words without regard to meaning usually form their plurals by adding an apostrophe and a roman -*s*.

> five *and*'s in one sentence
> all those *wherefore*'s and *howsoever*'s

When a word used as a word has become part of a fixed phrase, the plural is usually formed by adding a roman -*s* without the apostrophe.

> oohs and aahs
> dos and don'ts   *or*   do's and don't's

Possessives

The possessive case of most nouns is formed by adding an apostrophe or an apostrophe plus -*s* to the end of the word.

Common Nouns

1. The possessive case of singular and plural common nouns that do not end in an *s* or *z* sound is formed by adding an apostrophe plus *-s* to the end of the word.

> the boy's mother   children's books
> men's clothing   the potato's skin
> her dog's leash   the symposia's themes

2. The possessive case of singular nouns ending in an *s* or *z* sound is usually formed by adding an apostrophe plus *-s* to the end of the word. An alternative approach, although one less widely accepted, is to add an apostrophe plus *-s* to the word only when the added *-s* is easily pronounced; if adding the *-s* is felt to create a word that is difficult to pronounce, only an apostrophe is added.

> the press's books
> the boss's desk
> the index's arrangement
> the horse's saddle
> the princess's duties   *also*   the princess' duties

Even those who follow the pattern of adding an apostrophe plus *-s* to all singular nouns will often make an exception for a multisyllabic word that ends in an *s* or *z* sound if it is followed by a word beginning with an *s* or *z* sound.

> for convenience' sake
> for conscience' sake

3. The possessive case of plural nouns ending in an *s* or *z* sound is formed by adding only an apostrophe to the end of the word. One exception to this rule is that the possessive case of one-syllable irregular plurals is usually formed by adding an apostrophe plus -*s*.

horses' stalls
geese's calls
consumers' confidence
mice's habits

Proper Names

4. The possessive forms of proper names are generally made in the same way as they are for common nouns. The possessive form of singular proper names not ending in an *s* or *z* sound is made by adding an apostrophe plus -*s* to the name. The possessive form of plural proper names is made by adding just an apostrophe.

Mrs. Wilson's store
the Wattses' daughter
Utah's capital
the Cohens' house
Canada's rivers
Niagara Falls' location

5. As is the case for the possessive form of singular common nouns (see paragraph 2 above), the possessive form of singular proper names ending in an *s* or *z* sound may be formed either by adding an apostrophe plus -*s* or by adding just an apostrophe to the name. For the sake of consistency, most writers choose one pattern for forming the possessive of all singular names ending in an *s* or *z* sound, regardless of the pronunciation of individual names (for exceptions see paragraphs 6 and 7 below). Adding an apostrophe plus -*s* to all such names is more common than adding just the apostrophe.

Jones's car *also* Jones' car

Bliss's statue *also* Bliss' statue
Dickens's novels *also* Dickens' novels

6. The possessive form of classical and biblical names of two or more syllables ending in *-s* or *-es* is usually made by adding an apostrophe without an *-s*. If the name has only one syllable, the possessive form is made by adding an apostrophe and an *-s*.

Aristophanes' plays   Judas' betrayal
Achilles' heel   Zeus's anger
Odysseus' journey   Mars's help

7. The possessive forms of the names *Jesus* and *Moses* are always formed with just an apostrophe.

Jesus' time
Moses' law

8. The possessive forms of names ending in a silent *-s*, *-z*, or *-x* usually include the apostrophe and the *-s*.

Arkansas's capital
Camus's *The Stranger*
Josquin des Prez's music
Delacroix's painting

9. When the possessive ending is added to a name that is in italics, it is usually not italicized.

the U.S.S. *Constitution*'s cannons
Gone with the Wind's ending
the *Mona Lisa*'s somber hues
High Noon's plot

Pronouns

10. The possessive case of indefinite pronouns such as *anyone*, *everybody*, and *someone* is formed by adding an apostrophe and an *-s*.

anyone's	someone's
everybody's	somebody's

Some indefinite pronouns usually require an *of* phrase to indicate possession.

> the rights of each
> the inclination of many
> the satisfaction of all

11. Possessive pronouns do not include apostrophes.

mine	hers
ours	his
yours	theirs
its	

Phrases

12. The possessive form of a phrase is made by adding an apostrophe or an apostrophe plus -*s* to the last word in the phrase.

> board of directors' meeting
> his brother-in-law's sidecar
> from the student of politics' point of view
> after a moment or so's thought

Constructions such as these can become awkward, and it is often better to rephrase the sentence to eliminate the need for the possessive ending. For instance, the last two examples above could be rephrased as follows:

> from the point of view of the student of politics
> after thinking for a moment or so

Words in Quotation Marks

13. The possessive form of words in quotation marks can be formed in two ways, with the apostrophe plus -*s* placed either inside the quotation marks or outside them. Both arrangements look awkward, and this construction is best avoided.

> the "Today Show" 's cohosts
> the "Grande Dame's" escort
> *but more commonly*
> the cohosts of the "Today Show"
> escort to the "Grande Dame"

Abbreviations

14. Possessives of abbreviations are formed like those of nouns that are spelled out. The singular possessive is formed by adding an apostrophe plus -*s* to the abbreviation; the plural possessive, by adding an apostrophe only.

> the AMA's executive committee
> Itek Corp.'s Applied Technology Division
> the MPs' decisions

Numerals

15. The possessive form of nouns composed of numerals is made in the same way as for other nouns. The possessive of singular nouns is formed by adding an apostrophe plus -*s*; the possessive form of plural nouns is formed by adding an apostrophe only.

> 1995's most popular model
> the 1980s' most colorful figure

Individual and Joint Possession

16. Individual possession is indicated by adding an apostrophe plus -*s* to each noun in a sequence. Joint possession is most commonly indicated by adding an apostrophe or an apostrophe plus -*s* to the last noun in the sequence, but may also be

indicated by adding a possessive ending to each
name.

Kepler's and Clark's respective clients
John's, Bill's, and Larry's boats
Bissell and Hansen's law firm
Christine and James's vacation home
   or   Christine's and James's vacation home

Compounds

A compound is a word or word group that consists of
two or more parts that work together as a unit to express a specific concept. Compounds can be formed
by combining two or more words (as in *eye shadow,
graphic equalizer, farmhouse, cost-effective, blue-pencil,
around-the-clock,* or *son of a gun*), by combining prefixes or suffixes with words (as in *ex-president, shoeless,
presorted, uninterruptedly,* or *meaningless*), or by combining two or more word elements (as in *supermicro*
or *photomicrograph*). Compounds are written in one
of three ways: solid (as in *cottonmouth*), hyphenated
(*player-manager*), or open (*field day*).

Permanent compounds are compounds that are so
commonly used that they have become permanent
parts of the language; many of them are entered in
dictionaries. *Temporary compounds* are those created to
fit a writer's need at a particular moment (such as
quasi government); thus, they cannot be found in dictionaries. *Self-evident compounds* are compounds that
are readily understood from the meanings of the
words that make them up (such as *baseball game* or *economic policy*). Most self-evident compounds are not entered in dictionaries. Writers thus cannot rely wholly
on dictionaries to guide them in writing compounds,
but must develop an approach for dealing with those
that are not in the dictionary.

One approach is simply to leave open any compound that is not in the dictionary. Many writers do this, but there are drawbacks to this approach. A temporary compound may not be easily recognized as a compound when it is left open. For instance, if you need to use *wide body* as a term for a kind of jet airplane, a phrase like "the operation of wide bodies" may catch the reader unawares. And if you use the open style for a compound modifier, you may create momentary confusion (or even unintended amusement) with a phrase like "the operation of wide body jets."

Another possibility is to hyphenate all compounds not in the dictionary. Hyphenation gives your compound immediate recognition as a compound. But hyphenating all such compounds runs counter to some well-established American practice, and might thus call too much attention to the compound and momentarily distract the reader.

A third approach is to pattern your temporary compound after some other similar compound. This approach is likely to be more complicated, and usually will not free you from the need to make your own decisions. But it does have the advantage of making your compound less distracting or confusing by making it look like other more familiar compounds. The paragraphs that follow are aimed at helping you to use this third approach.

The symbol + in the following paragraphs can be interpreted as "followed immediately by."

Compound Nouns

Compound nouns are combinations of words that function in a sentence as nouns. They may consist of two or more nouns, a noun and a modifier, or two or more elements that are not nouns.

1. **noun + noun** Compounds composed of two nouns that are short, commonly used, and pronounced with falling stress—that is, with the most stress on the first noun and less or no stress on the second—are usually written solid.

teapot	birdbath
catfish	handsaw
cottonmouth	handmaiden
sweatband	farmyard

2. When a noun + noun compound is short and common but pronounced with nearly equal stress on both nouns, it is more likely to be open.

bean sprouts	beach buggy
fuel oil	duffel bag

3. Many short noun + noun compounds begin as temporary compounds written open. As they become more familiar and better established, there is a tendency for them to become solid.

data base	*has become*	database
chain saw	*is becoming*	chainsaw
lawn mower	*is becoming*	lawnmower

4. Noun + noun compounds that consist of longer nouns and are self-evident or temporary are usually written open.

wildlife sanctuary
football game
television camera
reunion dinner

5. When the nouns in a noun + noun compound describe a double title or double function, the compound is hyphenated.

city-state	secretary-treasurer

decree-law	player-manager
dinner-dance	author-critic

6. Compounds formed from a noun or adjective followed by *man, woman, person,* or *people* and denoting an occupation are normally solid.

salesman	salesperson
congresswoman	spokesperson
handyman	salespeople

7. Compounds that are units of measurement are hyphenated.

foot-pound	column-inch
kilowatt-hour	light-year

8. **adjective + noun** Most adjective + noun compounds are written open.

automatic weapons	minor seminary
religious freedom	modular arithmetic
pancreatic juice	graphic equalizer

9. Adjective + noun compounds consisting of two short words may be written solid when pronounced with falling stress. However, short adjective + noun compounds are often written open; a few are hyphenated.

shortcut	dry run
longhand	long haul
blueprint	red tape
drywall	yellow jacket
wetland	red-eye

10. **participle + noun** Most participle + noun compounds are written open.

running total
whipped cream

furnished apartment
nagging backache
shredded wheat

11. **noun's + noun** Compounds consisting of a possessive noun followed by another noun are usually written hyphenated or open.

crow's-feet	hornet's nest
cat's-paw	lion's share
cat's cradle	fool's gold

Compounds of this type that have become solid have lost the apostrophe.

foolscap
menswear
sheepshead

12. **noun + verb + -er; noun + verb + -ing** Temporary or self-evident compounds in which the first noun is the object of the verb to which the suffix has been added are most often written open. However, a hyphen may be used to make the relationships of the words immediately apparent. Permanent compounds like these are sometimes written solid as well.

temporary or self-evident:	opinion seeker	cost-cutter
	career planning	risk-taking
permanent:	data processing	bookkeeper
	bird-watcher	lifesaver
	fund-raising	copyediting

13. **object + verb** Noun compounds consisting of a verb preceded by a noun that is its object are written in various ways.

clambake	face-lift
car wash	turkey shoot

14. **verb + object** A few, mostly older compounds are formed from a verb followed by a noun that is its object; they are written solid.

tosspot	carryall
cutthroat	pinchpenny
breakwater	pickpocket

15. **noun + adjective** Compounds composed of a noun followed by an adjective are written open or hyphenated.

battle royal	heir apparent
sum total	president-elect
consul general	secretary-general

16. **particle + noun** Compounds consisting of a particle (usually a preposition or adverb) and a noun are usually written solid, especially when they are short and pronounced with falling stress.

downpour	undershirt
output	outpatient
offshoot	aftershock
inpatient	upkeep

A few particle + noun compounds, especially when composed of longer elements or having equal stress on both elements, may be hyphenated or open.

off-season	off year
cross-fertilization	down payment

17. **verb + particle; verb + adverb** These compounds may be hyphenated or solid. Compounds with two-letter particles (*by, to, in, up, on*) are usually hyphenated, since the hyphen aids quick comprehension. Compounds with three-letter particles (*off, out*) are hyphenated or solid with about equal

frequency. Those with longer particles or adverbs are more often solid.

flyby	turnoff
set-to	shoot-out
sit-in	dropout
letup	breakthrough
run-on	giveaway
show-off	gadabout

18. **verb + -*er* + particle; verb + -*ing* + particle** Except for *passerby,* these compounds are hyphenated.

hanger-on	talking-to
runner-up	falling-out
looker-on	goings-on

19. **Compounds of three or four elements** Compounds of three or four elements may be either hyphenated or open. Those consisting of noun + prepositional phrase are generally open, although some are hyphenated. Those formed from other combinations are usually hyphenated.

base on balls	jack-of-all-trades
lily of the valley	know-it-all
justice of the peace	pick-me-up

20. **letter + noun** Compounds formed from a single letter (or sometimes a combination of them) followed by a noun are either open or hyphenated.

A-frame	Rh factor
C ration	T-shirt
D day	T square
H-bomb	H and L hinge

Compounds That Function as Adjectives

Compound adjectives are combinations of words that work together to modify a noun—that is, they work as *unit modifiers*. As unit modifiers they should be distinguished from other strings of adjectives that may also precede a noun.

For instance, in "a low, level tract of land" or "that long, lonesome road" the two adjectives each modify the noun separately. We are talking about a tract of land that is both low and level and about a road that is both long and lonesome. These are *coordinate modifiers*.

In "a low monthly fee" or "suggested retail price" the first adjective modifies the noun plus the second adjective. In other words, we mean a monthly fee that is low and the retail price that has been suggested. These are *noncoordinate modifiers*.

But in "low-level radiation" we do not mean radiation that is low and level or level radiation that is low; we mean radiation that is at a low level. Both words work as a unit to modify the noun. Unit modifiers are usually hyphenated. The hyphens not only make it easier for the readers to grasp the relationship of the words but also avoid confusion. The hyphen in "a call for more-specialized controls" removes any ambiguity as to which word *more* modifies. By contrast, the lack of a hyphen in a phrase like "graphic arts exhibition" may give it an undesirable ambiguity.

21. **Before the noun (attributive position)** Most two-word permanent or temporary compound adjectives are hyphenated when placed before the noun.

> tree-lined streets
> well-intended advice
> a trumped-up charge
> fast-acting medication
> an input-output device
> a risk-free investment

22. Temporary or self-evident compounds formed of an adverb (such as *well, more, less, still*) followed by a participle (or sometimes an adjective) are usually hyphenated when placed before a noun.

> a well-funded project
> more-specialized controls
> a still-growing company
> these fast-moving times
> a just-completed survey
> a now-vulnerable politician

23. Compounds formed from an adverb ending in *-ly* followed by a participle may sometimes be hyphenated but are more commonly open, because adverb + adjective + noun is a normal word order.

> a widely-read feature
> internationally-known authors
> *but more often*
> a widely read feature
> internationally known authors

24. The combination of *very* + adjective is not a unit modifier.

> a very satisfied smile

25. Many compound adjectives are formed by using a compound noun—either permanent or temporary—to modify another noun. If the compound noun is an open compound, it is usually hyphenated to make the relationship of the words more immediately apparent.

> the farm-bloc vote
> a tax-law case
> a picture-framing shop
> a secret-compartment ring
> ocean-floor hydrophones

26. Some open compound nouns are so recognizable that they are frequently placed before a noun without a hyphen.

> a high school diploma *or* a high-school diploma
> a data processing course *or* a data-processing course
> a dry goods store *or* a dry-goods store

27. A proper name placed before a noun to modify it is not hyphenated.

> a Thames River marina
> a Korean War veteran
> a Huck Finn life
> a General Motors car

28. Compound adjectives of three or more words are hyphenated when they precede the noun. Many temporary compounds are formed by hyphenating a phrase and placing it before a noun.

> spur-of-the-moment decisions
> higher-than-anticipated costs

29. Compound adjectives composed of foreign words are not hyphenated when placed before a noun unless they are hyphenated in the foreign language itself.

> the per capita cost
> a cordon bleu restaurant
> an a priori argument
> a ci-devant professor

30. Chemical names used as modifiers before a noun are not hyphenated.

> a sodium hypochlorite bleach
> a citric acid solution

31. **Following the noun (as a complement or predicate adjective)**   When the words that make up a compound adjective follow the noun they modify, they tend to fall in normal word order and are no longer unit modifiers. They are therefore no longer hyphenated.

> arrested on charges that had been trumped up
> decisions made on the spur of the moment
> They were ill prepared for the journey.

32. Many permanent and temporary compounds keep their hyphens after the noun in a sentence if they continue to function as unit modifiers.

> Your ideas are high-minded but impractical.
> You were just as nice-looking then.
> metals that are corrosion-resistant
> tends to be accident-prone

33. Permanent compound adjectives are usually written as they appear in the dictionary, whether they precede or follow the noun they modify.

> The group was public-spirited.
> The problems are mind-boggling.
> is well-read in economics

34. Compound adjectives of three or more words are normally not hyphenated when they follow the noun they modify.

> These remarks are off the record.

35. Permanent compounds of three or more words may appear as hyphenated adjectives in dictionaries. In such cases the hyphens are retained as long as the phrase is being used as a unit modifier.

    the plan is still pay-as-you-go
      but a plan in which you pay as you go

36. It is possible that a permanent hyphenated adjective may appear alongside a temporary compound in a position where it would normally be open (such as "one who is both ill-humored and ill prepared"). In such cases, it is best to either hyphenate both compounds or leave both open.

37. When an adverb modifies another adverb that is the first element of a compound modifier, the compound may lose its hyphen. If the first adverb modifies the whole compound, however, the hyphen should be retained.

    a very well developed idea
    a delightfully well-written book
    a most ill-humored remark

38. Adjective compounds that are names of colors may be written open or hyphenated. Color names in which each element can function as a noun (such as *blue green* or *chrome yellow*) are almost always hyphenated when they precede a noun; they are sometimes open when they follow the noun. Color names in which the first element can only be an adjective are often not hyphenated before a noun and usually not hyphenated after.

    blue-gray paint
    paint that is blue-gray *also* paint that is blue gray
    bluish gray paint *or* bluish-gray paint

39. Compound modifiers that include a number followed by a noun are hyphenated when they precede the noun they modify. When the modifier follows the noun, it is usually not hyphenated.

    five-card stud

> 10-foot pole
> 12-year-old girl
> a child who is seven years old
> an 18-inch rule   *but*   a 10 percent raise

40. An adjective that is composed of a number followed by a noun in the possessive is not hyphenated.

> a two weeks' wait
> a nine days' wonder

Compounds That Function as Adverbs

41. Adverb compounds consisting of preposition + noun are almost always written solid. However, there are a few important exceptions.

> downtown
> upstairs
> onstage
> offhand
>   *but*
> in-house
> off-line
> on-line

42. Compound adverbs of more than two words are usually written open, and they usually follow the words they modify.

> every which way   hook, line, and sinker
> little by little   off and on
> high and dry   over and over

43. A few three-word adverbs are spelled like hyphenated adjectives and are therefore written with hyphens. But many adverbs are written open even if the adjective is hyphenated.

    back-to-back (adverb or adjective)
    face-to-face (adverb or adjective)
        but
    hand-to-hand combat
    fought hand to hand
    off-the-cuff remarks
    spoke off the cuff

Compound Verbs

44. Two-word verbs consisting of a verb followed by
an adverb or a preposition are written open.

get together	strike out
break through	run across
run around	put down
run wild	print out

45. A compound composed of a particle followed by
a verb is written solid.

upgrade	overcome
outflank	bypass

46. A verb derived from an open or hyphenated
compound noun is hyphenated.

blue-pencil	tap-dance
sweet-talk	poor-mouth
double-check	water-ski

47. A verb derived from a solid noun is written solid.

    bankroll
    roughhouse
    mainstream

Compounds Formed with Word Elements

Many new and temporary compounds are formed by
adding word elements to existing words or by com-

bining word elements. There are three basic word elements: prefixes (such as *anti-*, *re-*, *non-*, *super-*), suffixes (such as *-er*, *-ly*, *-ness*, *-ism*), and combining forms (such as *mini-*, *macro-*, *pseud-*, *ortho-*, *-ped*, *-graphy*, *-gamic*, *-plasty*). Prefixes and suffixes are usually attached to existing words; combining forms are usually combined to form new words.

48. prefix + word Except as specified in the paragraphs below, compounds formed from a prefix and a word are usually written solid.

precondition	suborder
interagency	overfond
refurnish	postwar
misshapen	unhelpful

49. If the prefix ends with a vowel and the word it is attached to begins with the same vowel, the compound is usually hyphenated.

anti-inflation
co-owner
de-emphasize

However, there are many exceptions.

cooperate
reentry
preempt

50. If the base word to which a prefix is added is capitalized, the compound is hyphenated.

anti-American	pre-Columbian
post-Victorian	inter-Caribbean

The prefix is usually not capitalized in such compounds. But if the prefix and the base word together form a new proper name, the compound may be solid with the prefix capitalized.

Postimpressionist
Precambrian

51. Compounds made with *self-* and *ex-* meaning "former" are hyphenated.

self-pity
ex-wife

52. If a prefix is added to a hyphenated compound, it may be either followed by a hyphen or closed up solid to the next element. Permanent compounds of this kind should be checked in a dictionary.

unair-conditioned   non-self-governing
ultra-up-to-date   unself-conscious

53. In typewritten and keyboarded material, if a prefix is added to an open compound, the prefix is followed by a hyphen. In typeset material, this hyphen is often represented by an en dash. (For more on this use of the en dash, see paragraph 13 on page 33.)

ex–Boy Scout
post–coup d'état

54. A compound that would be identical with another word if written solid is usually hyphenated to prevent misreading.

a multi-ply fabric
re-collect the money
un-ionized particles

55. A compound that might otherwise be solid may be hyphenated if it could be momentarily puzzling.

coed *or* co-ed
coworker *or* co-worker

overreact   *or*   over-react
interrow   *or*   inter-row

56. Temporary compounds formed from *vice-* are usually hypenated; however, some permanent compounds (such as *vice president* and *vice admiral*) are open.

57. When prefixes are attached to numerals, the compounds are hyphenated.

pre-1982 expenses
post-1975 vintages
non-20th-century ideas

58. Compounds created from combining forms like *Anglo-*, *Judeo-*, or *Sino-* are hyphenated when the second element is an independent word. They are written solid when it is a combining form.

Judeo-Christian   Anglophobe
Austro-Hungarian   Francophone
Sino-Soviet   Italophile

59. Prefixes that are repeated in the same compound are separated by a hyphen.

sub-subheading

60. Some prefixes and initial combining forms have related independent adjectives or adverbs that may be used where the prefix might be expected. A temporary compound with *quasi(-)* or *pseudo(-)* therefore may be written open as modifier + noun, or hyphenated as combining form + noun.

quasi intellectual   *or*   quasi-intellectual
pseudo liberal   *or*   pseudo-liberal

In some cases (such as *super, super-*), the independent modifier may not have quite the same meaning as the prefix.

61. Compounds consisting of different prefixes with the same base word and joined by *and* or *or* are shortened by pruning the first compound back to a hyphenated prefix, followed by a space.

> pre- and postoperative care
> anti- or pro-Revolutionary sympathies.

62. word + suffix Except as noted in the paragraphs below, compounds formed by adding a suffix to a word are written solid.

> Darwinist   landscaper
> fortyish   powerlessness

63. Permanent or temporary compounds formed with a suffix are hyphenated if the addition of the suffix would create a sequence of three identical letters.

> bell-like
> will-less
> a coffee-er coffee

64. Temporary compounds made with a suffix are often hyphenated if the base word is more than two syllables long, if the base word ends with the same letter the suffix begins with, or if the suffix creates a confusing sequence of letters.

> industry-wide   tunnel-like
> umbrella-like   jaw-wards
> American-ness   battle-worthy

65. Compounds made from a number + *odd* are hyphenated whether the number is spelled out or in numerals; a number + *-fold* is solid if the number is spelled out but hyphenated if it is in numerals.

> 20-odd   twenty-odd
> 12-fold   twelvefold

66. Most compounds formed from an open or hyphenated compound + a suffix do not separate the suffix by a hyphen. But such suffixes as *-like*, *-wide*, *-worthy*, and *-proof*, all of which exist as independent adjectives, are attached by a hyphen.

> good-humoredness
> dollar-a-yearism
> do-it-yourselfer
> a United Nations-like agency

Open compounds often become hyphenated when a suffix is added unless they are proper nouns.

> middle age *but* middle-ager
> tough guy *but* tough-guyese
> New Englandism
> Wall Streeter

67. combining form + combining form Many new terms in technical fields are created by adding combining form to combining form or combining form to a word or word part. Such compounds are generally intended to be permanent, even though many never get into the dictionary. They are normally written solid.

> macrographic
> pseudoserial

Miscellaneous Styling Conventions

68. Compounds that would otherwise be written solid according to the principles described above may be written open or hyphenated to avoid ambiguity, to ensure rapid comprehension, or to make the pronunciation clearer.

> re-utter   tri-city
> bi-level   un-iced
> umbrella-like   meat-ax *or* meat ax

69. When typographical features such as capitals or italics make word relationships in a sentence clear, it is not necessary to hyphenate an open compound.

> his America First sign
> a *Chicago Tribune* story
> an "eyes only" memo

70. Publications (such as technical journals) aimed at a specialized readership likely to recognize the elements of a compound tend to use open and solid stylings more frequently than general publications do.

> electrooculogram
> radiofrequency
> rapid eye movement

71. Words that are formed by reduplication and so consist of two similar-sounding elements (such as *hush-hush*, *razzle-dazzle*, or *hugger-mugger*) present styling questions like those of compounds. Words like these are hyphenated if each of the elements is made up of more than one syllable. If each element has only one syllable, the words are often written solid. However, for very short words (such as *no-no*, *go-go*, and *so-so*), words in which both elements may have primary stress (such as *tip-top* and *sci-fi*), and words coined in the twentieth century (such as *ack-ack* and *hush-hush*), the hyphenated styling is more common.

> goody-goody   peewee
> teeter-totter   knickknack
> topsy-turvy   singsong
> crisscross   boo-boo

Chapter 4

Abbreviations

Abbreviations are used for a variety of reasons: to save space, to avoid repetition of long words and phrases, to save time, or simply to conform to conventional usage.

Unfortunately, the contemporary styling of abbreviations is inconsistent and arbitrary. No set of rules can hope to cover all the possible variations, exceptions, and peculiarities encountered in print. The styling of abbreviations—capitalized vs. lowercased, closed-up vs. spaced, punctuated vs. unpunctuated—depends most often on a writer's preference or an organization's policy.

All is not complete confusion, however. Some abbreviations (such as *e.g., etc., i.e., No.,* and *viz.*) are almost always punctuated, while others that are pronounced as words (such as *NATO, NASA, NOW, OPEC,* and *SALT*) tend to be all-capitalized and unpunctuated. Punctuated abbreviations are always closed up except when each abbreviated word has two or more letters (as in *lt. gov.* and *rec. sec.*). Styling problems can be dealt with by consulting a good general dictionary such as *Merriam-Webster's Collegiate*

Dictionary, Tenth Edition, especially for capitalization guidance, and by following the guidelines of one's own organization. An abbreviations dictionary such as *Webster's Guide to Abbreviations* may also be helpful.

Punctuation

The paragraphs that follow provide a few broad principles that apply to abbreviations in general. However, there are many specific situations in which these principles will not apply. The section on Specific Styling Conventions, beginning on page 137, contains information on these situations and on particular kinds of abbreviations.

1. A period follows most abbreviations that are formed by omitting all but the first few letters of a word.

> bull. [for *bulletin*]
> bro. [for *brother*]
> fig. [for *figure*]
> Fr. [for *French*]

2. A period follows most abbreviations that are formed by omitting letters from the middle of a word.

> secy. [for *secretary*]
> mfg. [for *manufacturing*]
> agcy. [for *agency*]
> Mr. [for *Mister*]

3. Punctuation is usually omitted from abbreviations that are made up of initial letters of words that constitute a phrase or compound word. However, for some of these abbreviations, espe-

cially ones that are not capitalized, the punctuation is retained.

> GNP [for *gross national product*]
> EFT [for *electronic funds transfer*]
> PC [for *personal computer*]
> f.o.b. [for *free on board*]

4. Terms in which a suffix is added to a numeral, such as *1st, 2nd, 3d, 8vo,* and *12mo,* are not abbreviations and do not require a period.

5. Isolated letters of the alphabet used to designate a shape or position in a sequence are not abbreviations and are not punctuated.

> T square I beam
> A 1 V sign

6. Some abbreviations are punctuated with one or more slashes in place of periods.

> c/o [for *care of*]
> d/b/a [for *doing business as*]
> w/o [for *without*]
> w/w [for *wall to wall*]

Capitalization

1. Abbreviations are capitalized if the words they represent are proper nouns or adjectives.

> F [for *Fahrenheit*]
> NBC [for *National Broadcasting Company*]
> Nov. [for *November*]
> Brit. [for *British*]

2. Abbreviations are usually all-capitalized when they represent single letters of words that are

normally lowercased. There are, however, some very common abbreviations formed in this way that are not capitalized.

> TM [for *trademark*]
> ETA [for *estimated time of arrival*]
> CATV [for *community antenna television*]
> EEG [for *electroencephalogram*]
> FY [for *fiscal year*]
> a.k.a. [for *also known as*]
> d/b/a [for *doing business as*]

3. Most acronyms that are pronounced as words, rather than as a series of letters, are capitalized. If they have been assimilated into the language as words in their own right, however, they are most often lowercased.

> OPEC   quasar
> NATO   laser
> MIRV   sonar
> NOW account   scuba

Plurals, Possessives, and Compounds

1. Punctuated abbreviations of single words are pluralized by adding -*s* before the period.

> bldgs.   figs.
> bros.   mts.

2. Punctuated abbreviations that stand for phrases or compounds are pluralized by adding -*'s* after the last period.

> Ph.D.'s   J.P.'s
> f.o.b.'s   M.B.A.'s

3. Unpunctuated abbreviations that stand for phrases or compound words are usually pluralized by adding -s to the end of the abbreviation.

   COLAs   PCs
   CPUs   DOSs

4. The plural form of most lowercase single-letter abbreviations is made by repeating the letter. For the plural form of single-letter abbreviations that are abbreviations for units of measure, see paragraph 5 below.

   cc. [for *copies*]
   ll. [for *lines*]
   pp. [for *pages*]
   nn. [for *notes*]
   vv. [for *verses*]
   ff. [for *and the following ones*]

5. The plural form of abbreviations of units of measure is the same as the singular form. (For details on punctuation, see paragraph 48 on page 149.)

   30 sec.   20 min.
   30 d.   50 m
   24 ml   200 bbl.
   24 h.   10 mi.

6. Possessives of abbreviations are formed in the same way as those of spelled-out nouns: the singular possessive is formed by adding -'s, the plural possessive simply by adding an apostrophe.

   the CPU's memory
   Brody Corp.'s earnings
   most CPUs' memories
   Bay Bros.' annual sale

7. Compounds that consist of an abbreviation added to another word are formed in the same way as compounds that consist of spelled-out nouns.

a Kalamazoo, Mich.-based company
an AMA-approved medical school

8. Compounds formed by adding a prefix or suffix to an abbreviation are usually written with a hyphen.

an IBM-like organization
non-DNA molecules
pre-HEW years

Specific Styling Conventions

The following paragraphs, arranged alphabetically, describe practices commonly followed for specific kinds of situations involving abbreviations.

A and An

1. The choice of the article *a* or *an* before abbreviations depends on the sound with which the abbreviation begins. If an abbreviation begins with a consonant sound, *a* is normally used; if an abbreviation begins with a vowel sound, *an* is used. (For more on the use of *a* and *an*, see paragraphs 3–5 on page 200.)

a B.A. degree	an FCC report
a YMCA club	an SAT score
a UN agency	an IRS agent

A.D. and B.C.

2. The abbreviations A.D. and B.C. usually appear in typeset matter as punctuated, unspaced small capitals; in typed material they usually appear as punctuated, unspaced capitals.

3. The abbreviation A.D. usually precedes the date; the abbreviation B.C. follows the date. However, many writers place A.D. after the date as well. In references to whole centuries, A.D. follows the century. (For more details, see paragraph 14 on page 165.)

> A.D. 185   *but also*   185 A.D.
> 41 B.C.
> the fourth century A.D.

Agencies, Associations, and Organizations

4. The names of agencies, associations, and organizations are usually abbreviated after they have been spelled out on their first occurrence in a text. The abbreviations are usually all-capitalized and unpunctuated.

> EPA   NCAA
> SEC   USO
> NAACP   NOW

In contexts where the abbreviation will be recognized, it may be used without having its full form spelled out on its first occurrence.

Beginning a Sentence

5. Most writers avoid beginning a sentence with an abbreviation that is ordinarily not capitalized. Abbreviations that are ordinarily capitalized, on the other hand, are commonly used to begin sentences.

> Page 22 contains ...   *not*   P. 22 contains ...
> Doctor Smith believes ...   *or*   Dr. Smith believes ...
> OSHA regulations require ...

Books of the Bible

6. Books of the Bible are generally spelled out in running text but abbreviated in references to chapter and verse.

The minister based the sermon on Genesis.
In the beginning God created the heavens and the earth.—Gen. 1:1

Company Names

7. The styling of company names varies widely. Many writers avoid abbreviating any part of a company's name unless the abbreviation is part of the official name. However, others routinely abbreviate words such as *Company, Corporation,* and *Incorporated.* Words such as *Airlines, Associates, Fabricators,* and *Manufacturing,* however, are spelled out.

> McGraw-Hill Book Company
> *or* McGraw-Hill Book Co.

An ampersand (&) frequently replaces the word *and* in official company names. For more on this use of the ampersand, see paragraph 1 on page 2.

8. If a company is easily recognizable from its initials, its name is usually spelled out for the first mention and abbreviated in all subsequent references. Some companies have made their initials part of their official name, and in those cases the initials appear in all references.

> General Motors Corp. released its first-quarter earnings figures today. A GM spokesperson said . . .
> MCM Electronics, an Ohio-based company . . .

Compass Points

9. Compass points are abbreviated when occurring after street names; these abbreviations may be punctuated and may be preceded by a comma.

When a compass point precedes the word *Street,
Avenue,* etc., it is usually spelled out in full.

>   2122 Fourteenth Street, NW
>   *or*   2122 Fourteenth Street NW
>   *or*   2122 Fourteenth Street, N.W.
>   192 East 49th Street
>   1282 North Avenue

Contractions

10. Some abbreviations resemble contractions by including an apostrophe in place of omitted letters.
These abbreviations are not punctuated with a
period. (This style of abbreviation is usually
avoided in formal correspondence.)

>   sec'y [for *secretary*]
>   ass'n [for *association*]
>   dep't [for *department*]

Dates

11. The names of days and months should not be abbreviated in running text. The names of months
usually are not abbreviated in datelines of business letters, but they may be abbreviated in government or military correspondence.

>   the December issue of *Scientific American*
>   a meeting held on August 1, 1985
>   *not*   a meeting held on Aug. 1, 1985
>   *business dateline:*   November 1, 1985
>   *military dateline:*   1 Nov 85

Degrees

12. Except for a few academic degrees with highly
recognizable abbreviations (such as *A.B., M.S.,*
and *Ph.D.*), the names of degrees and profes-

sional ratings are spelled out in full when first mentioned. Often the name of the degree is followed by its abbreviation enclosed in parentheses, so that the abbreviation may be used alone later. When a degree or professional rating follows a person's name, it is usually abbreviated.

> Special attention is devoted to the master of arts in teaching (M.A.T.) degree.
> Julia Ramirez, J.D.

13. Like other abbreviations, abbreviations of degrees and professional ratings are often unpunctuated. In general, punctuated abbreviations are more common for academic degrees, and unpunctuated abbreviations are slightly more common for professional ratings, especially if the latter consist of three or more capitalized letters.

Ph.D.	R.Ph.
B.Sc.	CLU
M.B.A.	RDMS

14. The first letter of each element in abbreviations of all degrees and professional ratings is capitalized. Letters other than the first letter are usually not capitalized.

D.Ch.E.	M.F.A.
Litt.D.	D.Th.

Division of Abbreviations

15. Division of abbreviations at the end of lines or between pages should be avoided.

Full Forms

16. When using an abbreviation that may be unfamiliar or confusing to the reader, many writers give

the full form first, followed by the abbreviation in parentheses. In subsequent references, just the abbreviation is used.

first reference: At the American Bar Association (ABA) meeting in June . . .

subsequent reference: At that particular ABA meeting . . .

Geographical Names

17. U.S. Postal Service abbreviations for states, possessions, and Canadian provinces are all-capitalized and unpunctuated, as are Postal Service abbreviations for streets and other geographical features when these abbreviations are used on envelopes addressed for automated mass handling.

regular address style: 1234 Cross Blvd.
Sayville, MN 56789

automated handling: 1234 CROSS BLVD
SAYVILLE, MN 56789

18. Abbreviations of states are often used in running text to identify the location of a city or county. In this context the traditional state abbreviations are usually used, set off with commas. In other situations within running text, the names of states are usually not abbreviated.

John Slade of 15 Chestnut St., Sarasota, Fla., has won . . .

the Louisville, Ky., public library system

Boston, the largest city in Massachusetts, . . .

19. Terms such as *street, road,* and *boulevard* may be either abbreviated or unabbreviated in running text. When they are abbreviated, they are punctuated.

> an accident on Windward Road [*or* Rd.]
> our office at 1234 Cross Blvd. [*or* Boulevard]

20. Names of countries are usually spelled in full in running text. The most common exception is the abbreviation *U.S.* (see paragraph 22 below).

> Great Britain and the U.S. announced the agreement.

21. Abbreviations for the names of most countries are punctuated. Abbreviations for countries whose names include more than one word are often not punctuated if the abbreviations are formed from only the initial letters of the individual words.

> Mex.   Gt. Brit.
> Can.   U.K.   *or*   UK
> Ger.   U.S.   *or*   US
> Scot.

22. *United States* is often abbreviated when used as an adjective. When used as a noun, it is usually spelled out, or it is spelled on its initial use and then abbreviated in subsequent references.

> U.S. Department of Justice
> U.S. foreign policy
> The United States has offered to . . .

23. *Saint* is usually abbreviated when it is part of the name of a geographical or topographical feature. *Mount, Point,* and *Fort* may be either spelled out or abbreviated, according to individual preference. *Saint, Mount,* and *Point* are normally abbreviated when space is at a premium. (For more on the abbreviation of *Saint,* see paragraph 35 below.)

St. Louis, Missouri   Mount McKinley
St. Kitts   Point Pelee
Mount St. Helens   Fort Sumter

Latin Words and Phrases

24. Words and phrases derived from Latin are commonly abbreviated in contexts where readers can be expected to recognize them. They are punctuated, lowercased, and usually not italicized.

etc.   viz.
i.e.   et al.
e.g.   ibid.

Latitude and Longitude

25. Latitude and longitude are abbreviated in tabular data but written out in running text.

in a table: lat. 10°20′N   *or*   lat. 10-20N
in text: from 10°20′ north latitude to 10°30′
                 south latitude

Laws and Bylaws

26. Laws and bylaws are spelled in full when first mentioned; in subsequent references they may be abbreviated.

first reference: Article I, Section 1
subsequent reference: Art. I, Sec. 1

Military Ranks and Units

27. Military ranks are usually given in full when used with a surname only, but are abbreviated when used with a full name.

Colonel Howe
Col. John P. Howe

28. In nonmilitary correspondence, abbreviations for military ranks are often punctuated and set in capital and lowercase letters.

in the military:	BG John T. Dow, USA
	LCDR Mary I. Lee, USN
	Col S. J. Smith, USMC
outside the military:	Brig. Gen. John T. Dow, USA
	Lt. Comdr. Mary I. Lee, USN
	Col. S. J. Smith, USMC

29. Abbreviations for military units are capitalized and unpunctuated.

USA	SAC
USAF	NORAD

Number

30. The word *number,* when used with figures such as *1* or *2* to indicate a rank or rating, is usually abbreviated to *No.*

The No. 1 priority is to promote profitability.

31. The word *number* is usually abbreviated when it is part of a set unit (such as a contract number).

Contract No. N-1234-76-57
Policy No. 123-5-X
Publ. Nos. 12 and 13
Index No. 7855

Personal Names

32. First names are not usually abbreviated.

George S. Patterson   *not*   Geo. S. Patterson

33. Unspaced initials of famous persons are sometimes used in place of their full names. The initials may or may not be punctuated.

FDR   *or*   F.D.R.

34. When initials are used with a surname, they are spaced and punctuated.

> F. D. Roosevelt

Saint

35. The word *Saint* is often abbreviated when used before the name of a saint or when it is the first element of the name of a city or institution named after a saint. However, when it forms part of a surname, it may or may not be abbreviated. Surnames and names of institutions should follow the style used by the person or the institution.

> St. Peter   *or*   Saint Peter
> St. Cloud, Minnesota
> St. John's University
> Augustus Saint-Gaudens
> Louis St. Laurent
> Saint Joseph College

Scientific Terms

36. In binomial nomenclature, a genus name may be abbreviated with its initial letter after the first reference to it is spelled out. The abbreviation is always punctuated.

> *first reference:*   *Escherichia coli*
> *subsequent reference:*   *E. coli*

37. Abbreviations for the names of chemical compounds or mechanical or electronic equipment or processes are usually not punctuated.

> PCB   CPU
> OCR   PBX

38. The symbols for chemical elements are not punctuated.

H	Pb
Cl	Na

Time

39. When time is expressed in figures, the abbreviations that follow are most often written as punctuated lowercase letters; punctuated small capital letters are also common. (For more on the use of *a.m.* and *p.m.*, see paragraph 43 on page 175.)

   8:30 a.m.   *or*   8:30 A.M.
   10:00 p.m.   *or*   10:00 P.M.

40. In transportation schedules, *a.m.* and *p.m.* are generally written in capitalized, unpunctuated, unspaced letters.

   8:30 AM
   10:00 PM

41. Time-zone designations are usually written in capitalized, unpunctuated, unspaced letters.

   EST
   PST
   CDT

Titles

42. The only courtesy titles that are always abbreviated in written references are *Mr., Ms., Mrs.,* and *Messrs.* Other titles, such as *Doctor, Representative,* or *Senator,* may be either written out or abbreviated.

   Ms. Lee A. Downs
   Messrs. Lake, Mason, and Nambeth
   Doctor Howe   *or*   Dr. Howe

43. Despite some traditional objections, the titles *Honorable* and *Reverend* are often abbreviated, with and without *the* preceding the titles.

> the Honorable Samuel I. O'Leary
> *or* [the] Hon. Samuel I. O'Leary
> the Reverend Samuel I. O'Leary
> *or* [the] Rev. Samuel I. O'Leary

44. The designations *Jr.* and *Sr.* may be used with courtesy titles, with abbreviations for academic degrees, and with professional-rating abbreviations. They may or may not be preceded by a comma, according to the writer's preference. They are only used with a full name.

> Mr. John K. Walker, Jr.
> General John K. Walker Jr.
> The Honorable John K. Walker, Jr.
> John K. Walker Jr., M.D.

45. When an abbreviation for an academic degree, professional certification, or association membership follows a name, it is usually preceded by a comma. No courtesy title should precede the name.

> Dr. Jesse Smith   *or*   Jesse Smith, M.D.
> *but not*   Dr. Jesse Smith, M.D.
> Katherine Derwinski, CLU
> Carol Manning, M.D., FACPS

46. The abbreviation *Esq.* for *Esquire* is used in the United States after the surname of professional persons such as attorneys, architects, consuls, clerks of the court, and justices of the peace. It is not used, however, if a courtesy title such as *Dr., Hon., Miss, Mr., Mrs.,* or *Ms.* precedes the first name.

> Carolyn B. West, Esq.

Units of Measure

47. Measures and weights may be abbreviated in figure-plus-unit combinations. However, if the numeral is written out, the unit should also be written out.

> 15 cu ft *or* 15 cu. ft. *but* fifteen cubic feet
> How many cubic feet does the refrigerator hold?

48. Abbreviations for metric units are usually not punctuated. Abbreviations for traditional units are usually punctuated.

> | | |
> |---|---|
> | 14 ml | 8 ft. |
> | 12 km | 4 sec. |
> | 22 mi. | 20 min. |

Versus

49. *Versus* is usually abbreviated as "v." in legal contexts; it is either spelled out or abbreviated as lowercase roman letters "vs." in general contexts. For more on the use of *v.* in legal contexts, see paragraph 35 on page 78.

> | | |
> |---|---|
> | *in a legal context:* | Smith v. *Vermont* |
> | *in a general context:* | honesty versus dishonesty |
> | | *or* |
> | | honesty vs. dishonesty |

Chapter 5

Numbers

The styling of numbers presents special difficulties to writers because there are so many conventions to follow, some of which may conflict when applied to particular passages. Your major decision will be whether to write out numbers or to express them in figures, and usage varies considerably on this point.

Numbers as Words or Figures

At one extreme of styling, all numbers, sometimes even including dates, are written out. This usage is uncommon and is usually limited to proclamations, legal documents, and some other types of very formal writing. At the other extreme, some types of technical writing, such as statistical reports, contain no written-out numbers except sometimes at the beginning of a sentence.

In general, figures are easier to read than spelled-out numbers; however, the spelled-out forms are helpful in certain circumstances, such as in distinguishing different categories of numbers or in providing relief from an overwhelming cluster of numerals. Most writers follow one or the other of two common conventions combining numerals and written-out numbers. The conventions are described in this section, along with the exceptions to the general rules.

Basic Conventions

1. The first system requires that a writer use words for numbers up through nine and figures for exact numbers greater than nine. (A variation of this system sets the number ten as the dividing point.) In this system, numbers that consist of a whole number between one and nine followed by *hundred, thousand, million,* etc., may either be spelled out or expressed in figures.

> She performed in 22 plays on Broadway, seven of which won awards.
>
> The new edition will consist of 25 volumes, which will be issued at a rate of approximately four volumes per year.
>
> The cat show attracted an unexpected two thousand entries.
>
> They sold more than 2,000 units in the first year.

2. The second system requires that a writer use figures for all exact numbers 100 and above (or 101 and above) and words for numbers from one through ninety-nine (or one through one hundred) and for numbers that consist of a whole number between one and ninety-nine followed by *hundred, thousand, million,* etc.

> The artist spent nearly twelve years completing these four volumes, which comprise 435 hand-colored engravings.
>
> The 145 seminar participants toured the area's eighteen period houses.

In the course of four hours, the popular author signed twenty-five hundred copies of her new book.

Sentence Beginnings

3. Numbers that begin a sentence are written out, although some writers make an exception for dates. Avoid spelled-out numbers that are lengthy and awkward by restructuring the sentence so that the number appears elsewhere than at the beginning and may then be written as a figure.

> Sixty-two new models will be introduced this year.
> *or*
> There will be 62 new models introduced this year.
> Nineteen eighty-seven was our best earnings year so far.
> *or*
> 1987 was our best earnings year so far.
> One hundred fifty-seven illustrations, including 86 color plates, are contained in the book.
> *or*
> The book contains 157 illustrations, including 86 color plates.

Adjacent Numbers and Numbers in Series

4. Generally, two separate sets of figures should not be written adjacent to one another in running text unless they form a series. In order to avoid the juxtaposition of unrelated figures, either the sentence should be rephrased or one of the figures should be spelled out—usually the figure with the written form that is shorter and more easily read.

> sixteen ½-inch dowels
> twenty-five 11-inch platters
> twenty 100-point games

78 twenty-point games
By 1997, thirty schools . . .

5. Numbers paired at the beginning of a sentence are usually written alike. If the first word of the sentence is a spelled-out number, the second, related number is also spelled out. However, some writers prefer that each number be styled independently, even if that results in an inconsistent pairing.

> Sixty to seventy-five copies will be required.
> Sixty to 75 copies will be required.

6. Numbers that form a pair or a series referring to comparable quantities within a sentence or a paragraph should be treated consistently. The style of the largest number usually determines the style of the other numbers. Thus, a series of numbers including some that would ordinarily be spelled out might all be written as figures. Similarly, figures are used to express all the numbers in a series if one of those numbers is a mixed or simple fraction.

> The three jobs took 5, 12, and 4½ hours, respectively.
> We need four desks, three chairs, fourteen file cabinets, and six computers.

Round Numbers

7. Approximate or round numbers, particularly those that can be expressed in one or two words, are often written out in general writing; in technical and scientific writing they are more likely to be expressed as numerals.

> seven hundred people
> five thousand years

four hundred thousand volumes
but in technical writing
50,000 people per year
20,000 species of fish

8. For easier reading, numbers of one million and above may be expressed as figures followed by the word *million, billion,* and so forth. The figure may include a decimal fraction, but the fraction is not usually carried past the first digit to the right of the decimal point, and it is never carried past the third digit. If a more exact number is required, the whole amount should be written in figures.

about 4.6 billion years old
1.2 million metric tons of grain
the last 600 million years
but 200,000 years *not* 200 thousand years
$7.25 million
$3,456,000,000

Ordinal Numbers

1. Ordinal numbers generally follow the styling rules for cardinal numbers. In technical writing, however, ordinal numbers are usually written as figure-plus-suffix combinations. In addition, certain ordinal numbers—for example, those specifying percentiles and latitudinal lines—are usually set as figures.

the sixth Robert de Bruce
the ninth grade
the 9th and 14th chapters
the 98th Congress
the 7th percentile
the 40th parallel

2. The forms *second* and *third* may be written with figures as *2d* or *2nd*, *3d* or *3rd*, *22d* or *22nd*, *93d* or *93rd*, *102d* or *102nd*, etc. A period does not follow the suffix.

Roman Numerals

Roman numerals are generally used in the specific situations described below.

1. Roman numerals are traditionally used to differentiate rulers and popes with identical names.

> Elizabeth II   Innocent X
> Henry VIII   Louis XIV

2. Roman numerals are used to differentiate related males who have the same name. The numerals are used only with a person's full name and are placed after the surname with no intervening comma. Ordinals are sometimes used instead of Roman numerals.

> James R. Watson II
> James R. Watson 2nd *or* 2d

Possessives for these names are formed as follows:

> *singular:*   James R. Watson III's [*or* 3rd's *or* 3d's] house
> *plural:*   the James R. Watson IIIs' [*or* 3rds' *or* 3ds'] house

3. Lowercase Roman numerals (i, ii, iii, iv, etc.) are often used to number the pages of a publication that precede the regular Arabic sequence, as in a foreword, preface, or introduction.

4. Roman numerals are often used in outlines and in lists of major headings. For an example of an outline, see paragraph 20 on page 169.

5. Roman numerals are found as part of a few established technical terms such as blood-clotting factors, quadrant numbers, designations of cranial nerves, and virus or organism types. Also, chords in the study of music harmony are designated by capital and lowercase Roman numerals (often followed by small Arabic numbers). For the most part, however, technical terms that include numbers express them in Arabic form.

> blood-clotting factor VII
> quadrant III
> the cranial nerves II and IX
> Population II stars
> type I error
> vii$_6$ chord
> HIV-III virus
> > *but*
> adenosine 3′,5′-monophosphate
> cesium 137
> PL/1 programming language

Punctuation and Plurals

The paragraphs that follow provide general rules for the use of commas and hyphens in compound and large numbers, as well as the plural forms of numbers. For specific categories of numbers, such as dates, money, and decimal fractions, see the section on Specific Styling Conventions on page 161.

Commas in Large Numbers

1. In general writing, with the exceptions explained in paragraph 3 below, figures of four digits may

be written with or without a comma; the punctuated form is more common. If the numerals form part of a tabulation, commas are necessary so that four-digit numerals can align with numerals of five or more digits.

> 2,000 case histories
> *or less commonly*   1253 people

2. Whole numbers of five digits or more (but not decimal fractions) use a comma to separate three-digit groups, counting from the right.

> a fee of $12,500
> 15,000 units
> a population of 1,500,000

3. Certain types of numbers are treated differently. Decimal fractions and serial and multidigit numbers in set combinations, such as the numbers of policies, contracts, checks, streets, rooms, suites, telephones, pages, military hours, and years, do not contain commas.

> 2.5544   Room 1206
> Policy No. 33442   1650 hours
> check 34567   the year 1929

Hyphens

4. Hyphens are used with written-out numbers between 21 and 99.

> forty-one
> forty-first
> four hundred twenty-two

5. A hyphen is used between the numerator and the denominator of a fraction that is written out when that fraction is used as a modifier. A written-out fraction consisting of two words only

(such as *two thirds*) is usually left open, although the hyphenated form is also common. Multiword numerators and denominators are usually hyphenated. If either the numerator or the denominator is hyphenated, no hyphen is used between them. (For more on fractions, see the section beginning on page 169.)

> a two-thirds vote
> three fifths of her paycheck
> seven and four fifths
> forty-five hundredths
> four five-hundredths

6. Numbers that form the first part of a compound modifier expressing measurement are followed by a hyphen, except when the second part of the modifier is the word *percent*.

> a 5-foot board
> a 28-mile trip
> a 10-pound weight
> an eight-pound baby
> a 680-acre ranch
> a 75 percent reduction

7. An adjective or adverb made from a numeral plus the suffix *-fold* contains a hyphen, while a similar term made from a written-out number is closed up. (For more on the use of suffixes with numbers, see paragraphs 62 and 65 on page 129.)

> increased 20-fold
> a fourfold increase

8. Serial numbers, such as Social Security or engine numbers, often contain hyphens that make lengthy numerals more readable.

> 020-42-1691

9. Numbers should not be divided at the end of a line. If division is unavoidable, the break occurs only after a comma. End-of-line breaks do not occur at decimal points, and a name with a numerical suffix (such as Robert F. Walker III) is not divided between the name and the numeral.

Inclusive Numbers

10. Inclusive numbers—those which express a range—are separated either by the word *to* or by a hyphen or en dash, which means "(up) to and including" when used between dates and other inclusive numbers. (For more on the en dash, see paragraph 13 on page 33.)

> pages 40 to 98
> pages 40–98
> pp. 40–98
> the fiscal year 1987–88
> spanning the years 1915 to 1941
> the decade 1920–1930

Inclusive numbers separated by a hyphen or en dash are not used in combination with the words *from* or *between*, as in "from 1955–60" or "between 1970–90." Instead, phrases like these are written as "from 1955 to 1960" or "between 1970 and 1990."

11. Units of measurement expressed in words or abbreviations are usually used only after the second element of an inclusive number. Symbols, however, are repeated.

> an increase in dosage from 200 to 500 mg
> ten to fifteen dollars
> 30 to 35 degrees Celsius
> *but*

$50 to $60 million
45° to 48° F

12. Numbers that are part of an inclusive set or range are usually styled alike: figures with figures, spelled-out words with other spelled-out words. Similarly, approximate numbers are usually not paired with exact numbers.

from 8 to 108 absences
five to twenty guests
300,000,000 to 305,000,000
  not 300 million to 305,000,000

13. Inclusive page numbers and dates may be written in full or elided (i.e., shortened). However, inclusive dates that appear in titles and other headings are almost never elided. Dates that appear with era designations are also not elided (see also paragraph 14 on page 165).

467–68 *or* 467–468
203–4 *or* 203–204
1724–27 *or* 1724–1727
1463–1510
1800–1801
552–549 B.C.

Elided numbers are used because they save space. The most commonly used style for the elision of inclusive numbers is based on the following rules:

a. Never elide inclusive numbers that have only two digits: 33–37, *not* 33–7.

b. Never elide inclusive numbers when the first number ends in 00: 100–108, *not* 100–08 *and not* 100–8.

c. In other numbers, do not omit the tens digit from the higher number: 232–34. *Exception:* Where the tens digit of both numbers is zero,

write only one digit for the higher number:
103–4, *not* 103–04.

Plurals

14. The plurals of written-out numbers are formed
by adding *-s* or *-es*.

> Back in the thirties these roads were unpaved.
> Christmas shoppers bought the popular toy in twos
> and threes.

15. The plurals of figures are formed by adding *-s*.
Some writers prefer to add an apostrophe before
the *-s*. (For more on the plurals of figures, see
paragraphs 18 and 19 on page 104 and paragraph 5 on page 4.)

> This ghost town was booming back in the 1840s.
> The first two artificial hearts to be implanted in
> human patients were Jarvik-7s.
>> *but also*
> 1's and 7's that looked alike

Specific Styling Conventions

The following paragraphs, arranged alphabetically,
describe styling practices commonly followed for specific situations involving numbers.

Addresses

1. Arabic numerals are used for all building, house,
apartment, room, and suite numbers except for
one, which is written out.

> 6 Lincoln Road
> 1436 Fremont Street
>> *but*
> One Bayside Drive

When the address of a building is used as its name, the number in the address is often written out.

> Fifty Maple Street

2. Numbered streets have their numbers written as ordinals. There are two distinct styling conventions. Under the first, numbered street names from First through Twelfth are written out, and numerals are used for all numbered streets above Twelfth. Under the second, all numbered street names up to and including One Hundredth are spelled out.

> 167 Second Avenue
> 19 South 22nd Street
> 122 East Forty-second Street
> 145 East 145th Street
> in the Sixties [streets from 60th to 69th]
> in the 120s [streets from 120th to 129th]

When a house or building number immediately precedes a street number, a spaced hyphen may be inserted between the two numbers, or the street number may be written out.

> 2018 - 14th Street
> 2018 Fourteenth Street

3. Arabic numerals are used to designate highways and, in some states, county roads.

> Interstate 91   *or*   I-91
> U.S. Route 1   *or*   U.S. 1
> Massachusetts 57
> County 213

Dates

4. Year numbers are written as figures. If a number representing a year begins a sentence, it may be

spelled out or the sentence may be rewritten to avoid beginning it with a figure. (For additional examples, see paragraph 3 on page 152.)

> 1995
> 1888–96
> Fifteen eighty-eight marked the end to Spanish ambitions for the control of England.
>> *or*
> Spanish ambitions for the control of England ended in 1588.

5. A year number may be abbreviated, or cut back to its last two digits, in informal writing or when an event is so well known that it needs no century designation. In these cases an apostrophe precedes the numerals. (For more on this use of the apostrophe, see paragraph 5 on page 4.)

> He always maintained that he'd graduated from Korea, Clash of '52.
> the blizzard of '88

6. Full dates (month, day, and year) may be written in one of two ways. The traditional style is the month-day-year sequence, with the year set off by commas that precede and follow it. An alternative style is the inverted date, or day-month-year sequence, which does not require commas. This sequence is used in U.S. government publications and in the military.

> *traditional:* July 8, 1776, was a warm, sunny day in Philadelphia.
> the explosion on July 16, 1945, at Alamogordo
> *military style:* the explosion on 16 July 1945 at Alamogordo
> Lee's surrender to Grant on 9 April 1865 at Appomattox

7. Ordinal numbers are not used in full dates, even though the numbers may be pronounced as ordinals. Ordinals may be used, however, for a date without an accompanying year, and they are always used when preceded in a date by the word *the*.

> December 4, 1829
> on December 4th   *or*   on December 4
> on the 4th of December

8. Commas are usually omitted from dates that include the month and year but not the day. Alternatively, writers sometimes insert the word *of* between month and year.

> in November 1805
> back in January of 1981

9. Once a numerical date has been given, a reference to a related date may be written out.

> After the meeting on June 6 the conventioneers left for home, and by the seventh the hotel was virtually empty.

10. All-figure dating, such as 6-8-95 or 6/8/95, is inappropriate except in informal correspondence. For some readers, it may also create a problem of ambiguity; the examples above may mean either June 8, 1995, or (especially in Britain and many other countries) August 6, 1995.

11. References to specific centuries are often written out, although they may be expressed in figures, especially when they form the first element of a compound modifier.

> the nineteenth century

> a sixteenth-century painting
> *but also* a 16th-century painting

12. In general correspondence, the name of a specific decade often takes a short form. Although many writers place an apostrophe before the shortened word and a few capitalize it, both the apostrophe and the capitalization are often omitted when the context clearly indicates that a date is being referred to.

> in the turbulent seventies
> *but also*
> back in the 'forties
> in the early Fifties

13. The name of a specific decade is often expressed in numerals, usually in plural form. (For more on the formation of plural numbers, see paragraphs 14 and 15 on page 161.) The figure may be shortened with an apostrophe to indicate the missing numerals, but any sequence of such numbers should be styled consistently. (For more on this use of the apostrophe, see paragraph 5 on page 4.)

> the 1950s and 1960s *or* the '50s and '60s
> *but not*
> the 1950s and '60s *or* the '50's and '60's

14. Era designations precede or follow words that specify centuries or numerals that specify years. Era designations are unspaced and are nearly always abbreviated; they are usually typed as regular capitals and typeset as small capitals, and they may or may not be punctuated with periods. Any date that is given without an era designation or context is understood to mean A.D. The two most common abbreviations are B.C. (before Christ)

and A.D. (*anno Domini,* "in the year of our Lord").
The abbreviation B.C. is placed after the date,
while A.D. is usually placed before the date but
after a century designation.

> 1792–1750 B.C.
> between 600 and 400 B.C.
> from the fifth or fourth millennium to c. 250 B.C.
> 35,000 B.C.
> between 7 B.C. and A.D. 22
> c. A.D. 1100
> the second century A.D.
> the seventeenth century

15. Less commonly used era designations include
A.H. (*anno Hegirae,* "in the year of [Muhammad's]
Hegira," or *anno Hebraico,* "in the Hebrew year");
B.C.E. (before the common era; a synonym for
B.C.); C.E. (of the common era; a synonym for
A.D.); and B.P. (before the present; often used by
geologists and archeologists, with or without the
word *year*). The abbreviation A.H. in both its
meanings is usually placed before the year num-
ber, while B.C.E., C.E., and B.P. are placed after it.

> the tenth of Muharram, A.H. 61 (October 10,
>   A.D. 680)
> the first century A.H.
> from the first century B.C.E. to the fourth
>   century C.E.
> 63 B.C.E.
> the year 200 C.E.
> 5,000 years B.P
> two million years B.P.

Degrees of Temperature and Arc

16. In technical writing, quantities expressed in degrees are generally written as a numeral followed

by the degree symbol (°). In the Kelvin scale, however, neither the word *degree* nor the symbol is
used with the figure.

> a 45° angle
> 6°40′10″N
> 32° F
> 0° C
> Absolute zero is zero kelvins or 0 K.

17. In general writing, the quantity expressed in degrees may or may not be written out. A figure is
usually followed by the degree symbol or the
word *degree;* a written-out number is always followed by the word *degree.*

> latitude 43°19″N
> latitude 43 degrees N
> a difference of 43 degrees latitude
> The temperature has risen thirty degrees since this
> morning.

Enumerations and Outlines

18. Both run-in and vertical lists are often numbered.
In run-in enumerations—that is, lists that form
part of a normal-looking sentence—each item is
preceded by a number (or an italicized letter) enclosed in parentheses. The items in the list are
separated by commas if the items are brief and
have little or no internal punctuation; if the items
are complex, they are separated by semicolons.
The entire list is introduced by a colon if it is preceded by a full clause.

> We feel that she should (1) increase her administra-
> tive skills, (2) pursue additional professional edu-
> cation, and (3) increase her production.

The oldest and most basic word-processing systems consist of the following: (*a*) a typewriter for keyboarding information, (*b*) a console to house the storage medium, and (*c*) the medium itself.

The vendor of your system should (1) instruct you in the care and maintenance of your system; (2) offer regularly scheduled maintenance to ensure that the system is clean, with lubrication and replacement of parts as necessary; and (3) respond promptly to service calls.

19. In vertical enumerations, the numbers are usually followed by a period. Each item begins its own line, which is either flush left or indented. Run-over lines are usually aligned with the first word that follows the number, and figures are aligned on the periods that follow them. Each item on the list is usually capitalized if the items are syntactically independent of the words that introduce them; however, lowercase letters for such items are also fairly common. The items do not end with periods unless at least one of the items is a complete sentence, in which case a period follows each item. Items that are syntactically dependent on the words that introduce them begin with a lowercase letter and carry the same punctuation marks that they would if they were a run-in series in a sentence.

Required skills include the following:
1. Shorthand
2. Typing
3. Transcription

To type a three-column table, follow this procedure:
1. Clear tab stops.
2. Remove margin stops.
3. Determine precise center of the page. Set a tab stop at center.

The vendor of your system should
1. instruct you in the care and maintenance of your system;
2. offer regularly scheduled maintenance to ensure that the system is clean, with lubrication and replacement parts as necessary; and
3. respond promptly to service calls.

20. Outlines make use of Roman numerals, Arabic numerals, and letters.

I. Editorial tasks
   A. Manuscript editing
   B. Author contact
      1. Authors already under contract
      2. New authors
II. Production responsibilities
   A. Scheduling
      1. Composition
      2. Printing and binding
   B. Cost estimates and bids
      1. Composition
      2. Printing and binding

Fractions and Decimal Fractions

21. In running text, fractions standing alone are usually written out. Common fractions used as nouns are usually written as open compounds, but when they are used as modifiers they are usually hyphenated. (For more on written-out fractions, see paragraph 5 on page 157.)

two thirds of the paint
a two-thirds vote
three thirty-seconds
seventy-two hundredths
one one-hundredth

22. Mixed fractions (fractions with a whole number, such as 3½) and fractions that form part of a unit modifier are expressed in figures in running text. A -*th* is not added to a figure fraction.

> waiting 2½ hours
> 1¼ million population
> a ⅞-mile course
> a 2½-kilometer race

When mixed fractions are typed or keyboarded a space is left between the whole number and the fraction. The space is closed up when the number is set in type. Fractions that are not on the keyboard may be made up by typing the numerator, a slash, and the denominator in succession without spacing.

> waiting 2 3/4 hours   a 7/8-mile course

23. Fractions used with units of measurement are expressed in figures.

> ⅒ km
> ¼ mile

24. Decimal fractions are always set as figures. In technical writing, a zero is placed to the left of the decimal point when the fraction is less than a whole number. In general writing, the zero is usually omitted. A comma is never inserted in the numbers following a decimal point.

> An example of a pure decimal fraction is 0.375, while 1.402 is classified as a mixed decimal fraction.
> 0.142857
> 0.2 g
> received 0.1 mg/kg diazepam IV
> *but*
> a .22-caliber rifle

25. Fractions and decimal fractions are usually not mixed in a text.

5½ lb. and 2⅕ oz.   *or*   5.5 lb. and 2.2 oz.
  but not
5½ lb. and 2.2 oz.

Money

26. Sums of money are expressed in words or figures, as described in paragraphs 1 and 2 on page 151. If the sum can be expressed in one or two words, it is usually written out in running text. But if several sums are mentioned in the sentence or paragraph, all are usually expressed as figures. When the amount is written out, the unit of currency is also written out. If the sum is expressed in figures, the symbol of the currency unit is used, with no space between it and the numerals.

> Fifty dollars was stolen from my wallet.
> The price of a nickel candy bar seems to have risen to more like sixty cents.
> The shop charges $67.50 for our hand-knit sweaters.
> My change came to 87¢.
> We paid $175,000 for the house.

27. Monetary units of mixed dollars-and-cents amounts are expressed in figures.

> $16.75
> $307.02
> $1.95

28. Even-dollar amounts are often expressed in figures without a decimal point and zeros. But when even-dollar amounts appear near amounts that include dollars and cents, the decimal point and zeros are usually added for consistency. The dollar sign is repeated before each amount in a series or inclusive range; the word *dollar* may or may not be repeated.

> The price of the book rose from $7.95 in 1970 to $8.00 in 1971 and then to $8.50 in 1972.
>
> The bids were eighty, ninety, and one hundred dollars.
>
> *or*
>
> The bids were eighty dollars, ninety dollars, and one hundred dollars.

29. Sums of money given in round units of millions or above are usually expressed in a combination of figures and words, either with a dollar sign or with the word *dollars*. (For more on round numbers, see paragraphs 7 and 8 on pages 153–54.)

> 60 million dollars
> a $10 million building program
> $4.5 billion

30. In legal documents a sum of money is usually written out fully, with the corresponding figures in parentheses immediately following.

> twenty-five thousand dollars ($25,000)

Percentages

31. In technical writing, specific percentages are written as figure plus symbol %. In general correspondence, the percentage number may be expressed as a figure or spelled out. The word *percent* rather than the symbol is used in nonscientific texts.

> *technical:*   15%
>   13.5%
> *general:*   15 percent
>   87.2 percent

> Twenty-five percent of the office staff
> was out with the flu.
> a four percent increase

32. The word *percentage* or *percent,* used as a noun without an adjacent numeral, should never be replaced by a percent sign.

> Only a small percentage of the staff objected to the smoking ban.

33. In a series or unit combination, the percent sign should be included with all numbers, even if one of the numbers is zero.

> a variation of 0% to 10%

Proper Names

34. Numbers in the names of religious organizations and churches are usually written out in ordinal form. Names of specific governmental bodies may include ordinals, and these are written out if they are one hundred or below.

> Third Congregational Church
> Seventh-Day Adventists
> Third Reich
> First Continental Congress

35. Names of electoral, judicial, and military units may include ordinal numbers that precede the noun. Numbers of one hundred or below are usually written out.

> First Congressional District
> Twelfth Precinct
> Ninety-eighth Congress *or* 98th Congress
> Court of Appeals for the Third Circuit
> United States Eighth Army

36. Local branches of labor unions and fraternal organizations are generally identified by a numeral usually placed after the name.

> International Brotherhood of Electrical
>   Workers Local 42
> Elks Lodge No. 61
> Local 98 Operating Engineers

Ratios

37. Ratios expressed in figures use a colon, a hyphen, a slash, or the word *to* to indicate comparison. Ratios expressed in words use a hyphen or the word *to*.

> a 3:1 chance
> a 6-1 vote
> 22.4 mi/gal
> odds of 100 to 1
> a fifty-fifty chance
> a ratio of ten to four

Serial Numbers and Miscellaneous Numerals

38. Figures are used to refer to things that are numbered serially, such as chapter and page numbers, addresses, years, policy and contract numbers, and so forth.

> pages 420–515
> vol. 5, p. 202
> column 2
> Serial No. 5274
> Permit No. 63709

39. Figures are also used to express stock-market quotations, mathematical calculations, scores, and tabulations.

> $3\frac{1}{8}$ percent bonds
> $3 \times 15 = 45$

won by a score of 8 to 2
the tally: 322 ayes, 80 nays

Time of Day

40. In running text, the time of day is usually spelled out when expressed in even, half, or quarter hours.

> Quitting time is four-thirty.
> The meeting should be over by half past eleven.
> We should arrive at a quarter past five.

41. The time of day is also usually spelled out when it is followed by the contraction *o'clock* or when *o'clock* is understood.

> He should be here by four at the latest.
> My appointment is at eleven o'clock.
>   *or* My appointment is at 11 o'clock.

42. Figures are used to specify a precise time.

> The meeting is scheduled for 9:15 in the morning.
> Her plane is due at 3:05 this afternoon.
> The program starts at 8:30 in the evening.

43. Figures are also written when the time of day is used with the abbreviations *a.m. (ante meridiem)* and *p.m. (post meridiem).* The lowercase styling for these abbreviations is most common, but small capital letters are also frequently used. These abbreviations should not be used with the words *morning* or *evening* or the word *o'clock.*

> 8:30 a.m. *or* 8:30 A.M.
> 10:30 p.m. *or* 10:30 P.M.
> 8 a.m. *or* 8 A.M.
>   *but*
> 9:15 in the morning
> 11:00 in the evening
> nine o'clock

When twelve o'clock is written, it is helpful to add the designation *midnight* or *noon* rather than *a.m.* or *p.m.*

> twelve o'clock (midnight)
> twelve o'clock (noon)

44. For consistency, even-hour times should be written with a colon and two zeros when used in a series or pairing with any odd-hour times.

> He came at 7:00 and left at 9:45.

45. The 24-hour clock system—also called military time—uses no punctuation and is expressed without the use of *a.m.*, *p.m.*, or *o'clock*; the word *hours* sometimes replaces them.

> from 0930 to 1100
> at 1600 hours

Units of Measurement

46. Numbers used with units of measurement are treated according to the basic conventions explained in the first part of this chapter. However, in some cases writers achieve greater clarity by writing out all numbers (even those below ten) that express quantities of physical measurement as numerals.

> The car was traveling in excess of 80 miles an hour.
> The old volume weighed three pounds and was difficult to hold in a reading position.
> *but also in some general texts*
> 3 hours, 25 minutes
> saw 18 eagles in 12 minutes
> a 6-pound hammer
> weighed 3 pounds, 5 ounces

47. When units of measurement are written as abbreviations or symbols, the adjacent numbers are always figures.

6 cm	67.6 fl oz
1 mm	4′
$4.25	98.6°

48. When two or more quantities are expressed, as in ranges or dimensions or series, an accompanying symbol is usually repeated with each figure.

4″ × 6″ cards

temperature on successive days of 30°, 55°, 43°, and 58°

$400–$500

Chapter 6

Grammar and Composition

No guide to effective communication can ignore the basic components of writing: the word, the phrase, the clause, the sentence, and the paragraph. Each of these increasingly complex units contributes to the expression of a writer's ideas. Basic to all of them is the word.

Words have traditionally been classified into eight parts of speech: adjective, adverb, conjunction, interjection, noun, preposition, pronoun, and verb. This classification is based mainly on a word's inflectional features (or changes in form), its grammatical functions, and its position within a sentence. On the following pages, the parts of speech are discussed briefly in alphabetical order.

Adjective

An adjective is a word that describes or modifies the meaning of a noun. Adjectives serve to point out a quality of a thing named, indicate its quantity or extent, or specify a thing as distinct from something else.

Adjectives are often classified by the ways in which they modify or limit the meaning of a noun. The following paragraphs describe, in alphabetical order, the various types of adjectives and also outline situations involving adjectives that are sometimes troublesome for writers.

Absolute Adjectives

1. Some adjectives (such as *prior, maximum, optimum, minimum,* and *first*) normally cannot be used comparatively (see paragraphs 4 and 5 below), because they represent ultimate conditions. These adjectives are called *absolute* (or *nongradable*) *adjectives.* Some writers are careful to modify these adjectives with adverbs such as *almost, near,* or *nearly,* rather than *least, less, more, most,* or *very.*

    an *almost fatal* dose
    at *near maximum* capacity
    a *more nearly perfect* likeness

    However, many writers do compare and qualify this type of adjective in order to show connotations and shades of meaning they consider less than absolute.

a *more perfect* union
a *less complete* account

When in doubt about the comparability of an absolute adjective, check the definitions and examples of usage given in a dictionary.

Adjective/Noun Agreement

2. The number (singular or plural) of a demonstrative adjective *(this, that, these, those)* should agree with that of the noun it modifies. (See also paragraph 11 below.)

> *these kinds* of typewriters
>   *not*   *these kind* of typewriters
> *those sorts* of jobs   *not*   *those sort* of jobs
> *this type* of person   *not*   *these type* of people

Articles

3. An article is one of three words (*a, an,* and *the*) that are used with nouns to limit or give definiteness to the application of a noun.

Compared with Adverbs

4. Both adjectives and adverbs describe or modify other words; however, adjectives can only modify nouns, while adverbs can modify verbs, adverbs, and adjectives. For more on the differences between adjectives and adverbs, see paragraph 20 on page 184 and paragraphs 4–6 on page 187.

Comparison of Adjectives

5. A *gradable* adjective can indicate degrees of comparison (positive, comparative, superlative) by the addition of the endings *-er* and *-est* to the base word; the addition of *more, most, less,* and *least* before the base word; or the use of irregular forms.

positive	comparative	superlative
clean	cleaner	cleanest
meaningful	less meaningful	least meaningful
bad	worse	worst

6. The comparative degree is used to show that the thing being modified has more (or less) of a particular quality than the one or ones to which it is being compared. The superlative degree is used to show that the thing being modified has the most (or least) of a quality out of all those things to which it is being compared. The superlative degree is used when there are more than two things being compared.

comparative	superlative
prices *higher* than those elsewhere	the *highest* price in the area
a *better* report than our last one	the *best* report so far
the *more expensive* of the two methods	the *most expensive* of the three methods

7. The comparatives and superlatives of one-syllable adjectives are usually formed by adding *-er* and *-est* to the base word. The comparatives and superlatives of adjectives with more than two syllables are formed by adding *more, most, less,* and *least* before the base word. The comparatives and superlatives of two-syllable adjectives are formed by either adding *-er* and *-est* to the base word or using *more, most, less,* and *least* before the base word. When in doubt about the inflection of a particular adjective, consult a dictionary, which will show irregular forms. (If none are shown, the inflection is normal.)

positive	*comparative*	*superlative*
big	bigger	biggest
narrow	narrower	narrowest
complex	more complex	most complex
concise	less concise	least concise
important	more important	most important

8. Some adjectives are ordinarily not compared, because they are felt to represent ultimate conditions (see paragraph 1 above).

Coordinate and Noncoordinate Adjectives

9. Adjectives that share equal relationships to the nouns they modify are called *coordinate adjectives* and are separated from each other by commas.

> a *concise, coherent* essay
> a *soft, flickering* light

10. When the first of two adjectives modifies the noun plus the second adjective, the result is a pair of *noncoordinate adjectives*. Such adjectives are not separated by commas.

> a *low monthly* fee
> the *first warm* day

Demonstrative Adjectives

11. The demonstrative adjective *this* or *that* points to what it modifies in order to distinguish it from others. *This* and *that* are the only two adjectives with plural forms: *these* and *those*. (See also paragraph 2 above.)

Descriptive Adjectives

12. A descriptive adjective describes something or indicates a quality, kind, or condition.

a *brave* soldier
a *new* dress
a *sick* pony

Double Comparisons

13. Double comparisons should not be used.

an *easier* method   *not*   a *more easier* method
the *easiest* solution   *not*   the *most easiest* solution

Incomplete or Understood Comparisons

14. Some comparisons are left incomplete because the context clearly implies the comparison. However, the use of incomplete comparisons, especially for making vague claims of superiority such as commonly appear in advertising, is often considered careless or illogical in formal writing.

Older Americans vote in *larger* numbers.
Get *better* buys here!
We have *lower* prices.

Indefinite Adjectives

15. An indefinite adjective designates unidentified or not immediately identifiable persons or things.

some children
other hotels

Interrogative Adjectives

16. Interrogative adjectives are used in asking questions.

Whose office is this?
Which book do you want?

Nouns Used as Adjectives

17. Nouns are frequently used to describe other nouns, and in this way they act like adjectives. For more on the use of nouns as modifiers, see paragraph 7 on page 201 and paragraphs 25 and 26 on pages 120–21.

Placement within a Sentence

18. Adjectives may occur in the following positions within sentences: (1) preceding the nouns they modify, (2) following the nouns they modify, (3) following the verb *to be* (*am, is, are, was, were*, etc.) and other linking verbs in the predicate-adjective position, and (4) following some transitive verbs used in the passive voice.

> the *black* hat
> a *dark, shabby* coat
> painted the room *blue*
> a hat that is *black*
> while I felt *sick*
> a room that was painted *blue*
> passengers found *dead* at the crash site

Possessive Adjectives

19. A possessive adjective is the possessive form of a personal pronoun.

> *her* idea
> *my* car
> *our* paintings

Predicate Adjectives

20. A predicate adjective modifies the subject of a linking verb (such as *be, become, feel, taste, smell, seem*) which it follows.

She is *happy* with the outcome.

The milk tastes *sour*.

The student seems *puzzled*.

Because some linking verbs (such as *feel, look, smell, taste*) can also function as active verbs, which can in turn be modified by adverbs, writers are sometimes confused over whether they should use the adverbial or adjectival form of a modifier after the verb. The answer is that an adjective is used if the subject of the sentence is being modified. If the verb is being modified, an adverb is used. (For more examples, see paragraph 5 on page 187.)

adjective: Your memo looks *good*.

The colors feel *right*.

The engine smells *hot*.

adverb: They looked *quickly* at each item.

He felt *immediately* for his wallet.

She smelled the food *carefully* for spoilage.

Proper Adjectives

21. A proper adjective is derived from a proper noun and is usually capitalized.

Victorian furniture

a *Puerto Rican* product

Keynesian economics

Relative Adjectives

22. A relative adjective (*which, that, who, whom, whose, where*) introduces an adjectival clause or a clause that functions as a noun.

at the April conference, by *which* time the report should be finished

not knowing *whose* lead she should follow

Adverb

An adverb is a word or combination of words that typically serves as a modifier of a verb, an adjective, another adverb, a preposition, a phrase, a clause, or a sentence and expresses some relation of manner or quality, place, time, degree, number, cause, opposition, affirmation, or denial. Because of its many roles, the adverb can be one of the most confusing parts of speech.

Most adverbs are adjectives with an *-ly* ending added (*actually, congenially, madly, really*). There are many exceptions to this pattern, however. Adverbs based on adjectives ending in *-ly* (*cowardly, early, daily*) do not include an additional *-ly* ending but take the same form as the adjective. In addition, some adverbs do not end in *-ly* (*again, now, quite, too*).

Adverbs answer such questions as: *when?* ("Please reply *at once*"), *how long?* ("This is taking *forever*"), *where?* ("She works *there*"), *in what direction?* ("Move the lever *upward*"), *how?* ("They moved *quickly*"), and *to what degree?* ("It was *very* popular").

Basic Uses

1. Adverbs modify verbs, adjectives, and other adverbs.

   > She *carefully* studied the balance sheet.
   > She gave the balance sheet *very* careful study.
   > She studied the balance sheet *very* carefully.

2. Conjunctive adverbs join clauses or link sentences. (For more on this use of adverbs, see paragraphs 13–16 on pages 195–97.)

   > You're welcome to join our hiking club; *however,* the hikes are strenuous.
   > He thoroughly enjoyed the opera. *Indeed,* he was fascinated by the soprano.

3. In addition, adverbs may be essential elements of two-word verbs.

> Our staff will work *up* the specifications.
> We can farm them *out* later.

Compared with Adjectives

4. Adverbs but not adjectives modify action verbs.

> *not:*   He answered very *harsh.*
> *instead:* He answered very *harshly.*

5. A word referring to the subject of a sentence and occurring after a linking verb normally is an adjective rather than an adverb. (For more examples, see paragraph 20 on page 184.)

> *not:*   He looks *badly* these days.
>   The letter sounded *strongly.*
> *instead:* He looks *bad* these days.
>   The letter sounded *strong.*
> *and also:* He looks *good* these days.
>   He looks *well* these days.

In the last two examples, either *good* or *well* is acceptable, because both words are here functioning as adjectives in the sense of "healthy."

6. Adverbs but not adjectives modify adjectives and other adverbs.

> *not:*   She looked *dreadful* tired.
> *instead:* She looked *dreadfully* tired.

Comparison of Adverbs

7. Most adverbs have three different forms to indicate degrees of comparison: positive, comparative, and superlative. The *positive* form is the base word itself *(quickly, loudly, near)*. The *comparative*

form is usually shown by the addition of *more* or *less* before the base word *(more quickly, less quickly)*. The *superlative* form is usually shown by the addition of *most* or *least (most quickly, least quickly)*. However, a few adverbs (such as *fast, slow, loud, soft, early, late,* and *near*) may also be compared by the addition of the endings *-er* and *-est* to the base word *(near, nearer, nearest)*. For an explanation of the uses of the comparative and superlative forms, see paragraphs 5 and 6 on pages 180–81.

8. As a general rule, one-syllable adverbs add the *-er* and *-est* endings to show comparison. Adverbs of three or more syllables use *more/most* and *less/least*. Two-syllable adverbs take one form or the other. (For more details, see paragraph 7 on page 181.)

positive	comparative	superlative
fast	faster	fastest
easy	easier	easiest
madly	more madly	most madly
happily	more happily	most happily

9. Some adverbs (such as *quite* and *very*) cannot be compared.

Double Negatives and Similar Cases

10. A combination of two adverbs with negative meaning (such as *not, hardly, never,* and *scarcely*) to express a single negative idea should be avoided.

not:	We *cannot* see *hardly* any reason to buy this product.
instead:	We *cannot* see any reason to buy this product.
	We can see *hardly* any reason to buy this product.

Emphasis

11. Adverbs such as *just* and *only* are often used to emphasize other words. Various emphases can result from the positioning of an adverb in a sentence.

> He *just* nodded to me as he passed.
> He nodded to me *just* as he passed.

12. In some positions and contexts, these adverbs can be ambiguous.

> They will *only* tell it to you.

It is not clear whether this means that they will only tell it—that is, not put it in writing—or that they will tell no one else. If the latter interpretation is intended, a slight shift of position would remove the uncertainty.

> They will tell it *only* to you.

Placement within a Sentence

13. Adverbs are generally positioned as close as possible to the words they modify, if such a position will not result in misinterpretation.

> *unclear:*   A project that the board would support *completely* occupied her thinking.

Here it is unclear whether the writer means "would support completely" or "completely occupied her thinking." The adverb may be moved to another position, or the sentence may be rewritten.

> *clear:*   A project that the board would *completely* support occupied her thinking.
> Her thinking was *completely* occupied with a project that the board would support.

14. When an adverb separates *to* from the verbal element of an infinitive ("hope to really start"), the result is called a *split infinitive*. For a discussion of split infinitives, see paragraph 35 on page 229.

15. Adverbs sometimes modify an entire sentence rather than a specific word or phrase within the sentence. Such adverbs are referred to as *sentence adverbs,* and their position can vary.

> *Fortunately* they had already placed their order.
> They *fortunately* had already placed their order.
> They had already placed their order, *fortunately.*

Relative Adverbs

16. Relative adverbs (such as *when, where, why*) introduce subordinate clauses. (For more on subordinate clauses, see the section beginning on page 233.)

> They met at a time *when* prospects were good.
> I went into the room *where* they were sitting.
> Everyone knows the reason *why* she did it.

Conjunction

A conjunction is a word or phrase that joins together words, phrases, clauses, or sentences. Conjunctions may occur in many different positions in a sentence. There are three main types of conjunctions: *coordinating, correlative,* and *subordinating.* In addition, there are transitional adverbs and adverbial phrases called *conjunctive adverbs.* These function as conjunctions even though they are customarily classified as adverbs. A definition and discussion of the three types of conjunctions and of conjunctive adverbs follows.

Coordinating Conjunctions

1. Coordinating conjunctions (such as *and, because, but, for, or, nor, since, so,* and *yet*) join together grammatical elements of equal weight. The elements may be words, phrases, subordinate clauses, main clauses, or complete sentences. Coordinating conjunctions are used to join similar elements, to exclude or contrast, to offer alternatives, to propose reasons or grounds, or to specify a result.

   joining similar
   elements: She ordered pencils, pens, *and* erasers.

                   Sales were slow, *and* they showed no sign of improvement.

   excluding or
   contrasting: He is a brilliant *but* arrogant man.

                   They offered a promising plan, *but* it had not yet been tested.

   alternative: She can wait here *or* go on ahead.

   reason or
   grounds: The report is useless, *for* its information is no longer current.

   result: His diction is excellent, *so* every word is clear.

2. A comma is used before a coordinating conjunction linking coordinate clauses, especially when these clauses are lengthy. (For more on the use of commas between clauses, see paragraphs 1–4 on pages 12–14.)

   We encourage applications from all interested students, *but* we do have high academic standards that the successful applicant must meet.

3. Coordinating conjunctions should link equal grammatical elements—for example, adjectives

with other adjectives, nouns with other nouns, participles with other participles, clauses with other equal-ranking clauses, and so on. Combining unequal grammatical elements may result in unbalanced sentences.

> *unbalanced:*   Having become disgusted *and* because he was tired, he left the meeting.
>
> *balanced:*   Because he was tired *and* disgusted, he left the meeting.
>
>   Having become tired *and* disgusted, he left the meeting.

4. Coordinating conjunctions should not be used to string together a long series of elements, regardless of their grammatical equality.

> *loose:*   We have sustained enormous losses in this division, *and* we have realized practically no profits even though the sales figures indicate last-quarter gains, *and* we are therefore reorganizing the entire management structure as well as cutting back on personnel.
>
> *tightened:*   Because this division has sustained enormous losses and has realized only insignificant profits even with its last-quarter sales gains, we are totally reorganizing its management and cutting back on personnel.

5. The choice of the right coordinating conjunction is important: the right word will pinpoint the writer's true meaning and intent and will emphasize the most relevant idea or point of the sentence. The following three sentences show increasingly stronger degrees of contrast through the use of different conjunctions:

He works hard *and* doesn't progress.
He works hard *but* doesn't progress.
He works hard, *yet* he doesn't progress.

6. The coordinating conjunction *and/or* linking two elements of a compound subject often poses a problem: should the verb that follows be singular or plural? A subject consisting of singular nouns connected by *and/or* may be considered singular or plural, depending on the meaning of the sentence.

singular: All loss *and/or* damage [one or the other and possibly both] *is* to be the responsibility of the sender.

plural: John R. Westlake *and/or* Maria A. Artandi *are* hereby appointed as the executors of my estate. [Both executors are to act, or either of them is to act if the other dies or is incapacitated.]

Correlative Conjunctions

7. Correlative conjunctions are coordinating conjunctions that are used in pairs, although they are not placed adjacent to one another. Correlative conjunctions are used to link alternatives and equal elements.

Either you go *or* you stay.
He had *neither* looks *nor* wit.
Both typist *and* writer should understand the rules of punctuation.
Not only was there inflation, *but* there was *also* unemployment.

8. Because they link equal grammatical elements, correlative conjunctions should be placed as close as possible to the elements they join. What follows *either* should be parallel to what follows *or;* for example, if a verb immediately follows one of these words, a verb must immediately follow the other.

misplaced:	*Either* I must send a fax *or* make a long-distance call.
repositioned:	I must *either* send a fax *or* make a long-distance call.

9. The negative counterpart to *either . . . or* is *neither . . . nor*. The conjunction *or* should not be substituted for *nor*, because its substitution will destroy the negative parallelism. However, *or* may occur in combination with *no*.

not:	He received *neither* a promotion *or* a raise.
instead:	He received *neither* a promotion *nor* a raise.
	He received *no* promotion *or* raise.

Subordinating Conjunctions

10. Subordinating conjunctions join a subordinate or dependent clause to a main clause. They are used to express cause, condition or concession, manner, purpose or result, time, place or circumstance, and alternative conditions or possibilities.

cause:	*Because* she learns quickly, she is doing well in her new job.
condition or concession:	Don't call *unless* you are coming.
manner:	He looks *as though* he is ill.
	We'll do it *however* you tell us to.
purpose or result:	She routes the mail early *so that* they can read it.
time:	She kept meetings to a minimum *when* she was president.

> *place or cir-*
> *cumstance:* I don't know *where* he went.
> He tries to help out *wherever* it is pos-
> sible.
>
> *conditions or*
> *possibilities:* It was hard to decide *whether* I
> should go or stay.

11. The subordinating conjunction *that* introduces
    several kinds of subordinate clauses, including
    those used as noun equivalents (such as a subject
    or an object of a verb or as a predicate nomina-
    tive).

    > Yesterday I learned *that* he has been sick for over a
    > week.

12. In introducing subordinate clauses, subordinat-
    ing conjunctions de-emphasize less important
    ideas in favor of more important ideas. The
    writer should take care that the point to be em-
    phasized is in the main clause and that the points
    of less importance are subordinated.

    > We were just coming out of the door *when* the build-
    > ing burst into flames.
    > *As* we were coming out of the door, the building
    > burst into flames.

Conjunctive Adverbs

13. Conjunctive adverbs are transitional adverbs and
    adverbial phrases that express relationships be-
    tween two independent units (such as two main
    clauses, two complete sentences, or two or more
    paragraphs). Though classed as adverbs, they
    function as conjunctions when they are used as
    connectives. Some common conjunctive adverbs
    are listed below.

accordingly	hence	namely
also	however	nevertheless
besides	in addition	otherwise
consequently	indeed	still
finally	in fact	then
first	meanwhile	therefore
furthermore	moreover	thus

14. Conjunctive adverbs are used to express addition, to add emphasis, to express contrast or discrimination, to introduce illustrations or elaborations, to express or introduce conclusions or results, or to order phrases or clauses in terms of time, space, or priority.

addition: This employee deserves a substantial raise; *furthermore,* she should be promoted.

emphasis: He is brilliant; *indeed,* he is a genius.

contrast or discrimination: The major responsibility lies with the partners; *nevertheless,* associates should be competent in decision-making.

illustrations or elaborations: Losses were due to several negative factors; *namely,* inflation, foreign competition, and restrictive government regulation.

conclusions or results: Government overregulation in that country has reached a prohibitive level. *Thus,* we are phasing out all of our operations there.

time, space, or priority: *First,* we can remind them that their account is long overdue; *second,* we can say that we must consider consulting our attorneys if they do not meet their obligation.

15. Conjunctive adverbs are usually placed at the beginning of a clause or sentence. When they are placed later in the clause or sentence, they receive additional emphasis.

> The overdue shipment arrived this morning; *however*, we must point out that it was incomplete.
>
> The overdue shipment arrived this morning; we must point out, *however*, that it was incomplete.

16. A semicolon is used before a conjunctive adverb connecting two main clauses. Using a comma with conjunctive adverbs leads to a problem known as *comma fault*. (For more on comma fault and punctuation between main clauses, see paragraphs 1–4 on pages 12–14 and paragraph 5 on page 59.)

> *comma fault:*   The company had flexible hours, *however* its employees were expected to abide by their selected arrival and departure times.
>
> *corrected:*   The company had flexible hours; *however*, its employees were expected to abide by their selected arrival and departure times.

Interjection

Interjections are exclamatory or interrupting words or phrases that express an emotion. Interjections are usually independent clauses that lack grammatical connection with the rest of the sentence. They often stand alone.

1. Interjections may be stressed or ejaculatory words, phrases, or even short sentences.

> Absurd!   Get out!
> No, no!   Not now!

2. Interjections may also be so-called "sound" words, such as those representing shouts, hisses, or cries.

> Shh! The meeting has begun.
> Pssst! Come over here.
> Ouch! That hurts.
> Ugh! What a horrible flavor.

3. Emphatic interjections expressing forceful emotions use exclamation points. Mildly stressed words or sentences may be punctuated with commas and periods.

> Fire!
> What an awful time we had!
> *Ah,* that's my idea of a terrific beer.
> *Well, well,* so that's their story now.
> *Oh,* you're probably right.

4. Interjections should be sparingly used, and then only to signal genuine emotion or for strong emphasis.

Noun

A noun is the name of something (such as a person, animal, place, object, quality, concept, or action). Nouns are used as the subject or object of a verb, the object of a preposition, the predicate after a linking verb, an appositive name, or a name in an absolute construction.

Nouns have several characteristic features. They can take a possessive form; they have number (that is, they are either singular or plural); they are often preceded by determiners (such as *a, an, the; this, that, these, those; all, every; one, two, three; his, her, their*); a few still show gender differences (*host/hostess, actor/actress*); and many are formed by adding a suffix (such as *-ance, -ist, -ness,* or *-tion*) to a root or verb form.

Basic Uses

1. Nouns are used as subjects, direct objects, objects of prepositions, indirect objects, retained objects, predicate nominatives, objective complements, and appositives, and in direct address.

subject:	The *office* was quiet.
direct object:	He locked the *office*.
object of a preposition:	The file is in the *office*.
indirect object:	He gave his *client* the papers.
retained object:	His client was given the *papers*.
predicate nominative:	Mrs. Adams is the managing *partner*.
objective complement:	They made Mrs. Adams managing *partner*.
appositive:	Mrs. Adams, the managing *partner*, wrote that memo.
direct address:	*Mrs. Adams,* may I present Mr. Bonkowski.

Compound Nouns

2. Because English is not static and unchanging, many of its words undergo styling variations because of the changing preferences of its users. The styling of compound nouns (that is, as open, closed, or hyphenated) is especially subject to changing usage. No set of rules can cover every possible variation or combination; however, some consistent patterns of usage can be seen. For

more details, see the section beginning on page 113.

Indefinite Articles with Nouns

3. Before a word or abbreviation beginning with a consonant *sound*, the article *a* is used. This is true even if the word begins with a vowel.

a door	a human
a COD package	a union
a B.A. degree	a one
a hat	a U.S. Senator

4. Before *h-* in an unstressed or lightly stressed first syllable, the article *a* is generally used, although *an* is more usual in speech whether or not the *h-* is actually pronounced. Either is acceptable in both speech and writing.

a historian   *or*   an historian

a heroic attempt   *or*   an heroic attempt

a hilarious performance   *or*   an hilarious performance

5. Before a word or abbreviation beginning with a vowel *sound*, the article *an* is used. This is true even if the word or abbreviation actually begins with a consonant.

an icicle	an nth degree
an orange	an FCC report
an unknown	an MIT professor
an honor	an Rh factor

Nominals

6. Nominals are words or groups of words that function as nouns. Adjectives, gerunds, and infinitives may act as nominals. An example of an

adjective used as a noun is the word *good* in the clause "the good die young." Examples of gerunds and infinitives used as nouns are *seeing* in the clause "seeing is believing" and *to see* in the clause "to see is to believe." Noun phrases and noun clauses are also considered to be nominals. For more about gerunds and infinitives, see paragraphs 14 and 16 on pages 222–23. For information about noun phrases and noun clauses, see paragraphs 4 and 3 on pages 232 and 234 respectively.

Nouns Used as Adjectives

7. Nouns are frequently used as adjectives by placing them before other nouns, as in *school board* or *office management*. When two or more nouns are frequently combined in this way, they become familiar compounds like *profit margin, money market, box lunch*. Such compounds provide useful verbal shortcuts ("office management" is shorter than "management of an office"). However, care should be taken not to pile up so many of these noun modifiers that the reader has difficulty sorting out their meanings.

shorter but unclear: Management review copies of the Division II sales department machine parts file should be indexed.

longer but clear: Copies of the machine parts file from the Division II sales department should be indexed before being sent to management for review.

Both of these sentences could be made clearer by hyphenating the compound nouns used as adjectives. (For more about this kind of compound, see the section beginning on page 118.)

Management-review copies of the Division II sales department's machine-parts file should be indexed.

Plurals

8. The plurals of nouns are usually produced by adding *-s* or *-es* to the base word, although some nouns have irregular plurals. For more about the formation of plurals, see the section beginning on page 99.

Possessives

9. The possessives of nouns are usually formed by adding an apostrophe plus *-s* to singular nouns or just an apostrophe to plural words ending in *-s*. For more about possessives, see the section beginning on page 106.

Proper Nouns

10. Proper nouns are nouns that name a particular person, place, or thing. Proper nouns are almost always capitalized. For more about capitalizing proper nouns, see the section beginning on page 68.

Preposition

A preposition is a word that combines with a noun, pronoun, or noun equivalent (such as a phrase or clause) to form a phrase that usually acts as an adverb, adjective, or noun.

Prepositions have no inflections, number, case, gender, or identifying suffixes. They can be identified chiefly by their position within sentences and by their grammatical functions. Prepositions may be simple—that is, consisting of only one word (*against, from, near, of, on, out,* or *without*)—or compound—that is, composed of more than one element (*according to, by means of,* or *in spite of*).

Basic Uses

1. Prepositions are chiefly used to link nouns, pronouns, or noun equivalents to the rest of the sentence. A prepositional phrase usually functions as an adverb or an adjective.

> She expected resistance *on* his part.
> He sat down *beside* her.

Conjunctions vs. Prepositions

2. The words *after, before, but, for,* and *since* may function as either prepositions or conjunctions. Their position within the sentence identifies them as conjunctions or prepositions. Conjunctions link two words or sentence elements that have the same grammatical function. Prepositions normally precede a noun, pronoun, or noun phrase.

> *conjunction:* I was a bit concerned *but* not panicky. [*but* links two adjectives]
>
> *preposition:* I was left with nothing *but* hope. [*but* precedes a noun]
>
> *conjunction:* The device conserves fuel, *for* it is battery-powered. [*for* links two clauses]
>
> *preposition:* The device conserves fuel *for* residual heating. [*for* precedes a noun phrase]

Implied Prepositions

3. If two words combine idiomatically with the same preposition, that preposition need not be used after both.

We were antagonistic [*to*] and opposed *to* the whole idea.

but

We are interested *in* and anxious *for* raises.

Position

4. Prepositions may occur before nouns or pronouns ("*below* the desk," "*beside* them"), after adjectives ("antagonistic *to*," "insufficient *in*," "symbolic *of*"), and after the verbal elements of standard verb + preposition combinations ("take *for*," "get *after*," "come *across*").

5. There is no reason why a preposition cannot end a sentence, especially when it is an element in a common verb phrase.

His lack of organization is only one of the things I put up *with*.

What does all this add up *to*?

Use of *Between* and *Among*

6. Despite an unfounded notion to the contrary, the preposition *between* can be used of more than two items. It is especially appropriate to denote one-to-one relationships, regardless of the number of items.

Treaties established economic cooperation *between* nations.

This is *between* you and me and the lamppost.

Among is more appropriate where the emphasis is on overall distribution rather than individual relationships.

There was discontent *among* the peasants.

When *among* is automatically chosen for more than two, the results can sound strained.

The author alternates *among* quotes, clichés, and street slang.

Pronoun

A pronoun is a word that is used as a substitute for a noun or noun equivalent, takes noun constructions, and refers to persons or things named or understood in the context. The noun or noun equivalent for which it substitutes is called the *antecedent*.

Pronouns may exhibit the following features: case (nominative, possessive, objective); number (singular, plural); person (first, second, third person); and gender (masculine, feminine, neuter). Pronouns are divided into seven major categories, each with its own function; they are described alphabetically below.

Demonstrative Pronouns

1. The words *this, that, these,* and *those* are classified as pronouns when they function as nouns. (They are classified as demonstrative adjectives when they modify nouns.) Demonstrative pronouns point out a person or thing to distinguish it from others of the same type.

    These are the best designs we've seen to date.
    Those are strong words.

2. They also distinguish between a person or thing nearby and one farther away.

    This is my desk; *that* is yours.

3. A potentially troublesome situation occurs when a demonstrative pronoun introduces a sentence, referring back to something previously mentioned. The reference should always be clear.

    unclear: The heir's hemophilia, the influence of
                an unprincipled faith healer on the
                royal family, devastating military set-

backs, general strikes, mass outbreaks of typhus, and repeated crop failures contributed to the revolution. *This* influenced the course of history.

clear: The heir's hemophilia, the influence of an unprincipled faith healer on the royal family, devastating military setbacks, general strikes, mass outbreaks of typhus, and repeated crop failures—all these factors contributed to the revolution and thus influenced the course of history.

4. When demonstrative pronouns are used with the words *kind/sort/type* + *of* + noun, they should agree in number with both nouns.

not: We want *these kind* of *pencils.*

instead: We want *this kind* of *pencil.*
   We want *these kinds* of *pencils.*

Indefinite Pronouns

5. Indefinite pronouns designate an unidentified or not immediately identifiable person or thing. They are chiefly used as third-person references and do not distinguish gender. Examples of indefinite pronouns are listed below.

all	either	none
another	everybody	no one
any	everyone	one
anybody	everything	other
anyone	few	several
anything	many	some
both	much	somebody
each	neither	someone
each one	nobody	something

6. Indefinite pronouns should agree in number with their verbs. The following are singular and

take singular verbs: *another, anything, each one, everything, much, nobody, no one, one, other, someone, something.*

>*Much is* being done.
>*No one wants* to go.

7. The indefinite pronouns *both, few, many, several,* and a few others are plural and take plural verbs.

>*Many were* called; *few were* chosen.

8. Some indefinite pronouns (such as *all, any, none, some*) present problems because they may be either singular or plural, depending on whether they are used with mass nouns or count nouns. (A *mass noun* identifies something not ordinarily thought of in terms of countable elements; a *count noun* identifies things that can be counted.)

>| | |
>|---|---|
>| with mass noun: | *All* of the *property is* entailed. |
>| | *None* of the *ink was* erasable. |
>| | *Some* of the *sky was* visible. |
>| with count noun: | *All* of our *bases are* covered. |
>| | *None* of the *clerks were* available. |
>| | *Some* of the *stars were* visible. |

9. The pronouns *anybody, anyone, everybody, everyone, somebody, nobody,* and *no one* are singular in form and as such logically take singular verbs. However, because of the plural aspect of their meaning, plural pronoun references to them are common in informal speech.

>I knew *everybody* by *their* first names.
>Don't tell *anyone; they* might spread the rumor.

Even in more formal contexts, such plural pronoun references are used increasingly, especially to avoid sexism in language. (For more about avoiding sexism in the use of personal pronouns, see paragraph 23 on page 212.)

> We called *everyone* by *their* first *names* [rather than "his first name"].

10. Sometimes an apparently singular indefinite pronoun may take a plural verb if the context makes it seem plural. The following two sentences illustrate how a singular indefinite pronoun may take either a singular or a plural verb, depending on how the writer interprets the pronoun *either* (or *neither*):

> *Either* [*Neither*] of these pronunciations *is* acceptable.
> *Either* [*Neither*] of these pronunciations *are* acceptable.

The normal choice of verb would be *is*, because the subject of the sentence is the singular pronoun. However, the plural word *pronunciations*, together with the possibility of interpreting *either* and *neither* to refer alternatively to one or both, permits the writer to choose either a singular or a plural verb.

11. The indefinite pronouns *any* and *anyone* are usually followed by *other(s)* or *else* in a comparison of two individuals in the same class.

not:	Helen has more seniority than *anyone* in the firm.
instead:	Helen has more seniority than *anyone else* in the firm.
not:	Our house is older than *any* building on the block.
instead:	Our house is older than *any other* building on the block.

The addition of *else* and *other* in the preceding sentences avoids the logical impossibility that

Helen has more seniority than herself or that our house is older than itself. Likewise, it prevents the possible misreading that Helen is not a member of the firm or that our house is not on the block.

12. The antecedent of an indefinite pronoun—that is, the thing it is referring to—must be clearly stated, not implied. A good check for a clear reference is to see if there is an antecedent in the sentence that could be substituted for the pronoun; if there is none, the pronoun should be replaced by a noun or nominal.

> *unclear:* He's the author of a best-selling book on sailing, even though he's never set foot on *one.*
>
> *clear:* He's the author of a best-selling book on sailing, even though he's never set foot on a sailboat.

Interrogative Pronouns

13. The interrogative pronouns *what, which, who, whom,* and *whose,* as well as combinations of these words with the suffix *-ever,* are used to introduce direct and indirect questions.

> *Who* is she?
> He asked me *who* she was.
> *Whom* did the article accuse?
> She asked *whom* the article accused.
> *Whoever* can that be?
> We wondered *whoever* that could be.

Personal Pronouns

14. Personal pronouns refer to beings and objects and reflect their person, number, and gender. Most personal pronouns take different forms for the three cases.

	nominative	*possessive*	*objective*
first person			
singular:	I	my, mine	me
plural:	we	our, ours	us
second person			
singular:	you	your, yours	you
plural:	you	your, yours	you
third person			
singular:	he	his, his	him
	she	her, hers	her
	it	its, its	it
plural:	they	their, theirs	them

15. Though a personal pronoun agrees in person, number, and gender with the word it refers to, its case is determined by its function within a sentence. The nominative case is used for a pronoun that acts as a subject of a sentence or as a predicate nominative (but see paragraph 16 below). The possessive case is used for pronouns that express possession or a similar relationship. The objective case is used for pronouns that are direct objects, indirect objects, retained objects, objects of prepositions, or objective complements.

> *You* and *I* thought the meeting was useful.
> My assistant and *I* attended the seminar.
> Our new candidate will be *you*.
> We all had *our* own offices.
> He told my assistant and *me* about the seminar.
> She gave *me* the papers.
> Just between *you* and *me*, the meeting was much too long.
> I was given *them* yesterday.
> That makes our new candidate *her*.

16. The nominative case after the verb *to be* (as in "It is I" and "This is she") is preferred by strict grammarians, but the objective case (as in "It's me") may also be used, especially in spoken English.

> The only candidate left for that job may soon be *she* [or *her*].

17. When a personal pronoun follows *than* or *as*, and is the subject of an implied verb, it should be in the nominative case.

> He received a bigger bonus than *she* [did].
> She has as much seniority as *I* [do].

18. The suffixes *-self* and *-selves* combine only with the possessive case of the first- and second-person pronouns *(myself, ourselves, yourself, yourselves)* and with the objective case of the third-person pronouns *(himself, herself, itself, themselves)*. Other combinations (such as "hisself" and "theirselves") are nonstandard and should not be used.

19. Personal pronouns in the possessive case (such as *your, their, theirs, its*) do not contain apostrophes and should not be confused with similar-sounding contractions (such as *you're, they're, there's, it's*), which do contain apostrophes.

> Put the contract in *its* file.
> *It's* an extensive contract.
> *Whose* turn is it?
> *Who's* going to go?

20. When *I* or *me* is used with other pronouns or other people's names, it should be last in the series.

> Mrs. Smith and *I* were trained together.
> He and *I* were attending the meeting.
> The memorandum was directed to Ms. Montgomery and *me*.

21. Some companies prefer that writers use *we* and not *I* when speaking for their companies in business correspondence. *I* is more often used when a writer is referring only to himself or herself. The following example illustrates the use of both within one sentence:

> *We* [i.e., the company] have reviewed the manuscript that you sent to *me* [i.e., the writer] on June 1, but *we* [i.e., the company] feel that it is too specialized a work to be marketable by *our* company.

22. While the personal pronouns *it*, *you*, and *they* are often used as indefinite pronouns in spoken English, they can be vague or even redundant.

vague:	*They* said at the seminar that the economy would experience a third-quarter upturn. [Who exactly is *they*?]
explicit:	The economists on the panel at the seminar predicted a third-quarter economic upturn.
redundant:	In the graph *it* says that production fell off by 50 percent.
lean:	The graph indicates a 50 percent production drop.

23. Forms of the personal pronoun *he* and, less frequently, the indefinite pronoun *one* have long been the standard substitutes for antecedents whose genders are mixed or irrelevant.

> Present the letter to the executive for *his* approval.
> Each employee should check *his* W-2 form.
> If *one* really wants to succeed, *one* can.

Many writers today who are concerned about sexism in language recast such sentences to avoid the generic use of the masculine pronoun.

Present the letter to the executive for approval.
All employees should check *their* W-2 forms.
Each employee should check *his or her* W-2 form.

The phrases *he or she, him or her,* and *his or her* should be used sparingly, however, as they can easily become tiresome. (For more on avoiding the generic use of the masculine pronoun, see paragraph 9 on page 207.)

Reciprocal Pronouns

24. The reciprocal pronouns *each other* and *one another* are used in the object position to indicate a mutual action or cross-relationship.

> They do not quarrel with *one another.*
> Karen and Rachel spelled *each other* at the convention booth.

25. Reciprocal pronouns may also be used in the possessive case.

> The two secretaries borrowed *one another's* stationery.
> The president and his vice president depend on *each other's* ideas.

Reflexive Pronouns

26. Reflexive pronouns (formed by compounding the personal pronouns *him, her, it, my, our, them,* and *your* with *-self* or *-selves*) express reflexive action or add extra emphasis to the subject of a sentence, clause, or phrase. Reflexive pronouns are used when an object or subjective complement refers to the same thing as the foregoing noun or noun phrase.

> She dressed *herself.*
> The baby isn't *himself* this morning.

They asked *themselves* if they were being honest.
I *myself* am not concerned.
The cook told us to help *ourselves* to seconds.

Relative Pronouns

27. The relative pronouns are *that, what, which, who, whom,* and *whose,* as well as combinations of these with *-ever.* They introduce subordinate clauses acting as nouns or modifiers. While a relative pronoun itself does not exhibit number, gender, or person, it does determine the number, gender, and person of elements that follow it in the relative clause because of its implicit agreement with its antecedent. Consider, for instance, the following sentence:

> People *who are* ready to start *their* jobs should arrive at 8:00 a.m.

In this sentence, the relative pronoun "who" refers to the plural subject "people" and acts as the subject of the relative clause "who are ready to start their jobs." Because it refers to a plural word, it acts like a plural word within its clause and therefore calls for the plural verb "are" and the plural pronoun "their."

28. The relative pronoun *who* typically refers to persons and some animals; *which* refers to things and animals; and *that* refers to persons, animals, and things.

> a man *who* sought success
> a man *whom* we can trust
> Seattle Slew, *who* won horse racing's Triple Crown
> a book *which* sold well
> a dog *which* barked loudly
> a man *that* we can trust

a dog *that* barked loudly
a book *that* sold well

29. *Which,* preceded by a comma, is used to introduce nonrestrictive clauses—that is, clauses that are not essential to the meaning of the nouns they modify. Either *that* or *which* can introduce restrictive clauses—that is, clauses that are needed to define the nouns they follow. However, many writers prefer to use *which* only with nonrestrictive clauses. (For more on restrictive and nonrestrictive clauses, see the section on page 235.)

> The paneled doors, *which* cost less, were more popular.
> The doors *that* they had ordered were out of stock.

30. Relative pronouns can sometimes be omitted for the sake of brevity.

> The man [*whom*] I was talking to is the senator.

31. The relative pronoun *what* may usually be substituted for the longer and more awkward phrases "that which," "that of which," or "the thing which."

> *stiff:* He was blamed for *that which* he could not have known.
>
> *easier:* He was blamed for *what* he could not have known.

32. The problem of when to use *who* or *whom* has been blown out of proportion. The situation is very simple: standard written English makes a distinction between the nominative and objective cases of these pronouns when they are used as relatives or interrogatives. (For more on cases, see paragraph 15 on page 210.)

nominative case: *Who* is she?

                     Who does she think she is, anyway?

                     She thinks she is the one *who* ought to be promoted.

                     Give me a list of the ones *who* you think should be promoted.

objective case: *Whom* are you referring to?

                     To *whom* are you referring?

                     He's a man *whom* everyone should know.

                     He's a man with *whom* everyone should be acquainted.

In spoken English *who* is favored as a general substitute for all uses of *whom* except in set phrases such as "*To whom* it may concern." In speech, then, *who* may be used not only as the subject of the clause it introduces but also as the object of a verb in a clause that it introduces or as an interrogative.

> Let us select *who* we think will be the best candidate.
> See the manager, Mrs. Keats, *who* you should be able to find in her office.
> *Who* should we tell?

33. *Whom* is commonly used as the object of a preposition in a clause that it introduces.

> Presiding is a judge *about whom* I know nothing.
> He is a man *for whom* I would gladly work.

However, *who* is commonly used to introduce a question even when it is the object of a preposition.

> *Who* [rarely *whom*] are you going to listen to?
> *Who* [rarely *whom*] do you work for?

34. While in speech the nominative form *who* can often be used in the objective case, the reverse is not true: the objective form *whom* cannot be used in the nominative case in either spoken or written English. Avoid such usages as "*Whom* do you suppose is coming to the meeting?" which result from a mistaken notion that *whom* is somehow always more correct.

35. In formal writing, the relative pronouns *whoever* and *whomever* follow the same principles as *who* and *whom*.

> *nominative:*   Tell *whoever* is going to research the case that . . .
>
> He wants to help *whoever* needs it most.
>
> *objective:*   She makes friends with *whomever* she meets.

In speech, however, as with *who* and *whom*, case distinctions become blurred, and *whoever* is generally used (see also paragraph 32 above).

> *Whoever* did she choose?

Verb

A verb is usually the grammatical center of a predicate and expresses an act, occurrence, or mode of being. Verbs are inflected (that is, altered) for agreement with the subject and for mood, voice, or tense.

Verbs exhibit the following features: inflection (e.g., *help, helps, helping, helped*), person (first, second, third person), number (singular, plural), tense (present, past, future), aspect (time relations other than the simple present, past, and future), voice (active, passive), mood (indicative, subjunctive, imperative), and the addition of suffixes (such as *-ate, -en, -ify,* and *-ize*). Some of these features are described below.

Inflection

1. Regular verbs have four inflected forms, produced by adding the suffixes *-s* or *-es, -ed,* and *-ing.* The verb *help* as shown in the paragraph above is regular. Most irregular verbs have four or five forms (for example, *see, sees, seeing, saw, seen*); and one, the verb *be,* has eight *(be, is, am, are, being, was, were, been).* If you are uncertain about a particular inflected form, consult a dictionary that shows the inflections of irregular verbs and inflections resulting in changes in base-word spelling.

   blame; blamed; blaming
   spy; spied; spying
   picnic; picnicked; picnicking

   A dictionary should also show acceptable alternative inflected forms for any verbs with such forms.

   bias; biased *or* biassed; biasing *or* biassing
   travel; traveled *or* travelled; traveling *or* travelling

   All such forms may be found at their respective main entries in *Merriam-Webster's Collegiate Dictionary, Tenth Edition.* There are, however, a few rules that will aid you in determining the proper spelling patterns of certain verb forms, as shown in the paragraphs below.

2. Verbs ending in a silent *-e* generally retain the *-e* before consonant suffixes (such as *-s*) but drop the *-e* before vowel suffixes (such as *-ed* and *-ing*).

   arrange; arranges; arranged; arranging
   hope; hopes; hoped; hoping
   require; requires; required; requiring
   shape; shapes; shaped; shaping

   A few verbs ending in a silent *-e* retain the *-e* before suffixes beginning with vowels in order to avoid confusion with other words.

dye; dyes; dyed; dyeing [*vs*. dying]
singe; singes; singed; singeing [*vs*. singing]

3. One-syllable verbs ending in a single consonant preceded by a single vowel double the final consonant before suffixes beginning with vowels (such as *-ed* and *-ing*).

    brag; bragged; bragging
    grip; gripped; gripping
    pin; pinned; pinning

4. Verbs of more than one syllable that end in a single consonant preceded by a single vowel and have an accented last syllable double the final consonant before suffixes beginning with vowels (such as *-ed* and *-ing*).

    commit; committed; committing
    control; controlled; controlling
    occur; occurred; occurring

    The final consonant is not doubled when it is preceded by either two vowels or a consonant.

    retrain; retrained; retraining
    respect; respected; respecting

5. Verbs ending in *-y* preceded by a consonant normally change the *-y* to *-i* before all suffixes except *-ing*.

    carry; carried; carrying
    marry; married; marrying
    study; studied; studying

    If the final *-y* is preceded by a vowel, it remains unchanged.

    delay; delayed; delaying
    enjoy; enjoyed; enjoying
    obey; obeyed; obeying

6. Verbs ending in -c add a -k before a suffix beginning with -e or -i.

   > mimic; mimics; mimicked; mimicking
   > panic; panics; panicked; panicking
   > traffic; traffics; trafficked; trafficking

Tense and Aspect

7. Verbs generally exhibit their simple present and simple past tenses by single-word forms (for example, *do, did*).

8. The future tense is expressed by *shall* or *will* or by use of the simple present or present progressive forms in a context that makes the future meaning clear.

   > I *shall do* it.
   > He *will do* it.
   > I *leave* shortly for New York.
   > I *am leaving* shortly for New York.

9. *Aspect* involves the use of auxiliary verbs to indicate time relations other than the simple present, past, or future tenses. The *progressive tense* expresses action in progress or future action. The *present perfect tense* expresses action that began in the past and continues into the present, or that occurred at an indefinite time in the past. The *past perfect tense* expresses action that was completed before another past action or event. The *future perfect tense* expresses action that will be completed before some future action or event.

   > | *progressive:* | is seeing |
   > |---|---|
   > | *present perfect:* | has seen |
   > | *past perfect:* | had seen |
   > | *future perfect:* | will have seen |

The perfect and progressive aspects can also be combined to produce special verb forms, such as *had been seeing*.

Voice

10. Voice enables a verb to indicate whether the subject of a sentence is acting (*active* voice) or is being acted upon (*passive* voice).

active: He *respects* the other scientists.
            She *loved* the children.

passive: He is *respected* by the other scientists.
           She *was loved* by the children.

Sentences can be changed from active voice to passive voice by making the object of the verb its subject and by adding a form of the verb *be* to the original verb's past participle.

active: Napoleon *bit* the mail carrier.
            Conrad *will cook* the dinner.

passive: The mail carrier *was bitten* by Napoleon.
           The dinner *will be cooked* by Conrad.

Mood

11. Mood indicates manner of expression. The *indicative* mood states a fact or asks a question.

He *is* here.
Is he here?

The *imperative* mood expresses a command or request.

Come here.
Please *come* here.

The *subjunctive* mood expresses a condition contrary to fact. While it is not used often today, the subjunctive mood does appear in clauses following the verb *wish* and in clauses introduced by *if*.

I wish he *were* here.
If she *were* there, she could answer that.

Transitive and Intransitive Verbs

12. Verbs may be used transitively or intransitively. A
transitive verb acts upon a direct object.

> She *contributed* money.
> He *ran* the store.

An *intransitive* verb does not act upon a direct object.

> She *contributed* generously.
> He *ran* down the street.

As in these examples, many verbs are transitive in
one sense and intransitive in another.

Verbals

13. A group of words derived from verbs, called *verbals,* deserve added discussion. The members of
this group—the gerund, the participle, and the
infinitive—exhibit some but not all of the features of their parent verbs.

14. A gerund is an *-ing* verb form that functions
mainly as a noun. It has both active and passive
voices. In addition, a gerund has other characteristics of a verb: it conveys action, occurrence, or
being; it can take an object; and it can be modified by an adverb. In the following sentences,
"typing" and "driving" are gerunds, "data" and
"his workers" are their objects, and "daily" and
"hard" are adverbs modifying the gerund.

> *Typing* tabular *data daily* is a boring task.
> He liked *driving his workers hard.*

Since gerunds function as nouns, nouns and pronouns occurring immediately before gerunds should generally be in the possessive case.

> She is trying to improve *her skiing*.
> We objected to *their telling* the story to the press.
> I listened to the *bird's chirping*.

15. Participles, on the other hand, function as adjectives. They may occur alone ("a *broken* lawn mower") or in phrases that modify other words ("*Having broken the lawn mower*, he gave up for the day"). Participles, like gerunds, have active and passive forms.

> *active form:*   *Having failed* to pass the examination, he was forced to repeat the course.
>
> *passive form:*   *Having been failed* by his instructor, he was forced to repeat the course.

Participles, unlike gerunds, are not preceded by possessive nouns or pronouns.

> We saw *them telling* their story to the press. [i.e., we saw them as they told]
> We saw the *senator coming*. [i.e., we saw him as he arrived]

16. Infinitives may exhibit active *(to do)* and passive *(to be done)* voice and may indicate aspect *(to be doing, to have done, to have been doing, to have been done)*. Infinitives may take complements and may be modified by adverbs. In addition, they can function as nouns, adjectives, and adverbs.

> *noun use:*   *To be known* is *to be castigated*. [subject and predicate nominative]
>
>   He tried everything except *to bypass his superior*. [object of preposition "except"]

adjectival use: They had found a way *to increase profits greatly*. [modifies the noun "way"]

adverbial use: He was too furious *to speak*. [modifies "furious"]

Although *to* forms part of a complete infinitive, it may be merely understood rather than stated.

He helped [*to*] *complete* the marketing report.

Sequence of Tenses

17. If the main verb in a sentence is in the present tense, any other tense or compound verb form may follow it.

I *realize* that you *are leaving*.
you *left*.
you *were leaving*.
you *had left*.
you *will be leaving*.
you *will leave*.
you *may be leaving*.
you *must be leaving*.

18. If the main verb is in the past tense, subsequent verbs in the sentence may not use the present tense.

I *realized* that you *were leaving*.
you *left*.
you *had left*.
you *had been leaving*.
you *would be leaving*.
you *could be leaving*.
you *might be leaving*.
you *would leave*.

19. If the main verb is in the future tense, subsequent verbs in the sentence may not use the simple past tense.

He *will see* you because he *is going* to the meeting too.

    he *will be going* to the meeting too.

    he *will go* to the meeting too.

    he *has been going* to the meetings too.

    he *will have been going* to the meetings too.

20. Most writers try to maintain an order of tenses throughout their sentences that is consistent with natural or real time; that is, present tense for present-time matters, past tense for past matters, and future tense for future matters. However, there are two common exceptions. First, when the contents of printed material are being discussed, the present tense is often used.

> In *Etiquette,* Emily Post *discusses* forms of address.
> This analysis *gives* market projections for the next two years.
> In this latest position paper, the Secretary of State *writes* that . . .

Second, in order to convey a sense of immediacy to a particular sentence, the present tense may be used instead of the future.

> I *leave* for Tel Aviv tonight.

21. The sequence of tenses in sentences that express contrary-to-fact conditions is a common problem. The examples below show proper tense sequences.

> If he *were* on time, we *would leave* now.
> If he *had been* [not *would have been*] on time, we *would have left* an hour ago.

22. At one time, *shall* was considered the only correct form to use with the first person in simple future tenses (*I shall, we shall*), while *will* was limited to the second and third persons (*you will, it will, they will*). Today, however, either form is considered correct for the first person, *shall* being slightly more formal than *will*.

> We *shall* give your request special attention.
> We *will* send the agreement out tomorrow.

Subject-Verb Agreement

23. Verbs agree in number and in person with their grammatical subjects. At times, however, the grammatical subject may be singular in form but the thought it carries may have plural connotations. Here are some general guidelines for such situations. (For discussion of verb agreement with indefinite-pronoun subjects, see paragraphs 6–10 on pages 206–8. For discussion of verb number as affected by a compound subject whose elements are joined by *and/or*, see paragraph 6 on page 193.)

24. Plural and compound subjects take plural verbs, even if the subject is inverted.

> Both dogs and cats *were* tested for the virus.
> Grouped under the heading "fine arts" *are* music, theater, and painting.

25. Compound subjects or plural subjects working as a unit take singular verbs.

> Lord & Taylor *has* stores in the New York area.
> Macaroni and cheese *is* our best-selling product.
> Five hundred dollars *is* a stiff price for a ton.
> *but*
> Twenty-five milligrams of pentazocine *were* administered.

26. Compound subjects expressing mathematical relationships may be either singular or plural.

> One plus one *makes* [or *make*] two.
> Six from eight *leaves* [or *leave*] two.

27. Singular subjects joined by *or* or *nor* take singular verbs; plural subjects so joined take plural verbs.

> A freshman or sophomore *is* eligible for the scholarship.
> Neither freshmen nor sophomores *are* eligible for the scholarship.

If one subject is singular and the other plural, the verb agrees with the number of the subject that is closer to it.

> Either the assistants or the supervisor *has* to do the job.
> Either the supervisor or the assistants *have* to do the job.

28. Singular subjects introduced by *many a, such a, every, each,* or *no* take singular verbs, even when several such subjects are joined by *and.*

> Many an executive *has* gone to the top in that division.
> No supervisor and no assembler *is* excused from the time check.
> Every chair, table, and desk *has* to be accounted for.

29. The agreement of the verb with its subject ordinarily should not be changed because of an intervening phrase.

> One of my reasons for resigning *involves* purely personal considerations.
> The president of the company, as well as members of his staff, *has* arrived.
> He, not any of the proxy voters, *has* to be present.

30. The verb *to be* agrees with its subject but not necessarily with what follows.

> His mania *was* minimizing payrolls and maximizing profits.
>
> Women in the workforce *constitute* an important field of study.

The subject following *There is, There are,* etc., must agree in number with the verb.

> There *are* many complications here.
>
> There *is* no reason to worry about him.

31. Collective nouns—such as *orchestra, team, committee, family*—usually take singular verbs but can take plural verbs if the emphasis is on the individual members of the unit rather than on the unit itself.

> The committee *has agreed* to extend the deadline.
>   *but also*
> The committee *have been* at odds ever since the beginning.

32. The word *number* in the phrase *a number of* usually takes a plural verb, but in the phrase *the number of* it takes a singular verb.

> A number of errors *were* [also *was*] made.
>
> The number of errors *was* surprising.

33. A relative clause that follows the expression *one of the/those/these* + plural noun takes a plural verb in conventional English, but in informal English it may take a singular verb.

> He is one of those executives who *worry* [also *worries*] a lot.
>
> This is one of those new printers that *create* [also *creates*] perfect copies.

Linking and *Sense* Verbs

34. Linking verbs (such as the various forms of *to be*) and the so-called "sense" verbs (such as *feel, look, taste,* and *smell,* as well as particular meanings of *appear, become, continue, grow, prove, remain, seem, stand,* and *turn*) connect subjects with predicate nouns or adjectives.

> He *is* a vice president.
> He *became* vice president.
> The temperature *continues* cold.
> The future *looks* prosperous.
> I *feel* bad about the loss of jobs.
> He *remains* healthy.

Sense words often cause confusion, since writers sometimes mistakenly use adverbs instead of adjectives following these words.

not:	This scent *smells nicely.*
instead:	This scent *smells nice.*
not:	The new formula *tastes well.*
instead:	The new formula *tastes good.*

Split Infinitives

35. A split infinitive is an infinitive that has a modifier between the *to* and the verbal (as in "to really care"). Some grammarians disapprove of them, and many people avoid them whenever they can. However, the split infinitive has been around a long time and has been used by a wide variety of distinguished writers. It can be useful particularly if a writer wants to stress the verbal element of an infinitive. For example, in the phrase "to *thoroughly* complete the financial study," placing the adverb immediately before the verbal element strengthens its effect on the verbal. The position of an adverb may actually modify or change the meaning of an entire sentence.

original: He arrived at the office to *unexpectedly* find a new name on the door.

repositioned with new meaning: He arrived at the office *unexpectedly* to find a new name on the door.

Very long adverbial modifiers that interrupt an infinitive are clumsy and should be avoided or moved.

awkward: He wanted to *completely and without mercy* defeat his competitor.

smoother: He wanted to defeat his competitor *completely and without mercy.*

Dangling Participles

36. Dangling participles are participles that lack a normally expected grammatical relation to the rest of the sentence. The standard error occurs when the participial phrase with which a sentence begins is immediately followed by a noun or pronoun representing a person or thing different from the one described in the phrase. They are best avoided, as they may confuse the reader or seem ludicrous.

not: *Walking through the door,* her coat was caught.

instead: *While walking through the door,* she caught her coat.

Walking through the door, she caught her coat.

She caught her coat *while walking through the door.*

not:	*Caught in the act,* his excuses were unconvincing.
instead:	*Caught in the act,* he could not make his excuses convincing.
not:	*Having been told that he was incompetent and dishonest,* the executive fired the man.
instead:	*Having told the man that he was incompetent and dishonest,* the executive fired him.
	Having been told by his superior that he was incompetent and dishonest, the man was fired.

Participles should not be confused with prepositions that end in *-ing* (such as *concerning, considering, providing, regarding, respecting, touching*).

Concerning your complaint, we can tell you . . .

Considering all the implications, you have made a dangerous decision.

Touching the matter at hand, we can say that . . .

Phrases

A phrase is a brief expression that consists of two or more grammatically related words but that does not constitute a clause. (See also the section on Clauses beginning on page 233.)

Basic Types

There are seven basic types of phrases.

1. An *absolute phrase* consists of a noun followed by a modifier (such as a participle). Absolute phrases act independently within a sentence without modifying a particular element of the sentence. Absolute phrases are also referred to as *nominative absolutes*.

    He stalked out, *his eyes staring straight ahead.*

2. A *gerund phrase* includes a gerund and functions as a noun.

   Sitting on a patient's bed is bad hospital etiquette.

3. An *infinitive phrase* includes an infinitive and may function as a noun, adjective, or adverb.

noun:	*To do that* would be stupid.
adjective:	This was an occasion *to remember*.
adverb:	They struggled *to get free* of the mounting debt.

4. A *noun phrase* consists of a noun and its modifiers.

   The second warehouse is huge.

5. A *participial phrase* includes a participle and functions as an adjective.

   Listening all the time with great concentration, she began to line up her options.

6. A *prepositional phrase* consists of a preposition and its object. It may function as a noun, adjective, or adverb.

noun:	*Out of debt* is where we'd like to be!
adjective:	Here is the desk *with the extra file drawer*.
adverb:	He now walked *without a limp*.

7. A *verb phrase* consists of a verb and any other terms that either modify it or complete its meaning.

   She *will have arrived too late* for you to talk to her.

Usage Problems

8. Usage problems with phrases occur most often when a modifying phrase is not placed close enough to the word or words that it modifies. The phrase "on December 10" in the following

sentence, for example, must be repositioned to clarify just what happened on that date.

not:	We received your letter concerning the shipment of parts *on December 10*.
instead:	*On December 10* we received your letter concerning the shipment of parts.
	We received your letter concerning the *December 10* shipment of parts.

9. Dangling participial phrases represent a very common usage problem. For a discussion of dangling participles, see paragraph 36 on page 230.

Clauses

A clause is a group of words containing both a subject and a predicate. A clause functions as an element of a compound or complex sentence. There are two general types of clauses: the *main* or *independent clause* and the *subordinate* or *dependent clause*. A main clause (such as "it is hot") is an independent grammatical unit and can stand alone. A subordinate clause (such as "because it is hot") cannot stand alone, and must be either preceded or followed by a main clause.

Basic Types

Like phrases, clauses can perform as particular parts of speech within the sentence. There are three basic types of clauses that have part-of-speech functions.

1. The *adjective clause* modifies a noun or pronoun and normally follows the word it modifies.

> The circus clown, *who was also a trainer*, was multi-talented.
>
> I can't see the reason *why you're upset*.

He is a man *who will succeed*.
She brought the specialty *that you ordered*.

2. The *adverb clause* modifies a verb, an adjective, or another adverb and normally follows the word it modifies.

They made a valiant effort *because the children were in danger*.
When it rains, it pours.
I'm certain *that he is guilty*.
We accomplished less *than we did before*.

3. The *noun clause* fills a noun slot in a sentence and thus can be a subject, an object, or a complement.

subject:	*Whoever is qualified* should apply.
object of a verb:	I do not know *what his problem is*.
object of a preposition:	Route that journal to *whichever desk you wish*.
complement:	The trouble is *that she has no alternative*.

Elliptical Clauses

4. Some clause elements may be omitted if the context makes clear the understood elements.

I remember the first time [that] we met.
This view is better than that [view is].
When [she is] on the job, she is always competent and alert.

Placement of Clauses

5. A modifying clause should be placed as close as possible to the word or words it modifies so as to ensure maximum clarity and avoid the possibility of misinterpretation. If intervening words impair

the clarity of a sentence, it should be rewritten or recast.

> *awkward:*   The yellow flowers were arranged in the blue vase, *picked that morning*.
>
> *recast:*   *Picked that morning*, the yellow flowers were arranged in the blue vase.

Restrictive and Nonrestrictive Clauses

Clauses that modify are also referred to as *restrictive* or *nonrestrictive*. Whether a clause is restrictive or nonrestrictive has a direct bearing on sentence punctuation. (For more information on restrictive and nonrestrictive clauses, see paragraph 10 on page 16 and paragraph 29 on page 215.)

6. Restrictive clauses are essential to the meaning of the word or words they modify, and cannot be omitted without the meaning of the sentences being radically changed. They are not set off by commas.

   > Textbooks *that are not current* should be returned.

   In this example, the clause "that are not current" restricts the subject to a certain kind of "textbooks," and thus is essential to the meaning of the sentence. If the restrictive clause were omitted, "textbooks" would not be limited at all and the sentence would convey an entirely different idea.

   > Textbooks should be returned.

7. Nonrestrictive clauses are not inextricably bound to the word or words they modify but instead merely convey additional information about them. Nonrestrictive clauses may be omitted altogether without radically changing the meaning of the sentence. They are set off by commas.

Our guide, *who wore a green beret,* was an experienced traveler.

In this example, the nonrestrictive clause "who wore a green beret" does not limit the subject to a particular class of guide; it merely serves as a bit of incidental detail. Removal of the clause does not affect the basic meaning of the sentence.

Our guide was an experienced traveler.

Sentences

A sentence is a grammatically self-contained unit that (1) makes a statement (declarative sentence), (2) asks a question (interrogative sentence), (3) makes a request or command (imperative sentence), or (4) expresses an exclamation (exclamatory sentence).

Basic Types

Sentences are classified into three main types on the basis of their clause structure.

1. The *simple sentence* has one subject and one predicate (either or both of which may be compound).

   Clothing is costly.
   Silk and linen are costly.
   Silk and linen are costly and are sometimes scarce.

2. The *compound sentence* is made up of two or more main clauses.

   I could arrange to arrive late, or I could simply send my colleague.
   This commute takes 40 minutes by car, but we can make it in 20 by train.

A few of the teachers had Ph.D.'s, even more had B.A.'s, but the majority had both B.A.'s and M.B.A.'s.

3. The *complex sentence* combines a main clause with one or more subordinate clauses (italicized in the examples).

> The committee meeting began *when the business manager and the staff supervisor walked in.*
>
> *Although the city council made some reforms,* the changes came so late *that they could not prevent these abuses.*

Construction

Grammatically sound sentences can be constructed by following some general guidelines.

4. Use connectives to link phrases or clauses of *equal* rank. When a connective is used to link phrases or clauses that are not equal, the resulting sentence may sound careless or clumsy, and may even be confusing.

not:	I was sitting in on a meeting, and he stood up and started a long, rambling discourse on a new pollution-control device.
instead:	I sat in on a meeting during which he stood up and rambled on about a new pollution-control device.
	I sat in on that meeting. He stood up and rambled on about a new pollution-control device.
not:	This company employs a full-time research staff and was founded in 1945.
instead:	This company, which employs a full-time research staff, was founded in 1945.
	Established in 1945, this company employs a full-time research staff.

5. Create parallel, balanced sentence elements. When clauses having unparallel subjects are linked together, the resulting sentence can be unclear.

nonparallel:	The report gives market statistics, but he does not list his sources for these figures.
parallel:	The report gives market statistics, but it does not list the sources for these figures.
nonparallel:	We are glad to have you as our client, and please call on us whenever you need help.
parallel:	We are glad to have you as our client, and we hope that you will call on us whenever you need help.
in two sentences:	We are glad to have you as our client. We hope that you will call on us whenever you need help.

6. Link sentence elements tightly together. When elements are strung together by loose or excessive use of *and*, the sentence can become too lengthy and may lack any logical flow.

not:	This company is a Class 1 motor freight common carrier of general commodities and it operates more than 10,000 tractors, trailers, and city delivery trucks through 200 terminals, and serves 40 states and the District of Columbia.
instead:	This company is a Class 1 motor freight common carrier of general commodities. It operates more than 10,000 tractors, trailers, and city delivery trucks through 200 terminals, and serves 40 states and the District of Columbia.

7. Choose the proper conjunction to link clauses. *And* is used to achieve simple linkage. However, if one clause is being contrasted with another, or if a reason or result is being expressed, a more specific conjunction should be used. (For more on coordinating and subordinating conjunctions, see paragraphs 1–6 and 10–12 on pages 191–95.)

too general:	The economy was soft *and* we lost a lot of business.
specific:	We lost a lot of business *because* the economy was soft.
	The economy was soft, *so* we lost a lot of business.
	The soft economy has cost us a lot of business.

8. Avoid unnecessary or unexpected grammatical shifts, which can interrupt the reader's train of thought and needlessly complicate the material.

shift from active to passive voice:	As we *finished* our tennis match, other players *were seen* coming onto the court.
rephrased:	As we *finished* our tennis match, we *saw* other players coming onto the court.
shift in person:	*One* can use either erasers or correction fluid to remove typographical errors; however, *you* should make certain that *your* corrections are clean.
rephrased:	*You* can use either erasers or correction fluid to eradicate errors; however, *you* should make certain that *your* corrections are clean.

shift from phrase *to clause:*	*Because of the current parts shortage and we are also experiencing a strike, we cannot fill any orders now.*
rephrased:	*Because of a parts shortage and a strike, we cannot fill any orders now.*

9. Order the sentence elements rationally and logically. Place closely related elements as close together as possible.

related elements *separated:*	We would appreciate your sending us the instructions on shipping by mail or fax.
joined:	We would appreciate your sending us by mail or by fax the shipping instructions.
	We would appreciate your mailing or faxing us the shipping instructions.

10. Be sure that your sentences form complete, independent units containing both a subject and a predicate.

incomplete:	During the last three years, our calculator sales soared. While our conventional office-machine sales fell off.
complete:	During the last three years, our calculator sales soared, but our conventional office-machine sales fell off.
	While our conventional office-machine sales fell off during the last three years, our calculator sales soared.

In dialogue or specialized copy, fragmentation may be used for particular reasons (for example, to attract the reader's attention).

See it now. The car for the Nineties ... A car you'll want to own.

Sentence Length

11. Sentence length is directly related to the writer's purpose; there is no magic number of words that guarantees a good sentence. An executive covering broad but complex topics in a long memo may use concise, succinct sentences for the sake of clarity, impact, and readability. An essayist who wants the reader to reflect on what is being said may employ longer, more involved sentences. A speechwriter may use a series of long sentences that build up to a climactic and forceful short sentence, in order to emphasize an important point.

Sentence Strategy

12. **Coordination and subordination** Coordination involves linking independent sentences and sentence elements by means of coordinating conjunctions, while subordination involves transforming elements into dependent structures by means of subordinating conjunctions. Coordination tends to promote loose sentence structure; subordination tends to tighten the structure and to emphasize a main clause.

coordination: During the balance of 1995, this Company expects to issue $100 million of long-term debt and equity securities *and* may guarantee up to $200 million of new corporate bonds.

subordination: While this Company expects to issue $100 million of long-term debt and equity securities during the balance of 1995, it may also guarantee up to $200 million of new corporate bonds.

13. Interrupting elements Interrupting the normal flow of a sentence by inserting comments can be a useful way to call attention to an aside, to emphasize a word or phrase, to convey a particular tone (such as forcefulness), or to make the prose a little more informal.

> His evidence, if reliable, could send our client to prison.
>
> These companies—ours as well as theirs—must show more profits.
>
> This, ladies and gentlemen, is the prime reason for your cost overruns. I trust it will not happen again?

Interrupting elements should not be overused, however, since too many of them may distract the reader.

14. Parallelism and balance Parallelism and balance work together to maintain an even, rhythmic flow of thought. Parallelism means a similarity in construction of adjacent phrases and clauses that are equivalent, similar, or opposed in meaning.

> These ecological problems are of crucial concern *to* scientists, *to* businesspeople, *to* government officials, and *to* all citizens.
>
> Our attorneys have argued *that* the trademark is ours, *that* our rights have been violated, and *that* appropriate compensation is required.
>
> He was respected not only *for his intelligence* but also *for his integrity.*
>
> The thing that interested me ... about New York ... was the ... contrast it showed between the dull and the shrewd, the strong and the weak, the rich and the poor, the wise and the ignorant....
>
> —Theodore Dreiser

Balance involves the symmetrical use of two or more parallel phrases or clauses that contain similar, contrasting, or opposing ideas.

> To err is human; to forgive, divine.
> —Alexander Pope

> Ask not what your country can do for you—ask what you can do for your country.
> —John F. Kennedy

15. **Periodic and cumulative sentences** Longer sentences can often be classified as either periodic or cumulative. The periodic sentence is structured so that its main idea or thrust is suspended until the very end, thereby drawing the reader's eye and mind along to an emphatic conclusion. In the example below, the main point follows the final comma.

> Although the Commission would like to give its licensees every encouragement to experiment on their own initiative with new and innovative means of providing access to their stations for the discussion of important public issues, it cannot justify imposing a specific right of access by government fiat.

The cumulative sentence, on the other hand, is structured so that its main point appears first, followed by other phrases or clauses expanding on or supporting it. In the following example, the main point precedes the first comma.

> The balance must be finely crafted, lest strategists err too much on the side of technological sophistication only to find that U.S. military forces can be defeated by overwhelming mass.

The final phrase or clause in a cumulative sentence theoretically could be deleted without changing the essential meaning of the sentence. A cumulative sentence is therefore more loosely structured than a periodic sentence.

16. **Reversal** A reversal of customary or expected sentence order can be an effective stylistic strategy when used sparingly.

> *customary or*
> *expected order:*   These realities are indisputable: the economy has taken a dramatic downturn, costs on all fronts have soared, and jobs are at a premium.
>
> *reversal:*   That the economy has taken a dramatic downturn; that costs on all fronts have soared; that jobs are at a premium—these are indisputable realities.

17. **Rhetorical questions** The rhetorical question is yet another device to focus the reader's attention on a problem or an issue. The rhetorical question requires no specific response from the reader but often merely sets up the introduction of the writer's own view. A rhetorical question may serve as a topic sentence in a paragraph, or a series of rhetorical questions may spotlight pertinent issues.

> What can be done to correct the problem? Two things, to begin with: never discuss cases out of the office, and never allow a visitor to see the papers on your desk.

18. **Variety** Any kind of repetitious pattern may create monotony. As a means of keeping the reader's attention, try to maintain a balance of different kinds of sentences. Use a combination of simple, compound, and complex sentences in a paragraph, including a variety of short and long sentences. Vary the beginnings of your sentences so

that every sentence in a paragraph does not begin directly with the subject. Through judicious use of combinations of sentence patterns and the sentence strategies discussed in the preceding paragraphs, you can attain an interesting, diversified style.

Paragraphs

The underlying structure of any written communication must be controlled by the writer if the material is to be clear, coherent, and effective. Since good paragraphing is a means to this end, the writer should be able to recognize various kinds of paragraphs and their functions, as well as problems that might arise from faulty paragraphing and discrepancies that could cause misinterpretation or detract from the effect of the communication.

1. A paragraph is a subdivision in writing that consists of one or more sentences, deals with one or more ideas, or quotes a speaker or a source. The first line of a paragraph is indented in reports, studies, articles, theses, and books; in business letters and memos it may or may not be indented, depending on the style being followed.

2. Paragraphs should not be considered as isolated, self-contained units that can be mechanically lined up without transitions or interrelationship of ideas. Rather, they should be viewed as components of larger sections that are tightly interlinked and that interact in the sequential development of a major idea or cluster of ideas. The overall coherence of a communication depends on this interaction.

Developing Paragraphs

3. Depending on the writer's intentions, paragraph development may take any of several directions. A paragraph may:

- Move from the general to the specific.
- Move from the specific to the general.
- Exhibit an alternating order of comparison and contrast.
- Chronicle events in order.
- Describe something (such as a group of objects) in a particular spatial order—for example, from near to far, or vice versa.
- Follow a climactic sequence, with the least important facts or examples described first, leading to the most important facts or examples. Or the facts or issues that are easy to comprehend or accept may be set forth first, followed by those that are more difficult to comprehend or accept. In this way the easier material makes the reader receptive and prepares him or her for the more difficult points.
- Follow an anticlimactic order, setting forth the most persuasive arguments first so that the reader, having been influenced in a positive way, is carried along by the rest of the argument with a growing feeling of assent.

Effective Paragraphing

The following material outlines some ways of building effective paragraphs.

4. A topic sentence—a key sentence to which the other sentences in the paragraph are related—may be placed either at the beginning or at the end of a paragraph. A lead-in topic sentence should present the main idea of the paragraph

and set the tone of the material that follows. A terminal topic sentence should be an analysis, conclusion, or summation of what has gone before it.

5. A single-sentence paragraph can be used to achieve an easy transition from a preceding to a subsequent paragraph (especially when the paragraphs are long and complex) if it repeats an important word or phrase from the preceding paragraph, contains a pronoun reference to a key individual mentioned in a preceding paragraph, or is introduced by an appropriate conjunction or conjunctive adverb that tightly connects the paragraphs.

6. **Opening paragraph** The very first paragraph should set the tone, introduce the subject, and lead into the discussion. It should be worded so as to immediately attract attention and arouse interest. Opening paragraphs of the following kinds can be effective:

  - a succinct statement of purpose or point of view
  - a concise definition of a problem
  - a lucid statement of a key issue or fact

Openings of the following kinds, by contrast, can blunt the point of the rest of the material:

  - an apology for the material to be presented
  - a querulous complaint or a defensive posture
  - a detailed account of material presented earlier
  - a presentation of self-evident facts
  - a group of sentences rendered limp and meaningless by clichés

7. **Closing paragraph** The last paragraph should tie together the ideas and points that have been set

forth earlier and reemphasize the main thrust of the communication. Effective endings can be of several types:

- a setting forth of the most important conclusions drawn from the preceding discussion
- a final analysis of the main problems under discussion
- a lucid summary of the individual points brought up earlier
- a final, clear statement of opinion or position
- concrete suggestions or solutions, if applicable
- specific questions asked of the reader, if applicable

Endings of the following kinds, by contrast, can reduce the effect of a communication:

- apologies for a poor presentation
- qualifying remarks that blunt or negate incisive points made earlier
- insertion of minor details or afterthoughts
- a meaningless closing couched in clichés

Criteria

8. The following are tests of good paragraphs:

- Does the paragraph have a clear purpose, or is it there just to fill up space? Does it simply restate in other terms what has been said before?
- Does the paragraph clarify rather than cloud the main ideas of the piece?
- Is the paragraph adequately developed, or does it merely raise other questions that it does not attempt to answer? If a position is being taken, are supporting information and statistics essential to its defense included?
- Are the length and wording of the paragraphs sufficiently varied, or is the same language used again and again?

- Is the sentence structure within each paragraph coherent?
- Is each paragraph unified and coherent? Do all the sentences really *belong* there, or do they digress into areas that would have been better covered in another paragraph or omitted altogether? Does each sentence lead clearly and logically to the next?
- Are the transitions between paragraphs achieved by transitional phrases that indicate the relationship between them and indicate the direction in which the presentation is moving?

Chapter 7

Problems in Word Usage

In your writing you will frequently have to decide between alternative words and terms, not to mention alternative spellings, some of which may be more correct or appropriate in given contexts than others. Here are brief discussions (many adapted from *Merriam-Webster's Collegiate Dictionary*) of a number of words and terms that represent usage or spelling problems for many writers.

a, an   For the use of these articles, see paragraphs 3–5 on page 200.

above   The use of *above* as both a noun ("none of the *above*") and an adjective ("Please refer to the *above* table") has long been established as standard usage.

adapt, adopt   *Adopt* suggests taking something over as it is ("The committee voted to *adopt* a new set of rules"). *Adapt* suggests changing something to meet new needs ("*adapt* a short story for television"). When you start a new job, you'll have to *adapt* to the way your new company does things. You may like one of their procedures well enough to *adopt* it as your own.

adverse, averse   These words are similar in meaning, but *adverse* is the more generally useful word. It is commonly used to modify a following noun ("*adverse* circumstances," "an *adverse* reaction"). *Adverse to* is freely used of things as a predicate adjective ("testimony that was *adverse to* our cause"). When used of people, *adverse to* and *averse to* are essentially the same. A subtle distinction in which *adverse* refers to opinion or intention and *averse* to feelings or inclination is sometimes observed ("senators *adverse* to the nomination"; "*averse* to long engagements"). *Averse* is very commonly used in negative constructions ("I am not *averse* to hearing myself praised").

affect, effect   These verbs have been getting muddled for about five hundred years, but they are not synonyms. There are even two verbs *affect* ("*affected* an air of worldly indifference," "how the news will *affect* the stock market"), and *effect* has been mistakenly put in place of both. *Effect* means approximately "to bring about" ("the steps necessary to *effect* a change in government policy"). If you have doubts about which spelling to use, see your dictionary. The nouns are likewise confused, but *effect* is usually the one you'll want, as *affect* is a specialized term in psychology.

aggravate   *Aggravate* is used chiefly in two meanings: "to make worse" ("*aggravated* her shoulder injury," "their financial position was *aggravated* by the market downturn") and "to irritate, annoy" ("The President was *aggravated* by French intransigence"). In published prose you are much more likely to meet the first use than the second. The same is not true, however, for *aggravation*, which means "irritation" more often than not, and *aggravating*, which almost always expresses annoyance.

allusion, illusion   If these words are confused, someone has made a spelling mistake, because the words have nothing in common except their last seven letters. A quick check in your dictionary will dispel all confusion (*allusion* is an indirect reference; *illusion* is a misleading image).

almost, most *Most* is often used like *almost* ("*Most* everyone was there"). This is basically a speech form and is commonly put into advertising copy to create a homey everyday atmosphere. You won't need it in most writing.

alot, a lot There are a lot of people who wish that *a lot* were a single word, quicker to write or type, and one space shorter than the two-word form. But most of the people responsible for turning words into print—in books, in magazines, in letters—insist on two words. You might as well resign yourself to two words: you won't have a lot of success in slipping the single-word form past their watchful eyes.

alright Even though the business community has been using the one-word *alright* since the 1920s, the world of publishing has preferred *all right*. *Alright* is only gradually gaining acceptance, and that most often in business publications and newspaper writing. *All right* is still more common in print.

amount, number *Number* is regularly used with nouns that can form a plural and can be used with a numeral ("a large *number* of orders," "any *number* of times"). *Amount* is mainly used with nouns that denote a substance or concept that can't be divided and counted up ("the annual *amount* of rainfall," "a large *amount* of money"). The use of *amount* with count nouns has been criticized; it is usually used when the number of things can be thought of as a mass or collection ("a substantial *amount* of job offers"), but you'll probably want to avoid it in most of your writing.

anymore, any more Although both *anymore* and *any more* are found in written use, in this century *anymore* is more common. *Anymore* is regularly used with negatives ("Don't get around much *anymore*"), to ask a question ("Do you jog *anymore*?") and in the conditional ("If you do that *anymore*, I'll leave"), and sometimes appears in positive constructions ("I'm too old to believe in Santa Claus *anymore*"). The use of *anymore* to mean "now" or "these days" is widespread in speech in all areas of the United States except New England ("Hardly a day passes without rain *anymore*"), but it is not likely to appear in formal writing.

apt, liable   Both *liable* and *apt* when followed by an infinitive are used nearly interchangeably with *likely* ("He was more *liable* [*likely*] to get tired easily," "The roads are *apt* [*likely*] to be slippery when wet"). This use of *apt* is widely accepted. Some people think *liable* should be limited to situations having an undesirable outcome ("If you speed, you're *liable* to be caught") and it is most often used this way in writing.

as, as if, like   *Like* used as a conjunction in the sense of *as* ("just *like* I used to do") or in the sense of *as if* ("It looks *like* it will rain") has been frequently criticized, especially since its use in a widely publicized cigarette commercial slogan. *Like* has been so used for nearly six hundred years, although it was not as common in written works in the past as it has been in the twentieth century. There is no real grammatical basis for objecting to these uses of *like*, but you can avoid controversy by using *as* or *as if*.

as far as   "*As far as* clothes, young people always know best." This sentence, from a newspaper article, shows *as far as* used as a preposition. Prepositional use developed from the more common conjunction ("*as far as* clothes are concerned") by omission of the following verb or verb phrase, and it is mostly confined to spoken use, although we sometimes find it in journalistic writing.

as regards, in regard to, in regards to   The first two terms, along with their cousins *with regard to* and *re-*

garding, have been criticized in many handbooks as jargonistic or excessively wordy. You can often replace them with such alternatives as *about* or *concerning,* but if a writer prefers the longer phrases, there is no solid reason to change them. *In regards to,* with *regards* pluralized, is a spoken form only and should not be used except in a direct quotation.

assure, ensure, insure   You can distinguish between these words by using *insure* for money and guarantees ("*Insure* that package before sending it"), *ensure* for things ("Send the package overnight express to *ensure* its arrival in the morning"), and *assure* for people ("I *assure* you that the package will arrive tomorrow morning"). Current American English does reserve *assure* for people, but *insure* is usual for both the other uses; it is perfectly acceptable to write "Send the package overnight express to *insure* its arrival in the morning."

awful   It has been traditional to criticize any use of *awful* and *awfully* that doesn't convey the original sense of being filled with awe. However, *awful* has long been acceptable in the meanings "extremely objectionable" ("What an *awful* color") and "exceedingly great" ("an *awful* lot of money") in speech and casual writing. Use of the adverbs *awful* and *awfully* as intensifiers ("I'm *awful* tired," "he's *awfully* rich") is likewise common in informal prose. But you probably won't want to use any of these where a formal tone is called for.

awhile   The use of the adverb *awhile* as the object of a preposition is standard ("After *awhile* I felt better," "For *awhile* she was silent"). But some people are sticklers for the spelling *a while* after a preposition.

between, among   For the use of these prepositions, see paragraph 6 on page 204.

bimonthly, biweekly These words can cause confusion because they both have two meanings—"twice a week (or month)," and "once every two weeks (or months)." A memo that announces that from now on committee meetings will be biweekly may not be too helpful to the recipients. If you have to draw up such a memo, try to include a hint (*"Biweekly* meetings will be held every Tuesday and Friday"). Or you could skip the *bi*-word altogether and try "every Tuesday and Friday" or "every other Wednesday." Confusion will result if the writer and reader of *biweekly* or *bimonthly* don't both have the same meaning in mind. It's the writer's duty to make sure that there is no confusion.

can, may Both *can* and *may* are used to refer to possibility (*"Can* the deal still go through?" "It *may* still happen"). Since the possibility of someone's doing something may depend on someone else's agreeing to it, the two words have become interchangeable when they refer to permission ("You *can* [*may*] go now if you like"). Though the use of *can* to ask or grant permission has been common since the last century, *may* is often thought to be more appropriate in formal correspondence. This meaning of *may* is relatively rare in negative constructions, where *cannot* and *can't* are more usual ("They *cannot* [*may not*] use it without paying").

center The intransitive verb *center* (meaning "to focus") is most commonly used with the prepositions *at, in, on,* and *around. At* appears to be favored in mathematical contexts, while the others are found in a broad range of contexts. Some people object to *center around* as illogical, though it is a standard idiom. If you should need to avoid *center around,* you can use *center on* (or *in*) or try *revolve around.*

complement, compliment The confusion of these words is purely a matter of spelling, since they have no meanings in common, either as noun or verb. The most frequent mistake is to use the more common *compliment* in place of the less common *complement*. A quick look in a collegiate dictionary will clear up any doubts as to which word is needed. Take the same precautions for the adjectives *complimentary* and *complementary*.

comprise The sense of *comprise* meaning "to compose or constitute" ("the branches that *comprise* our government") rather than "to include or be made up of" ("Our government *comprises* various branches") has been attacked as wrong, for reasons that are unclear. Until recently, it was used chiefly in scientific and technical writing; today, it enjoys literary and business use as well, and this sense of *comprise* has become the most widely used sense. But you may prefer to choose a safe synonym such as *compose* or *make up*.

consensus The phrase *consensus of opinion* has been so often claimed to be redundant that many writers avoid it. It is not, in fact, a redundancy, since it uses a sense of *consensus* that means "general agreement." However, you can avoid the phrase by using *consensus* alone in its stead; many writers in fact do so.

contact The use of *contact* as a verb, especially to mean "get in touch with" ("*Contact* your local dealer"), has long been standard.

data *Data* has firmly established itself with a meaning independent of its use as the plural form of *datum*. It is used in one of two ways: as a plural noun (like *earnings*), taking a plural verb and plural modifiers (such as *these* or *many*) but not cardinal numbers ("These *data* show that we're out of the recession"); or as an abstract mass noun (like *information*), taking a

singular verb and singular modifiers (such as *this,
much,* or *little*) ("The *data* on the subject is plentiful").
Both constructions are standard, but many people
are convinced that only the plural form is correct,
and in consequence the plural form is somewhat
more common in print. What you want to avoid is
mixing in signs of the singular (like *this* or *much*) when
you use a plural verb.

different from, different than   Both of these phrases
are standard, in spite of some people's disliking *different than*. Each form has its particular virtues. *Different
from* works best when you can take advantage of its
preposition *from* ("The new proposal is very *different
from* the old one"). *Different than* works best when a
clause follows ("very *different* in size *than* it was two
years ago"). *Different than* can be used in place of *different from* ("*different than* the old proposal"), but you
must rephrase a sentence to change *different than* to
different from when a clause follows ("very *different* in
size *from* what it was two years ago").

disinterested, uninterested   *Disinterested* has basically
two uses: an ethical one, in the sense of "unbiased" ("a
disinterested decision," "*disinterested* intellectual curios-
ity"), and a neutral one that it shares with *uninterested,*
"not interested." Some people object to the neutral
use, but it is standard, and may even be chosen for
purposes of emphasis ("trying to lecture a wriggling
and *disinterested* child") or to suggest a loss of interest,
which *uninterested* does not ("became *disinterested* in
the subject").

due to   When the *due* of *due to* is clearly an adjective
("absences *due to* the flu") no one complains about the
phrase. When *due to* is a preposition ("*Due to* the holi-
day, our office will be closed"), some people object
and call for *owing to* or *because of*. Both uses of *due to*

are entirely standard, but in formal writing you may prefer one of the alternatives to the latter.

each other, one another The traditional rules call for *each other* to be used in reference to two ("The two girls looked at *each other* in surprise") and *one another* to be used in reference to three or more ("There will be time for people to talk with *one another* after the meeting"). In actual use, they are employed interchangeably. (For more examples, see paragraphs 24–25 on page 213.)

enormity Some people would limit *enormity* to the meaning "great wickedness" and not allow it to be used to denote large size. But the word has many interesting uses. When *enormity* is used to refer to large size, either literally or figuratively, it usually suggests something so large as to be overwhelming ("the *enormity* of the Grand Canyon," "the *enormity* of the problem of the homeless"). *Enormity* can also suggest both great size and deviation from morality ("the *enormity* of our stockpiles of nuclear weapons"). It can emphasize the importance of an event ("the *enormity* of the war") or of its consequences ("the *enormity* of the destruction"). *Enormity* can also suggest a considerable departure from the expected or the normal ("After the hurricane, the *enormity* of the situation set in"). These uses are all perfectly standard.

enthuse The use or avoidance of *enthuse* is entirely a matter of taste. *Enthuse* is solidly established as standard, especially in journalism. Some may feel it to be a bit informal for serious prose.

farther, further *Farther* and *further* have been used more or less interchangeably throughout most of their history, but currently they are showing signs of diverging. As adverbs they are interchangeable whenever spatial, temporal, or metaphorical distance is involved ("lived *farther* [*further*] from town," "The news spread even *farther* [*further*]"). Where there is no notion of distance, *further* is used ("Our techniques can be *further* refined"). *Further* is also used as a sentence modifier ("*Further*, there is no evidence"), but *farther* is not. As adjectives, their use is also diverging, with *farther* taking over the meaning of distance ("the *farther* shore") and *further* the meaning of addition ("needed no *further* invitation").

finalize   *Finalize* occurs most frequently in business and government contexts ("The budget will be *finalized*," "*finalizing* the deal"). See the entry for *-ize* below.

flaunt, flout   *Flaunt* acquired its meaning "to treat with contempt" ("*flaunting* the rules") from confusion with *flout*, which has the same meaning ("*flouting* the rules"). Although this meaning is well established, many people believe it is an error. *Flout* is sometimes used to mean "display ostentatiously" ("*flouted* their wealth"), but the standard term in such contexts is actually *flaunt*. The compromise spelling *flount* is also not standard.

formally, formerly   There is no reason to confuse these words, although they are likely to sound pretty similar. *Formally* means only "in a formal way" ("dressed *formally*," "a *formally* constituted committee"). *Formerly* means "at an earlier time" ("B&F Corporation, *formerly* doing business as Binns & Franks"). Notice that you could put *formally* into this last context, but it would not make very much sense.

fortuitous   The sense of *fortuitous* meaning "lucky" ("Our acquisition of the stock at that time was *fortuitous*") is standard, but is sometimes objected to. A newer sense, "coming by a lucky chance" ("There was a *fortuitous* cab at the corner just as the storm broke") is halfway between the "lucky" sense and the original "occurring by chance" sense. Only the original sense is likely to occur in a negative sentence ("Its happening five times in a row cannot have been *fortuitous*").

fulsome   The adjective *fulsome* can present a problem of ambiguity: two of its most frequently used senses mean very different things. In expressions such as "fulsome praise" or "a fulsome tribute," it can be hard to tell whether *fulsome* means "generous in amount, extent, or spirit" or "excessively complimentary or flattering." To avoid misinterpretation, be sure that the context in which you use it makes the intended meaning clear.

good   Both *good* and *well* are acceptable when used to express good health ("I feel *good*," "I feel *well*"). *Good* may also connote good spirits. However, the adverb *good* has been much criticized, with people insisting that *well* be used instead. This has resulted in a split in connotation so that *well* is used in neutral informal contexts ("The orchestra played *well* this evening") and *good* in those that are emotionally charged and emphatic ("He hit the ball *good*"). The adverb *good* is mainly a spoken form, and should be avoided in writing unless in direct quotation.

hanged, hung   In the sense "to suspend by the neck until dead," both *hanged* and *hung* are standard as either the past tense or the past participle. *Hanged* is most appropriate for official executions ("was *hanged*, drawn, and quartered") but *hung* is also used ("ordered the traitor *hung*"). *Hung* is used in all other senses ("was *hung* in effigy," "*hung* the clothes out to dry," "*hung* my head in shame").

hardly   *Hardly* meaning "certainly not" is sometimes used with *not* for added emphasis ("Just another day at the office? Not *hardly*"). *Hardly* is also used like *barely* or *scarcely* to emphasize a minimal amount ("I *hardly* knew her," "Almost new—*hardly* a scratch on it"). When *hardly* is used with a negative verb (such as *can't, couldn't, didn't*) it is often called a double negative, but it is really a weaker negative: "I can't hardly hear you" means that I can hear you, but with difficulty; "I can't hear you" means just what it says. *Hardly* with a negative is a spoken form; you should avoid using it in writing unless you are quoting someone directly.

hone in This is a recently established term of uncertain origin that many people regard as a mistake for the synonymous *home in*. You might want to consider *home in* or *zero in* as possible substitutes.

hopefully When used to mean "I hope" or "We hope" ("*Hopefully*, they'll reach an agreement"), as opposed to "full of hope" ("We continued our work *hopefully* and cheerfully"), *hopefully* is often criticized. However, other similar sentence adverbs (such as *frankly, clearly,* and *interestingly*) are accepted by everyone. Despite the objections, this sense of *hopefully* is now in standard use.

I, me It is all right to use *me* after forms of the verb *be* ("It's *me*"), *than* ("Susan is taller than *me*"), and *as* ("He's as big as *me*"), in absolute uses ("Who, *me*?"), and in emphatic positions ("*Me* too") in speech and in informal or casual contexts. But in more formal contexts many people prefer *I* after *be* ("It was *I* who discovered the mistake") and after *as* and *than* when the first term of the comparison is the subject of the sentence ("Susan is taller than *I*," "He is as big as *I*").

imply, infer Discussions of the proper uses of *infer* and *imply* generally center on logic. But there are no logical problems involved. *Infer* is mostly used to mean "to draw a conclusion, conclude" and is commonly accompanied by *from* ("I *infer* from your comments that you were not pleased with our service"). *Imply* is used to mean "suggest" ("The letter *implies* that our service has not been satisfactory"). The use of *infer* that the fuss is about always has a personal subject and resembles that of *imply* ("Are you *inferring* that I made a mistake?"). This use is mostly spoken, although it does turn up in letters to the editor, and is not found in logical discourse.

importantly A number of critics have objected to the use of *importantly* to modify a sentence ("More *importantly*, I got my job back"), and have suggested using *important* instead. Either word can be used in this way. *Important* is always used with *more* or *most* ("Second, and most *important*, we must increase our market share"). *Importantly* can be used with or without *more* or *most* ("sticks easily, and just as *importantly*, is easily removed").

irregardless *Irregardless*, though a real word (and not uncommon in speech), is still a long way from general acceptance. In writing, be sure to use *regardless* instead.

its, it's It's easy to keep these forms separate as each has its own function. *It's* is a contraction of *it is* or *it has*, and *its* is a possessive pronoun ("*It's* been a long time since I've seen *its* equal"). Back in the eighteenth century, people used *it's* for the pronoun. But let's not go back to the eighteenth century. Use *its* for the pronoun and *it's* for the contraction.

-ize Almost any noun or adjective can be made into a verb by adding *-ize* ("hospitalize," "familiarize," "idolize"). Many technical terms are formed this way ("oxidize," "crystallize") as are verbs of ethnic derivation ("Americanize") and verbs derived from proper names ("bowdlerize," "mesmerize"). People have always complained about new words formed this way and they still do: *finalize* and *prioritize* are two fairly recent ones that have been criticized. Remember that some *-ize* words are special or technical terms regularly used in a particular field or profession. No matter how strange these may seem, they should not be avoided in materials intended for the specialists.

kudo, kudos *Kudos* was introduced as a singular noun into English from Greek. As it became more popular, it was used in contexts ("She deserves *kudos* for her efforts") where a person unfamiliar with Greek could not tell whether it was a singular or plural. Many people took it to be a plural and used it with a plural verb ("Her *kudos* are well deserved"), and eventually someone removed the *-s* to make a singular *kudo*. This same sort of word formation has given us such common words as *cherry* and *pea*. The form *kudos* with either a plural or singular verb is still standard, however.

lay, lie *Lay* has long been used as an intransitive verb meaning "lie" ("tried to make the book *lay* flat," "*lay* down on the job"), but it has been condemned by schoolteachers and grammarians for years. These critics have been largely successful in removing the intransitive *lay* from most formal writing, but it has persisted in the spoken language. In relatively formal writing, stick to *lie* for intransitive uses. *Lay* and *lie* have similar but distinct inflected forms. Check your dictionary for the appropriate ones.

lend, loan Some people still object to the use of *loan* as a verb ("*loaned* me the book") and insist on *lend*. *Loan* is in standard use, however. You should remember that *loan* is used only literally ("*loans* large sums of money"), while *lend* can be both literal ("*lends* large sums of money") and figurative ("Would you please *lend* me a hand?").

less, fewer The traditional view is that *less* is used for matters of degree, value, or amount, and that it modifies nouns that refer to uncountable things ("*less* hostility," "*less* clothing") while *fewer* modifies numbers and plural nouns ("*fewer* students," "*fewer* than eight trees"). However, *less* has been used to modify plural nouns for centuries. Today *less* is actually more likely than *fewer* to modify plural nouns when distances, sums of money, and certain common phrases are involved ("*less* than 100 miles," "*less* than $2000," "in 25 words or *less*") and just as likely to modify periods of time ("in *less* [*fewer*] than four hours").

like, such as Should you write "cities *like* Chicago and Des Moines" or "cities *such as* Chicago and Des Moines"? In fact you can use either one, or change the latter to "*such* cities *as* Chicago and Des Moines." These expressions have been subjected to objections so diverse that it is plain there is nothing objectionable about any of them.

literally *Literally* means "in a literal sense or manner" or "actually" ("took the remark *literally*," "was *literally* insane"). It is also used to mean "in effect" or "virtually" as an intensifier ("She *literally* flew up the stairs," "The performance *literally* brought the house down"). This use is often criticized as nonsensical, but it is not supposed to make sense, only add emphasis. It is often used, however, where no additional emphasis is really needed.

masterful, masterly *Masterly* means "suitable to or resembling that of a master" ("a *masterly* performance"). *Masterful* has several meanings, one of which is "masterly." It has been argued that since *masterly* has only one meaning, it rather than *masterful* should be used whenever that meaning is intended. However, *masterful* is in reputable use in this sense, so there is no real need to prefer *masterly*.

media *Media* is the plural of *medium*. With all the references to the mass media today, *media* is often used as a singular mass noun ("The *media* always wants a story"). This singular use is not as well established as the similar use of *data,* and you will probably want to keep *media* plural in most writing. An exception must be recognized for the world of advertising, in which *media* has long been singular and is sometimes given the plural *medias*.

memorandum *Memorandum* is a singular noun with two acceptable plurals: *memorandums* and *memoranda*. *Memoranda* is not established as a singular form.

militate, mitigate *Militate* means "to have weight or effect" ("Current economic conditions *militate* against expansion at this time"). *Mitigate,* which means "to make less severe," is sometimes used with *against* in place of *militate*. You will want to avoid this use in writing.

nauseating, nauseous *Nauseous* is most frequently used to mean "physically affected with nausea" ("The ride made me *nauseous*"), while *nauseating* is used to mean "causing nausea or disgust" ("the *nauseating* violence on TV").

neither The use of *neither* to refer to more than two nouns, though sometimes criticized, has been standard for centuries ("*Neither* the post office, the bank, nor City Hall is open today"). Traditionally, the pronoun *neither* is used with a singular verb ("*Neither* is ideal"). However, when a prepositional phrase follows *neither,* a plural verb is common and acceptable ("*Neither* of those solutions are ideal"). (For more details, see paragraph 9 on page 194.)

one The use of *one* to indicate a generic individual lends formality to writing since it suggests distance between the writer and the reader ("*One* never knows" is more formal than "You never know"). Consequently, *one* is rarely used in informal English. The use of *one* to replace a first-person pronoun ("I'd like to read more but *one* doesn't have the time") is common in British English but may be thought odd or objectionable in American English. (For more details, see paragraph 23 on page 212.)

people, persons *People* is used to designate an unspecified number of persons ("*People* everywhere are talking about the new show"), and *persons* is commonly used when a definite number is specified ("Occupancy by more than 86 *persons* is prohibited"). However, the use of *people* where numbers are mentioned is also acceptable nowadays ("Ten *people* were questioned").

per *Per*, meaning "for each," is most commonly used with figures, usually in relation to price ("$150 *per* performance"), vehicles ("25 miles *per* gallon," "55 miles *per* hour"), or sports ("15 points *per* game"). Avoid inserting words like "a" or "each" between *per* and the word or words it modifies ("could type seventy words *per* each minute").

phenomena *Phenomena* is the usual plural of *phenomenon*. Use of *phenomena* as a singular ("St. Elmo's Fire is an eerie *phenomena*") is encountered in speech and now and then in writing, but is not established as standard.

plus The use of *plus* to mean "and" ("a hamburger *plus* french fries for lunch") or "besides which" ("We would've been on time, but we lost the car keys. *Plus*, we forgot the map") is found in speech and in informal writing, but is not used in formal writing.

precede, proceed The basic idea is that *precede* means "to come or go before" and *proceed* means "to go along." A more specific guide to their meanings can be quickly found in your dictionary. Confusion between the two words is really just a matter of spelling—it's not uncommon to find the tail end of *precede* tacked on to the front end of *proceed*. Your dictionary will keep you straight here too. And while we are on the subject, take note of *procedure*—no double *e*.

presently The use of *presently* to mean "at the present time" ("I am *presently* working up a report") rather than "soon" ("He'll be with you *presently*"), while often criticized, is standard and acceptable.

pretty *Pretty* is used to tone down or moderate a statement ("*pretty* cold weather"). Although it is not restricted to informal writing, it is most commonly found there.

principle, principal Avoid confusing *principle* and *principal*. *Principle* is only a noun; *principal* is both an adjective and a noun. If you are unsure which noun you need, consult your dictionary.

prior to *Prior to*, a synonym of "before," most often appears in fairly formal contexts. It is especially useful in suggesting anticipation ("If all specifications are finalized *prior to* system design, cost overruns will be avoided").

proved, proven Both *proved* and *proven* are past participles of *prove*. Earlier in this century, *proved* was more common than *proven*, but today they appear with nearly equal frequency. As a past participle, either is acceptable ("has been *proved* [*proven*] effective"). *Proven* is more frequent in adjectival use ("*proven* gas reserves").

providing, provided Although *providing* in the sense of "if" or "on condition that" has occasionally been disapproved ("*providing* he finds a buyer"), both *providing* and *provided* are well established as standard, and either may be used. *Provided* is somewhat more often used.

real The adverb *real* is used interchangeably with *really* only as an intensifier ("a *real* tough assignment"). This use is very common in speech and casual writing, but you should not use it in anything more formal.

set, sit In general, *set* takes an object ("*Set* the lamp over there") and *sit* does not ("*sat* for an hour in the doctor's office"). But *set* has exceptions: the sun *sets* and so does a hen (intransitive use). So does *sit:* "I *sat* her down by her grandfather" (transitive use). When used of people, intransitive *set* is a spoken use that should be avoided in writing except in direct quotation.

shall, will *Shall* and *will* are generally interchangeable in present-day American English. In recent years, *shall* has been regarded as somewhat affected; *will* is much more common. However, *shall* is more appropriate in questions to express simple choice ("*Shall* we go now?") because *will* in such a context suggests prediction ("*Will* the prototype be ready next week?").

slow, slowly Some commentators claim that use of *slow* as an adverb (meaning "slowly") is an error. But there is really not much of a usage problem with *slow* and *slowly* because in actual practice each has its own use. *Slow* is almost always used with verbs indicating motion or action, and it typically follows the verb it modifies ("a stew cooked long and *slow*"). *Slowly* can be used in the same way ("drove *slowly*"), but it also is used before the verb ("The winds *slowly* subsided"), with adjectives formed from verbs ("the *slowly* sinking sun"), and in places where *slow* would sound inappropriate ("turned *slowly* around").

so The intensive use of the adverb *so* to mean "very" or "extremely" has been condemned by many commentators but has long thrived especially in speech and informal writing ("He loves her *so*"). No one disapproves of it, though, when it is used in negative contexts ("not *so* long ago") or followed by an explaining clause ("cocoa *so* hot that I burned my tongue").

Use of the conjunction *so* to introduce clauses of result ("The acoustics are good, *so* every note is clear") and purpose ("Be quiet *so* I can sleep") is sometimes criticized, but these uses are standard. In the latter case (when used to mean "in order that"), *so that* is the more common form in formal and business writing ("to cut spending *so that* the deficit will be reduced").

some When the adverb *some* (meaning "about") is used to modify a number, it is usually a round figure ("*Some* 2000 fans packed the stadium"). It is also used with other numbers, though, as it is more emphatic than the alternatives *about* or *approximately* ("ate *some* 14 pies to win the contest"). Many people prescribe *somewhat* instead of *some* when used without a number; however, *somewhat* is only a good substitute when *some* modifies an adjective forming a comparison ("I feel *some* better today" or "I feel *somewhat* better today"). It is not a good idea to substitute *somewhat* for *some* automatically in many contexts ("The divorce forced me to mature *some*") because the resulting sentence would be awkward.

such Some people disapprove of the use of *such* as a pronoun ("*such* was the result") ("have to sort out glass and newspapers and *such*"). All dictionaries, however, recognize it as standard.

that, which, who For the use of these relative pronouns, see paragraphs 28–29 on pages 214–15.

transpire Numerous critics have condemned the use of *transpire* to mean "to come to pass" or "occur" ("the events that *transpired* last night"); however, it is firmly established as standard English, in both informal and formal prose.

unique Much hullabaloo is made of the use of *unique* with words of comparison ("somewhat *unique*," "very *unique*"); critics argue that either a thing is unique or it isn't. This objection is based on the mistaken assumption that there are only two senses of *unique*: "sole," and "unequaled." When *unique* is used in these senses it is not qualified. However, when it is used in its other meanings—"distinctively characteristic" ("a condition *unique* to dogs") or "unusual" ("a very *unique* work of art")—words of comparison and qualification are widespread and standard. This last use is common in advertising copy.

whom For the use of *whom* or *who*, see paragraph 32 on page 215.

The following list consists of other frequently confused and misused words. Review the list periodically, and consult your dictionary about any that give you trouble.

access, excess	band, banned
addition, edition	bare, bear
advice, advise	bazaar, bizarre
aesthetic, ascetic	bloc, block
allude, elude	boarder, border
altar, alter	boom, boon
alumnae, alumni	born, borne
amend, emend	brake, break
appraise, apprise	breadth, breath
ascent, assent	bridal, bridle
aural, oral	buy, by
bail, bale	capital, capitol

cite, sight, site
coarse, course
commiserate,
 commensurate
complacent,
 complaisant
concert, consort
corespondent,
 correspondent
council, counsel
councillor, counselor
currant, current
decree, degree
defuse, diffuse
deluded, diluted
denote, donate
desert, dessert
device, devise
died, dyed
disassemble, dissemble
disburse, disperse
discreet, discrete
elicit, illicit
elusive, illusive
eminent, imminent
ethically, ethnically
extant, extend, extent
fair, fare
feat, feet
flair, flare
foreword, forward
foul, fowl
generic, genetic
genteel, gentile
gibe, jibe
guarantee, guaranty
hail, hale

hardy, hearty
healed, heeled
hear, here
hoard, horde
install, instill
jibe, jive
kibbutz, kibitz
lead, led
lean, lien
load, lode
loose, lose
median, medium
might, mite
ordinance, ordnance
pair, pare, pear
palate, pallet, palette
parish, perish
parlay, parley
peace, piece
pedal, peddle
personal, personnel
perspective, prospective,
 prospectus
pole, poll
pore, pour
portend, portent
pray, prey
preclude, prelude
premier, premiere
prescribe, proscribe
profit, prophet
purser, bursar
raise, raze
reality, realty
rebound, redound
reign, rein
right, rite

role, roll
sheaf, sheath
shear, sheer
stationary, stationery
tack, tact
tail, tale
taught, taut
their, there, they're
threw, through

to, too
toe, tow
track, tract
trooper, trouper
vial, vile
wail, whale
waive, wave
wrap, rap
wreak, wreck

to attract the reader's attention).

Chapter 8

Notes and Bibliographies

Writers and editors often need to provide readers with documentation of the source of a quotation or a piece of information. Authors may also wish to provide additional information and commentary or cross-references. This type of information is usually included in a note, which may take the form of a foot-note at the bottom of a page, an endnote at the end of a chapter or work, or a note in parentheses. The information from all the notes is often compiled into an alphabetically arranged bibliography, normally provided at the end of the entire text.

Thorough documentation—whether by means of footnotes, endnotes, or parenthetical references—is the mark of scholarly writing. Serious scholarship requires that source citations be rigorously provided, for several reasons: (1) to demonstrate to the reader the research that has been done, so that he or she may judge its quality, (2) to lead the reader to the writer's sources for further study if desired, (3) to give other scholars due credit for their work, and (4) to make plagiarism by the writer more difficult, and easier to spot.

Most published nonfiction omits references of any kind. Omitting references gives a more relaxed feel to a book or magazine, and most readers prefer not to deal with references. Books and especially magazines intended to be read for pleasure rarely require serious documentation, and good writers often avoid the need for notes by gracefully working into their prose any necessary bibliographic material. Only when references are needed does the question of which type of reference to use arise.

Footnotes can be more convenient than endnotes for the serious reader, who is thereby spared the need of constantly turning to the end of a chapter or work to see what sources are being cited. Word-processing and computer-typesetting programs today have largely freed typists and typesetters from the time-consuming task of positioning footnotes on a page. However, a footnote reference that falls near the end of a page can still present difficulties in page makeup. Footnotes are sometimes thought to make pages less attractive, and a heavily footnoted work may have ungainly pages that consist more of footnotes than of normal text. For these reasons, endnotes and parenthetical references may still be preferred over footnotes by keyboarders and publishers, though this is no longer likely to be the decisive reason for choosing one or another form of documentation.

Parenthetical references do not allow for incidental discussions or material. If parenthetical references are used but such incidental material has to be accommodated, footnotes or endnotes must be used as well.

The choice of reference type is actually rarely left to the writer. Professors usually require one or another kind of reference in term papers and theses; a scholarly journal will almost always adopt a single type of reference for all its articles; a publisher of books for a particular audience may similarly have a general policy on documentation that it applies to all its books; a large corporation may specify a single mode of documentation for its in-house publications; and law firms follow the standard style of the legal profession.

In works related to the social and natural sciences, writers usually rely on parenthetical references. In works related to the humanities, the footnote and endnote forms have traditionally been preferred; in recent years these two forms have become slightly less popular, as some style manuals have urged writers in the humanities to adopt parenthetical references.

This chapter describes each of these systems, and the examples illustrate generally acceptable styles. However, many professions and academic disciplines have developed their own styles, some of which differ in details from those illustrated in this chapter.

Footnotes and Endnotes

A footnote or endnote keys full bibliographical information about a source (author, title, place of publication, publisher, date, and page number) to a specific text passage making use of that source. The text passage is marked with a number. All such notes are set aside from the rest of the text. Notes that appear at the bottom of the page are called *footnotes;* notes that appear at the end of an article, a chapter, or an entire book are called *endnotes*.

The use of parenthetical references to document sources results in fewer footnotes or endnotes and allows authors to treat notes that provide strictly bibliographical information differently from notes that provide commentary, cross-references, or additional information. For more on parenthetical references, see the section beginning on page 290.

Placement of the Elements

Footnotes and endnotes to a text are usually indicated by unpunctuated Arabic superior numbers placed immediately after the quotation or information with no intervening space. The number is usually placed at the end of a sentence or clause, or at some other natural break in the sentence. The number follows all marks of punctuation except the dash. The numbering is consecutive throughout an article. In a book-length work, it normally begins again with each new chapter.

The text of the note itself is introduced with the corresponding number. Depending on the word-processing program used, it may be a superior numeral or set on the line. The latter form is more common for typeset material.

> [3] Jones, 223.
>
> *or*
>
> 3. Jones, 223.

The indention of footnote and endnote text varies according to individual preference. Indenting the first line of the footnote to a paragraph indent with runover lines returning to flush left (as shown on pages 279 and 284) is probably most common. However, the flush-left and flush-and-hang styles are also found.

flush left:	1. Guy Davenport, *The Geography of the Imagination* (San Francisco: North Point, 1981), 51.
flush and hang:	1. Guy Davenport, *The Geography of the Imagination* (San Francisco: North Point, 1981), 51.

that the recent books in the field of business writing all agree on. As one puts it, "Although some writers apparently believe that length impresses readers, it is brevity that readers most appreciate."[5] Another calls for writing that is "direct, clear, simple, explicit, and to the point," a goal that "flies in the face of an unfortunate tradition of pompous, jargon-ridden, sexist language, antiquated and wordy phrases, and redundancy."[6] Still another observes that "nobody ever complained that a memo or report wasn't long enough."[7]

These books agree not only on the goal but also on the steps needed to realize it. One book states that a basic rule is to use short words: "Prefer the smaller word to the larger word when both say essentially the same thing."[8]

---

5. Ray E. Barfield and Sylvia S. Titus, *Business Communications* (New York: Barron's, 1992), 14.

6. Gary Blake and Robert W. Bly, *The Elements of Business Writing* (New York: Collier–Macmillan, 1991), 35.

7. John Tarrant, *Business Writing with Style* (New York: John Wiley, 1991), 130.

8. Blake and Bly, 39.

Text with footnotes

When preparing footnotes with a word-processing program, consult your user's manual for directions; footnotes in manuscripts to be typeset may require other instructions from the typesetter. Footnotes and endnotes are usually set in type that is one or two points smaller than the text type.

Endnotes are styled exactly like footnotes, but all of the notes are gathered together in a single list (as shown on page 279) either at the end of the article or chapter or at the end of the book-length work. In the latter case, the section is usually divided with chapter headings to indicate where the notes of a particular chapter begin and end.

First References

Both footnotes and endnotes provide full bibliographic information for a source the first time it is cited; in subsequent references, this information is abbreviated. The following paragraphs describe specific elements of first references; subsequent references are discussed on pages 285–88. (For entries in bibliographies and lists of references, see the section beginning on page 297.)

Books   A footnote or endnote that refers to a book contains as many of the following elements as are relevant. Examples of the elements described below are also listed in the box on page 279.

1. *Author's name*   The author's first name comes first and the last name after, followed by a comma. If there are more than three authors, the first author's name is followed by the phrase *et al.*, an abbreviation for *et alii* or *et aliae*, meaning "and others."

1. Elizabeth Bishop, *The Complete Poems: 1927–1979* (New York: Farrar, Straus & Giroux, 1983), 46.

2. Randolph Quirk et al., *A Comprehensive Grammar of the English Language* (London: Longman, 1985), 135.

3. Commission on the Humanities, *The Humanities in American Life* (Berkeley: Univ. of California Press, 1980), 46.

4. *Information Please Almanac: 1995* (Boston: Houghton Mifflin, 1994), 324.

5. Ernst Mayr, "Processes of Speciation in Animals," *Mechanisms of Speciation*, ed. C. Barigozzi (New York: Alan R. Liss, 1982), 1–3.

6. Simone de Beauvoir, *The Second Sex*, trans. and ed. H. M. Parshley (New York: Knopf, 1953; Vintage, 1974), 446.

7. Arthur S. Banks, ed., *Political Handbook of the World: 1992* (Binghamton, N.Y.: CSA Publications, 1992), 293–95.

8. George W. Stocking, Jr., ed., *Functionalism Historicized: Essays on British Social Anthropology*, vol. 2, History of Anthropology Series (Madison: Univ. of Wisconsin Press, 1984), 173–74.

9. Ronald M. Nowak, *Walker's Mammals of the World*, 5th ed., 2 vols. (Baltimore: Johns Hopkins Univ. Press, 1991), 2: 661.

Endnotes for book references

1. Elizabeth Bishop, *The Complete Poems: 1927–1979* (New York: Farrar, Straus & Giroux, 1983), 46.

2. Randolph Quirk et al., *A Comprehensive Grammar of the English Language* (London: Longman, 1985), 135.

If a publication is issued by a group or organization and no individual is mentioned on the title page, the name of the group or organization—the corporate author—may be used in place of an author's name.

3. Commission on the Humanities, *The Humanities in American Life* (Berkeley: Univ. of California Press, 1980), 46.

2. *Title of the work* The title is italicized in keyboarded and typeset manuscripts (underlined in typed or handwritten material). Each word of the title is capitalized except for articles and short prepositions other than the first word (see also paragraph 77 on page 90). Where no author's name is used in the note, the title comes first; this is the usual form for well-known reference books and for publications with corporate authors that are better known by their titles.

4. *Information Please Almanac: 1995* (Boston: Houghton Mifflin, 1994), 324.

3. *Portion of the book* If a reference is to one portion of a book (such as an essay, a short story, or a poem within a collection), the title is included and enclosed in quotation marks. The titles of chapters within nonfiction works by a single author are usually not part of a footnote reference.

5. Ernst Mayr, "Processes of Speciation in Animals," *Mechanisms of Speciation,* ed. C. Barigozzi (New York: Alan R. Liss, 1982), 1–3.

4. *Editor, compiler, or translator*   The name of an editor, compiler, or translator is preceded by the abbreviation *ed., comp.,* or *trans.* or some combination of them joined by *and.*

> 6. Simone de Beauvoir, *The Second Sex,* trans. and ed. H. M. Parshley (New York: Knopf, 1953; Vintage, 1974), 446.

If no author is mentioned on the title page, the name of the editor, compiler, or translator is placed first in the note, followed by the abbreviation *ed., comp.,* or *trans.*

> 7. Arthur S. Banks, ed., *Political Handbook of the World: 1992* (Binghamton, N.Y.: CSA Publications, 1992), 293–95.

5. *Name of the series*   If a book is part of a series, the name of the series should be included. If the book corresponds to a specific volume in that series, the volume number is also included, separated from the book title by a comma. The series name is separated from the volume title or number by a comma, and is capitalized but not italicized.

> 8. George W. Stocking, Jr., ed., *Functionalism Historicized: Essays on British Social Anthropology,* vol. 2, History of Anthropology Series (Madison: Univ. of Wisconsin Press, 1984), 173–74.

6. *Edition*   If a work is other than the first edition, the number or the nature of the edition is indicated (see example in paragraph 7 below).

7. *Volume number*   If a work has more than one volume, the total number of volumes is given after the title and edition. In addition, the number of the volume cited should precede the page num-

ber. The abbreviation *vol.* or *vols.* may precede the volume number, but it is often omitted.

> 9. Ronald M. Nowak, *Walker's Mammals of the World,* 5th ed., 2 vols. (Baltimore: Johns Hopkins Univ. Press, 1991), 2: 661.

8. *Publishing data*   The city of publication, the short name of the publisher, and the year of publication, in that order, are enclosed in parentheses; a colon follows the city name, and a comma follows the publisher's name (see examples above). If the city is a small one, the abbreviated state name (or country name) should be included. If the city or publisher is not known, use "n.p." *(no place/publisher)*. If the year is not given, use "n.d." *(no date)*.

9. *Page number*   The number of the page on which the quotation or piece of information can be found is included. The abbreviation *p.* or *pp.* may precede the page number or numbers, but it is usually omitted (see examples above).

Periodicals   A footnote or endnote describing an article in a periodical should include all of the following information that is relevant. Examples of each element described below can also be found in the listed references on page 284.

1. *Author's name*   The author's name is treated just as in a reference to a book. Writers of letters to a periodical and writers of book reviews are treated like authors.

> 1. Gordon A. Craig, review of *The Wages of Guilt: Memories of War in Germany and Japan,* by Ian Buruma, *New York Review of Books,* July 14, 1994: 43–45.

2. *Title of the article*   The title of the article is enclosed in quotation marks, capitalized like a book title (see paragraph 2 on page 280), and followed by a comma.

> 2. Carol J. Loomis, "A Whole New Way to Run a Bank," *Fortune,* 7 Sept. 1992: 78–79.

3. *Name of the periodical*   The name of the periodical is treated like the title of a book (see paragraph 2 on page 280).

4. *Volume and number of the periodical*   If a periodical uses both volume and number designations to identify an issue, both should be used.

> 3. Roseann Duenas Gonzalez, "Teaching Mexican American Students to Write: Capitalizing on the Culture," *English Journal* 71, no. 7 (Nov. 1982): 22–24.

A periodical in which pages are numbered consecutively through a volume needs only a volume number.

> 4. John Heil, "Seeing Is Believing," *American Philosophical Quarterly* 19 (1982): 229–39.

Most weekly and monthly magazines for general readers have a volume and number designation, but they are more commonly referred to by month and year.

> 5. John Lukacs, "The End of the Twentieth Century," *Harper's,* Jan. 1993: 40.

5. *Issue date*   Periodicals variously use months, days, and years to identify issues. The date is written in whatever form the periodical uses, but the name of the month may be abbreviated. When a volume number is included, the date is enclosed in parentheses (see paragraph 4 above); it is preceded only by a comma when no volume number is used.

> 6. William J. Broad, "Big Science Squeezes Small-Scale Researchers," *New York Times*, Dec. 29, 1992: C1–2.

6. *Page number* The number of the page on which the quotation or piece of information can be found is included. The abbreviation *p.* or *pp.* is usually omitted (see paragraphs 7 and 9 on pages 281–82). The volume number and page number are separated by a colon (see paragraph 4 above).

---

1. Gordon A. Craig, review of *The Wages of Guilt: Memories of War in Germany and Japan*, by Ian Buruma, *New York Review of Books*, July 14, 1994: 43–45.

2. Carol J. Loomis, "A Whole New Way to Run a Bank," *Fortune*, 7 Sept. 1992: 78–79.

3. Roseann Duenas Gonzalez, "Teaching Mexican American Students to Write: Capitalizing on the Culture," *English Journal* 71, no. 7 (Nov. 1982): 22–24.

4. John Heil, "Seeing Is Believing," *American Philosophical Quarterly* 19 (1982): 229–39.

5. John Lukacs, "The End of the Twentieth Century," *Harper's*, Jan. 1993: 40.

6. William J. Broad, "Big Science Squeezes Small-Scale Researchers," *New York Times*, Dec. 29, 1992: C1–2.

7. Clive Johnson, letter to Elizabeth O'Hara, 9 Nov. 1916, Johnson Collection, item 5298, California State Historical Society, San Marino, Calif.

Endnotes for periodicals and unpublished sources

Unpublished materials   A note referring to an unpublished work should include as many of the following elements as are known or are relevant.

1. *Author's name*   The author's name is treated in the same way as for a book (see paragraph 1 on page 278).

2. *Title of the work*   The title is enclosed in quotation marks and capitalized like a book title (see paragraph 2 on page 280).

3. *The nature of the material*   The reference should include a description of the document ("letter," "dissertation," etc.); see the example in paragraph 6 below.

4. *Date*   Include the date of the material if it is known (see paragraph 8 on page 282).

5. *Folio number or other identification number*   Include whatever kind of identification number is conventionally used with the material.

6. *Geographical location of the material*   Include the name and city of the institution where the materials can be found.

> 7. Clive Johnson, letter to Elizabeth O'Hara, 9 Nov. 1916, Johnson Collection, item 5298, California State Historical Society, San Marino, Calif.

Subsequent References

Two systems are used to refer to a source that has already been cited. One uses shortened footnotes; the other uses Latin abbreviations.

Shortened footnotes   When the same source is cited repeatedly with intervening footnotes, shortened footnotes may be used. The following style is generally acceptable for most publications.

1. *Author's name*   If the author's name occurs in the running text, it need not be repeated in footnote or endnote references to the work after the first one.

> *first*
> *reference:*   1. Albert H. Marckwardt, *American English* (New York: Oxford Univ. Press, 1980), 94.

> *repeated*
> *reference:*   2. *American English*, 95.

If the author's name does not appear in the running text prior to a repeated reference, either of the following styles may be used. However, the style of note 3 should be followed if more than one work by the same author is cited within the text.

> *repeated*
> *reference:*   3. Marckwardt, *American English*, 95.
>   *or*
>   4. Marckwardt, 95.

2. *More than one author*   In repeated references to books by more than one author, the authors' names may be shortened. The style of note 6 should be followed if more than one work by the same authors is cited within the text. In addition, a long title may be shortened if it has already been given in full in an earlier note.

> *first*
> *reference:*   5. Albert C. Baugh and Thomas Cable, *A History of the English Language*, 3d ed. (Englewood Cliffs, N.J.: Prentice Hall, 1978), 14.

> *repeated*
> *reference:* 6. Baugh and Cable, *English Language*, 17.
>
> *or*
>
> 7. Baugh and Cable, 17.

3. *Article in a periodical* A shortened reference to an article in a periodical should include the author's last name; the title of the article, which can be shortened; and the page number.

> *first*
> *reference:* 8. Roseann Duenas Gonzalez, "Teaching Mexican American Students to Write: Capitalizing on the Culture," *English Journal* 71, no. 7 (Nov. 1982): 22–24.
>
> *repeated*
> *reference:* 9. Gonzalez, "Teaching Mexican American Students," 23.

Latin abbreviations While the shortened note style has gained wide currency, some writers still prefer the traditional Latin abbreviation *ibid.*, and occasionally the abbreviations *loc. cit.* and *op. cit.*, for repeated references to sources cited earlier. These Latin abbreviations are not italicized and are capitalized only when they appear at the beginning of a footnote or endnote.

The abbreviation *ibid.* (for *ibidem*, "in the same place") is used when the writer is referring to the work cited in the immediately preceding note. The abbreviation may be used several times in succession.

> 10. Simone de Beauvoir, *The Second Sex*, trans. and ed. H. M. Parshley (New York: Knopf, 1953; Vintage, 1974), 600.
>
> 11. Ibid., 609.
>
> 12. Ibid.

When *ibid.* is used without a page number, it indicates that The same page of the same source is being cited as in the note immediately preceding. Thus, note 12 above cites page 609 of *The Second Sex*.

The abbreviations *loc. cit.* (for *loco citato,* "in the place cited") and *op. cit.* (for *opere citato,* "in the work cited") are rarely used today but are often encountered in older works. Both can easily be replaced by notes in shortened form.

The abbreviation *loc. cit.* is used only when referring to the same page or pages of the same source cited earlier with footnotes intervening.

> *first*
> *reference:*   13. Bert Hölldobler and Edward O. Wilson, *The Ants* (Cambridge, Mass.: Belknap–Harvard Univ. Press, 1990), 119–33.

> *repeated*
> *reference:*   15. Hölldobler and Wilson, loc. cit.

Note 15, with no page number, indicates that pages 119–33 are being cited again.

The abbreviation *op. cit.* is used to refer to a source cited earlier but not to the same page or pages of that source.

> *first*
> *reference:*   1. Albert H. Marckwardt, *American English* (New York: Oxford Univ. Press, 1980), 94.

> *repeated*
> *reference:*   24. Marckwardt, op. cit., 98.

Other Footnotes and Endnotes

Notes providing additional information, commentary, or cross-references that the author does not want to include in the main text are keyed to the text like bibliographical notes, as shown by notes 2, 3, and 5 below.

1. Lyon Richardson, *A History of Early American Magazines* (New York: Thomas Nelson, 1931), 8.

2. Total average circulation per issue of magazines reporting to the Bureau of Circulation rose from 96.8 million in 1939 to 147.8 million in 1945.

3. For a particularly compelling account of this episode, see James P. Wood, *Magazines in the United States* (New York: Ronald Press, 1949), 92–108.

4. Richardson, 42.

5. For more details, see Appendix.

Texts that use parenthetical references for bibliographical notes can still include footnotes or endnotes for other notes. When a nonbibliographical note mentions the name of a book or article that is not the source of a quotation or piece of information in the text, a footnote or endnote is used to describe it; see note 3 above.

Certain nonbibliographical notes in some publications are not keyed to the text with any kind of symbol, particularly notes placed at the beginning of each part of a collection of works by different authors to provide information about the individual author, state where the selection was originally published, or acknowledge those who gave assistance or contributed to the writing of the work. These notes are not keyed because the only logical place to put the reference mark or number would be on the title or the name of the author, where most editors and designers are reluctant to use such symbols. These unnumbered notes are conventionally placed at the bottom of the first page.

Reference Marks

In texts with few footnotes or endnotes, writers occasionally substitute reference marks for reference numbers. The traditional marks are listed below in the order in which they are usually used.

```
*   (asterisk)
†   (dagger)
‡   (double dagger)
§   (section mark)
‖   (parallels)
¶   (paragraph mark)
#   (number sign)
```

This sequence can begin anew with each page or with each chapter. If more than seven notes are needed in a sequence, the subsequent marks are doubled (**, ††, etc.); however, if such a large number of notes is needed, numbers rather than symbols should be used. When only two or three notes are needed, a common alternative is to use one asterisk for the first note, two for the second, and three for the third. A variation that works for up to four notes is to use the asterisk and dagger in the order *, **, †, ††.

Parenthetical References

Parenthetical references present very abbreviated bibliographic information (typically the name of the author followed by a page number, but sometimes just a page number) enclosed in parentheses in the main body of the text. They refer the reader to a list of references at the end of the article, chapter, or book. A list of references is a form of bibliography; they are discussed in the section beginning on page 297. A sample list of references is included on page 300, and all information about parenthetical references in this section refers to it.

Parenthetical formats have the advantage of providing essential information within the text, without providing so much information that reading the text is impeded. They can help the reader decide whether to turn to the list of references for further information.

The practice of using parenthetical references originated in the social and natural sciences; however, its adoption for writing in the humanities, and for all general writing that includes numerous bibliographical references, is now widely encouraged. Most systems of parenthetical references are similar, but differences in detail do exist among the various academic disciplines and professional organizations. The examples in this section generally follow the precepts of the *MLA Handbook for Writers of Research Papers,* to which readers are referred for a more detailed treatment. A discussion of a different system used in the sciences begins on page 295.

Placement of the Reference

Parenthetical references are placed immediately after the quotation or piece of information whose source they refer to. The sample on page 292 reproduces the text of the sample on page 277 to show how it would appear using parenthetical references instead of footnotes. Note especially that punctuation not associated with a quotation is placed after the reference; thus, periods and commas following a quotation are placed outside of quotation marks.

Content and Style

The reference's content and style are determined by (1) the first element of the corresponding entry in the list of references, and (2) the bibliographic information included in the text around it.

This is illustrated in the example on page 292. The first parenthetical reference reads "(Barfield and Titus 14)" because, in the list of references, the entry for this source begins "Barfield, Ray E., and Sylvia S. Titus." In the last sentence, the parenthetical reference "(39)" is sufficient because it is clear from the text that Blake and Bly are the authors.

that the recent books in the field of business writing all agree on. As one puts it, "Although some writers apparently believe that length impresses readers, it is brevity that readers most appreciate" (Barfield and Titus 14). Another calls for writing that is "direct, clear, simple, explicit, and to the point," a goal that "flies in the face of an unfortunate tradition of pompous, jargon-ridden, sexist language, antiquated and wordy phrases, and redundancy" (Blake and Bly 35). Still another observes that "nobody ever complained that a memo or report wasn't long enough" (Tarrant 130).

These books agree not only on the goal but also on the steps needed to realize it. Blake and Bly state that a basic rule is to use short words: "Prefer the smaller word to the larger word when both say essentially the same thing" (39).

Text with parenthetical references

Sometimes a reference is supported by citations to two separate sources. In such cases, the two citations are enclosed in the same parentheses, separated by a semicolon; for example, "(Blake and Bly 37; Tarrant 135)." However, lengthy references should be avoided because they interrupt the flow of text. Authors can avoid them by incorporating as much bibliographical information within the text itself as can be smoothly absorbed.

Matching the list of references The name in a parenthetical reference must correspond to a name that begins an entry in the list of references. The author's last name is usually sufficient. However, if there had been another author with the last name Tarrant in the list of references, it would have been necessary to include a first initial; for example, "(J. Tarrant 188)." If the list of references had included two different books by John Tarrant, it would have been necessary to include the book's title (shortened) in the parenthetical reference; for example, "(Tarrant, *Business Writing* 188)." The following paragraphs explain some other special cases.

1. *A work with two or three authors* The list of references on page 300 includes an entry for a book by Charles Brusaw, Gerald Alred, and Walter Oliu. A parenthetical reference to that work would take the following form:

   (Brusaw, Alred, and Oliu 182–84)

2. *A work with more than three authors* A work with more than three authors appears under the name of the first author followed by the phrase *et al.* (see also paragraph 1 on page 278).

   (Quirk et al. 135)

3. *A work by a corporate author* A corporate author, such as the Commission on the Humanities, can be treated like any other author. The corporate name may be abbreviated.

   (Commission on the Humanities 46)
        or
   (Comm. on Humanities 46)

4. *A work listed by its title* When a work has no official author, a parenthetical reference to it should refer to it by its title, which may be shortened.

> (*Information Please Almanac* 14)
> *or*
> (*Almanac* 14)

Locators Usually the only locator required is a page number. However, sometimes additional or alternative information is needed to help the reader find the original source. The following paragraphs describe some of these special situations. Note that no punctuation separates the author's name or the title from the locator and that no abbreviation is used to identify the locator unless confusion would result from its omission.

1. *A multivolume work* The list of references on page 300 includes a reference to the three-volume *Letters of Samuel Johnson,* edited by Bruce Redford. A reference to that work would have to include both a volume number and a page number, separated by an unspaced colon.

   > (Redford 1:45)

   If an entire volume of a multivolume work is being referred to, the abbreviation *vol.* is used to make it clear that the number is not a page number.

   > (Redford, vol. 1)

2. *A reference book* A reference to an entry in a dictionary or encyclopedia often begins with the name of the entry being cited, followed by the book title, edition, and date, as in the entry for "Aristotle" on page 300; the publishing data is usually omitted for well-known reference books. A parenthetic reference need only mention the name of the entry; no page number is needed either there or in the list of references. The name

of the reference book should be mentioned in the text so that the reader is not forced to consult the list of references to learn what source is being cited.

> As noted in the *Encyclopaedia Britannica*, the philosopher was the son of a court physician ("Aristotle"). . . .

3. *Literary works*   Parenthetical references to literary works often include references to stanzas, lines, verses, chapters, books, parts, and the like. This is useful to readers using a different edition of the work. For more on references to literary works, see the section on page 318.

References to unpublished sources   Parenthetical references are also used to cite unpublished sources that are not listed in a bibliography, such as letters to the author or telephone interviews. The reference should include the name of the person providing the information, the type of source, and the date; for example, "(Paul Roberts, letter to the author, Sept. 1984)." If any of these elements is included in the text, it may be omitted from the reference.

Author-Date System in the Sciences

Another system of parenthetical citation that is used mostly in the social and natural sciences is the *author-date system* (also called the *name-year system*). The following paragraphs describe specific elements of this system. The combination of humanities and sciences references in the examples is for illustration only; many of these would not be found together in the same list of references.

1. *Author's name*   In the author-date system the parenthetical reference contains the author's last

name and the date of publication with no intervening punctuation. A page number is optional.

(Nowak 1991)

  or

(Nowak 1991, 32)

If the author's name is mentioned in the introductory text, only the date and possibly the page
number are needed within the parentheses.

(1991, 32)

By referring to the list of references, the reader
can find complete bibliographic information about
the work. However, lists of references or bibliographies written in connection with the author-
date system must also follow the scientific styling
of placing the date after the author's name in
each entry (for examples, see page 301).

2. *Two or more authors* A book or article by two,
three, or more than three authors would be represented by the following stylings, respectively:

(Barfield and Titus 1992)
(Brusaw, Alred, and Oliu 1993)
(Quirk et al. 1985)

3. *Corporate author or editor* A corporate author
name or a title may be substituted when there are
no individual authors.

(Commission on the Humanities 1980)

An editor's last name may also be substituted,
without the abbreviation *ed.*

(Redford 1992)

4. *Locators* A page number or other number indicating a division of the work is often added to the
date, preceded by a comma. For citations to the

short articles so prevalent in the scientific literature, page numbers are often unnecessary, but
for books, page references are certainly helpful
to the reader.

(Quirk et al. 1985, 147–49)

Volumes are indicated by Arabic numerals with
an unspaced colon between volume and page
numbers.

(Redford 1992, 1:86–87)

5. *Multiple works*   More than one work by the same
author can be shown by adding a second date
after the first.

(Redford 1992, 1994)

Two or more separate citations can be included
within one parenthesis if they are separated by a
semicolon.

(Redford 1992; Nowak 1991)

More than one work published in the same year
by the same author can be indicated by adding an
a, b, or *c* to the date. The same letters should be
used in the list of references.

(Redford 1994a)

Bibliographies and Lists of References

A *bibliography* lists all of the works that a writer has
found relevant in writing the text. A *list of references*
includes only works specifically mentioned in the text
or from which a particular quotation or piece of information was taken. In all other respects, bibliographies and lists of references are identical. They both

appear at the end of an article, chapter, or book, where they list sources of information relevant to the text. They are punctuated and capitalized in the same way. They both differ from a section of bibliographic endnotes (see page 279) in that their entries are arranged alphabetically (as in the sample on page 300) and use different patterns of indention and punctuation. References to bibliographies in the following pages should be understood to include lists of references as well.

For each kind of entry described below, two examples are given, one in a style used in the humanities and general writing, the other in a style standard in the social and natural sciences.

In general, bibliographic stylings used in the sciences differ from those used in general writing in that (1) the author's first and middle names are expressed with initials only, (2) the date, which is important in scientific writings, immediately follows the author's name, (3) less capitalization is used, (4) titles of articles are not enclosed in quotation marks, (5) dates are usually written in the order day-month-year, and (6) more abbreviations are used. For a sample bibliography in the sciences, see page 301.

The examples used in this section by no means exhaust the possible variations on these two basic systems. Other alternatives are found in print, several of them recommended by various professional organizations and academic disciplines within the social and natural sciences. For example, in the sciences the author's first and middle initials are often closed up without any punctuation, and the book or periodical title may be unitalicized.

Books

Style and content of entries A bibliographic entry for a book should include all of the following elements that are relevant. The elements are listed here in the order in which they appear in entries written in humanities style. In each numbered paragraph, the first example illustrates humanities style (*h*); the second, the style used in the natural and social sciences (*s*).

1. *Author's name* The author's name or authors' names come first, whether the author is a single individual, a group of individuals, or an organization. Names of coauthors are listed in the order found on the title page. For a work with an editor rather than an author, the editor's name comes first, followed by a comma and *ed.* (see paragraph 4 below). The name of the first author is inverted so that the surname comes first and can be alphabetized. The names of additional authors are written in normal order (first, middle, last). In bibliographies that follow humanities style, the author's name is written as it appears on the title page. In sciences style, the last name and first two initials are always used, regardless of how the author's name is printed on the title page.

   (*h*) Hölldobler, Bert, and Edward O. Wilson. *The Ants*. Cambridge, Mass.: Belknap–Harvard Univ. Press, 1990.

   (*s*) Hölldobler, B., and E. O. Wilson. 1990. *The ants*. Cambridge, Mass.: Belknap–Harvard Univ. Press.

In the humanities and in some of the social and natural sciences, if there are more than three authors the first author's name is followed by *et al.* (for an example, see page 300).

2. *Title of the work* In the humanities, the title is italicized. In the sciences, the title is usually but not always italicized. Capitalization is either *headline-style* (all words capitalized except for internal articles and prepositions) or *sentence-style*

"Aristotle." *The New Encyclopaedia Britannica*. 15th ed. 1985.

Barfield, Ray E., and Sylvia S Titus. *Business Communications*. New York: Barron's, 1992.

Blake, Gary, and Robert W. Bly. *The Elements of Business Writing*. New York: Collier–Macmillan, 1991.

Brusaw, Charles T., Gerald J. Alred, and Walter E. Oliu. *The Business Writer's Handbook*. 4th rev. ed. New York: St. Martin's, 1993.

Commission on the Humanities. *The Humanities in American Life*. Berkeley: Univ. of California Press, 1980.

Hölldobler, Bert, and Edward O. Wilson. *The Ants*. Cambridge, Mass.: Belknap–Harvard Univ. Press, 1990.

Information Please Almanac: 1995. Boston: Houghton Mifflin, 1994.

Mayr, Ernst. "Processes of Speciation in Animals." *Mechanisms of Speciation*. Ed. C. Barigozzi. New York: Alan R. Liss, 1982.

Nowak, Ronald M. *Walker's Mammals of the World*. 5th ed. 2 vols. Baltimore: Johns Hopkins Univ. Press, 1991.

Quirk, Randolph, et al. *A Comprehensive Grammar of the English Language*. London: Longman, 1985.

Redford, Bruce, ed. *The Letters of Samuel Johnson*. 3 vols. Princeton, N.J.: Princeton Univ. Press, 1992.

Stocking, George W., Jr., ed. *Functionalism Historicized: Essays on British Social Anthropology*. Vol. 2. History of Anthropology Series. Madison: Univ. of Wisconsin Press, 1988.

Tarrant, John. *Business Writing with Style*. New York: John Wiley, 1991.

Bibliography/List of References (humanities style)

"Aristotle." 1985. *The new encyclopaedia Britannica.* 15th ed.

Barfield, R. E., and S. S. Titus. 1992. *Business communications.* New York: Barron's.

Blake, G., and R. W. Bly. 1991. *The elements of business writing.* New York: Collier–Macmillan.

Brusaw, C. T., G. J. Alred, and W. E. Oliu. 1993. *The business writer's handbook.* 4th rev. ed. New York: St. Martin's.

Commission on the Humanities. 1980. *The humanities in American life.* Berkeley: Univ. of California Press.

Hölldobler, B., and E. O. Wilson. 1990. *The ants.* Cambridge, Mass.: Belknap–Harvard Univ. Press.

Information please almanac: 1995. 1994. Boston: Houghton Mifflin.

Mayr, E. 1982. Processes of speciation in animals. *Mechanisms of speciation.* Ed. C. Barigozzi. New York: Alan R. Liss.

Nowak, R. M. 1991. *Walker's mammals of the world.* 5th ed. 2 vols. Baltimore: Johns Hopkins Univ. Press.

Quirk, R., et al. 1985. *A comprehensive grammar of the English language.* London: Longman.

Redford, B., ed. 1992. *The letters of Samuel Johnson.* 3 vols. Princeton, N.J.: Princeton Univ. Press.

Stocking, G. W., Jr., ed. 1984. *Functionalism historicized: Essays on British social anthropology.* Vol. 2. History of anthropology series. Madison: Univ. of Wisconsin Press.

Tarrant, J. 1991. *Business writing with style.* New York: John Wiley.

Bibliography/List of References (sciences style)

(only the first word and proper nouns and adjectives capitalized). In the humanities, headline-style capitalization is used; in the social and natural sciences, both styles are used. The titles of sample references in the sciences in this chapter are italicized and use sentence-style capitalization. Another difference is that titles in the humanities include any subtitles, whereas subtitles are often omitted in bibliographies for the sciences. Subtitles match the styling of the titles that precede them.

(*h*) Stocking, George W., Jr., ed. *Functionalism Historicized: Essays on British Social Anthropology.* Vol. 2. History of Anthropology Series. Madison: Univ. of Wisconsin Press, 1988.

(*s*) Stocking, G. W., Jr., ed. 1988. *Functionalism historicized.* Vol. 2. History of anthropology series. Madison: Univ. of Wisconsin Press.

3. *Portion of the book*   Some bibliography entries cite only one portion of a book, such as an essay within a collection or an article from a symposium. For these entries, the name of that portion is given first as a title, either enclosed in quotation marks or, in sciences style, unenclosed. The title of the book follows. The titles of chapters within nonfiction works by a single author are usually not included in the entry.

(*h*) Mayr, Ernst. "Processes of Speciation in Animals." *Mechanisms of Speciation.* Ed. C. Barigozzi. New York: Alan R. Liss, 1982. 1–19.

(*s*) Mayr, E. 1982. Processes of speciation in animals. *Mechanisms of speciation.* Ed. C. Barigozzi. New York: Alan R. Liss. 1–19.

4. *Editor, compiler, or translator*   In entries for books that have an author, the name of an editor, com-

piler, or translator comes after the title and is preceded or followed by the abbreviation *ed.*, *comp.*, or *trans.* or some combination of these. If no author is listed, the name of the editor, compiler, or translator is placed first, followed by a comma and the lowercase abbreviation *ed.*, *comp.*, or *trans.* For examples, see paragraph 2 above.

5. *Edition*   If a book is other than the first edition, the number or other description of the edition ("2d ed.," "1986 ed.," etc.) is written after the title. If the edition is identified by a word instead of a numeral, its first letter is capitalized (for example, "Rev. ed.").

> (*h*) Nowak, Ronald M. *Walker's Mammals of the World.* 5th ed. 2 vols. Baltimore: Johns Hopkins Univ. Press, 1991.
>
> (*s*) Nowak, R. M. 1991. *Walker's mammals of the world.* 5th ed. 2 vols. Baltimore: Johns Hopkins Univ. Press.

6. *Volume number or number of volumes*   In an entry that cites a multivolume work, the total number of volumes is given before the publication information (for example, "9 vols."). There is no need to cite the volumes actually used, since this information will be in a note or parenthetical reference. If only one of the volumes was consulted, however, that volume alone is listed as an entry, so that the text references need cite only page numbers, not volume numbers as well. For examples, see paragraphs 2 and 5 above.

7. *Name of the series*   If the book is part of a series, the series name should be included, as well as the book or volume number if the book represents a specific numbered volume in that series. The

series name is not italicized. For an example, see paragraph 2 above.

8. *Publication data* The city of publication (with the state abbreviation if the city is not well known), the name of the publisher, and the year of publication together form the grouping called the publication data. If the place or publisher is not known, use "n.p." (*no place/publisher*). If the date is not given, use "n.d." (*no date*). A colon follows the city name, and a comma follows the name of the publisher. A period after the date ends a bibliographical entry in humanities style; in the sciences, the date appears after the author's name. For examples, see paragraphs 1–3 above.

All of this information comes from the title page and the copyright page. If the title page lists more than one city, only the first is mentioned in the bibliography. Some books are published under a special imprint name, which is usually printed on the title page above the publisher's name. In a bibliographical entry, the imprint name is joined to the publisher's name with a hyphen (for example, "Golden Press–Western Publishing Co."). Short forms of publishers' names are often used in bibliographies and are acceptable if all such names are consistently shortened. The word *and* and the ampersand are equally acceptable within publishers' names if one or the other is used consistently.

For a multivolume work published over a period of several years, inclusive numbers are given for those years. The phrase *in press* is substituted for the date in works that are about to be published.

9. *Locators* Page numbers are added to book entries in a bibliography only when the entry cites a

portion of a book, such as a story or essay in an anthology or an article in a collection (see paragraph 3 above). If that portion is in a volume of a multivolume work, both volume and page number are given.

Articles in Journals or Other Periodicals

Style and content of entries   A bibliography entry for an article in a journal or other periodical or in a newspaper includes as many of the following elements as are relevant. Examples of humanities (*h*) and sciences (*s*) styles illustrate many of the elements.

1. *Author's name*   The author's name is written as it appears on the printed page and is styled just as for a book entry (see page 299). Names of people who write letters to a periodical or who contribute signed reviews are treated like names of authors.

2. *Title of the article*   The title of the article is written in full as it appears in the printed article. In humanities style, the title and subtitle are enclosed in quotation marks and capitalized headline-style. In sciences style, titles of articles omit the quotation marks, use sentence-style capitalization, and generally omit subtitles.

    (*h*)   Gould, Stephen Jay, and Niles Eldredge. "Punctuated Equilibria: The Tempo and Mode of Evolution Reconsidered." *Paleobiology* 3 (1977): 121.
    (*s*)   Gould, S. J., and N. Eldredge. 1977. Punctuated equilibria. *Paleobiology* 3:121.

3. *Name of the periodical*   The name of the periodical is usually italicized and treated in the same way as described above for a book (see paragraph 2 on

page 299), for both the humanities and the sciences. However, unlike book titles, periodical titles are fully capitalized in bibliographies in both the humanities and the sciences.

(h) Heil, John. "Seeing Is Believing." *American Philosophical Quarterly* 19 (1982): 229–39.

(s) Heil, J. 1982. Seeing is believing. *American Philosophical Quarterly* 19:229–39.

In addition, there are special principles for the styling of periodical names in both categories. One is the omission of an initial article. Whereas the initial article is included in a book title but ignored in alphabetizing, the initial article of a journal title is dropped completely (for example, *American Poetry Review*, for *The American Poetry Review*). Another is the use of abbreviations for journal titles of more than one word. Outside of the sciences, journal titles are written without abbreviations; the examples in this section show journal titles in this unabbreviated form. However, abbreviations are widely used in technical writing. Each discipline has its own set of abbreviations for the journals used in that discipline.

Am. Philos. Q. [for *American Philosophical Quarterly*]
New Engl. J. Med. [for *The New England Journal of Medicine*]

Journal titles that begin with the words *Transactions, Proceedings,* and *Annals* are often reversed for the purpose of alphabetizing so that these words come last.

American Philosophical Society Proceedings [for *Proceedings of the American Philosophical Society*]

Names of newspapers are treated as they appear on the masthead, except that initial articles are omitted. A place-name is added in brackets after the newspaper's name if it is needed to identify the paper.

   (*h*) Pitts, Gail. "Money Funds Holding Own." *Morning Union* [Springfield, Mass.], 23 Aug. 1982, 6.

   (*s*) Pitts, G. 1982. Money funds holding own. *Morning Union* [Springfield, Mass.], 23 Aug.:6.

4. *Volume and number of the periodical* This information comes after the name of the periodical and identifies the particular issue cited. An issue identified by both volume and number should be identified in that way in a bibliography entry (for example, "3(2):25–37" for vol. 3, no. 2, pp. 25–37). If the issue is identified in some other manner (for example, by a full date), that method is used in the entry. Issue numbers are not commonly used unless the issue is paginated independently of the volume as a whole and the number is needed to identify the issue. If the volume number corresponds to a particular year, as in the examples, the year in parentheses follows the volume number—but not in the sciences, where the year is placed after the author's name.

   (*h*) Gonzalez, Roseann Duenas. "Teaching Mexican American Students to Write: Capitalizing on the Culture." *English Journal* 71.7 (November 1982): 22–24.

   (*s*) Gonzalez, R. D. 1982. Teaching Mexican American students to write. *English Journal* 71.7 (Nov.):22–24.

Some periodicals use a seasonal designation in addition to a volume and number designation; the pages are often numbered independently of the volume as a whole. Issues of popular monthly magazines are commonly referred to by date rather than by volume or issue number. Newspapers are always identified by date.

(*h*) Lukacs, John. "The End of the Twentieth Century." *Harper's,* January 1993: 39–58.

(*s*) Lukacs, J. 1993. The end of the twentieth century. *Harper's,* Jan.:39–58.

5. *Issue date* Periodicals issued daily, weekly, monthly, and bimonthly are usually designated by date of issue. The date follows the unpunctuated day-month-year order ("27 May 1984") rather than the punctuated month-day-year order ("May 27, 1984"). Names of months having more than four letters are usually abbreviated.

(*h*) Preston, Richard. "A Reporter at Large: Crisis in the Hot Zone." *New Yorker,* 26 Oct. 1992: 58.

(*s*) Preston, R. 1992. A reporter at large: Crisis in the hot zone. *New Yorker,* 26 Oct.:58.

6. *Page numbers* Inclusive pages for the whole article are provided at the end of the entry. For newspaper entries, it may be necessary to add a section number or edition identification number as well (for example, "B6"). Articles that are continued on later pages are styled thus: "38–41, 159–60." The abbreviations *p.* and *pp.* are omitted.

Unpublished Materials

Bibliography entries for unpublished materials include as many of the following elements as are known or are relevant.

1. *Author's name* The author's name is treated in the same way as for a book (see paragraph 1 on page 299).

2. *Title of the work* If there is an official title, it is copied as it appears on the work, enclosed in quo-

tation marks, and capitalized like a book title (see example under paragraph 6 below). If the work has no official title, a descriptive title is used (not enclosed in quotation marks).

(*h*) Johnson, Clive. Letter to Elizabeth O'Hara. 9 Nov. 1916. Johnson Collection, item 5298. California State Historical Society, San Marino, Calif.

(*s*) Johnson, C. 1916. Letter to Elizabeth O'Hara. 9 Nov. Johnson collection, item 5298. Located at California State Historical Society, San Marino, Calif.

3. *The nature of the material* The entry should include a description of the document, such as "letter to the author" or "doctoral dissertation." For works without official author or title, this element is the first part of the entry.

4. *Date* The date must be included if it is known; if it is not, use *n.d.* If the date is known but does not appear on the document, it is enclosed in brackets.

5. *Name of collection and identification number* Whatever information is necessary to completely identify the document is included (see examples under paragraph 2 above).

6. *Geographical location* The name of the institution and the city where the materials can be located are often listed last in this kind of bibliographical entry.

(*h*) Velasquez, Joyce A. "The Format of Formal Reports." Report prepared for the Southern Engineering Company. Johnson City, Miss., May 29, 1994.

    (s) Velasquez, J. A. 1994. The format of formal reports. Report prepared for the Southern Engineering Co. 29 May. Johnson City, Miss.

Format of a Bibliography

Bibliographies are arranged alphabetically and indented flush-and-hang to set off the alphabetical sequence. Initial articles are ignored in determining the alphabetical order. All the entries are usually listed together alphabetically, whether the first word is an author's surname or the title of an anonymous work. Bibliographies are sometimes divided into categories by date of publication or by subject matter, but such divisions are not recommended unless the single-list form proves unmanageable.

More than one work by an author   After the first listing of an entry by an author (or group of coauthors) who has more than one work listed, the name is replaced in succeeding adjacent entries by a long dash. In typed or keyboarded bibliographies, the dash is usually represented by six hyphens; this is typeset as a three-em dash. The dash is followed by a period, or by a comma and an abbreviation such as *ed.*, just as a name would be.

    The dash substitutes for the author's full name (or the full names of the coauthors) but no more. Thus, the dash may be used only when the name or names are exactly the same in adjacent entries. For example, if an entry for a work by Richard Crawford is followed by an entry for a work coauthored by Crawford and someone else, the second entry would be spelled out. But if Crawford wrote more than one book, the dash would be used to replace his name in the second reference. A work by a single author precedes a work by that author and another; and works edited by an author usually follow works written by the same person.

> Crawford, Richard. *The American Musical Landscape.* . . .
> ———. *Studying American Music.* . . .
> Crawford, Richard, and Jeffrey Magee. *Jazz Standards on Record, 1900–1942.* . . .
> Crawford, Richard, et al., eds. *A Celebration of American Music.* . . .

In the humanities, the various works by an author or group of coauthors are arranged alphabetically by title. In the social and natural sciences, however, they are arranged by date of publication. If an author has published more than one article during a year, each can be distinguished by a letter (often italicized) that follows the year (1987, 1989a, 1989b, 1990, etc.).

Heading Depending on its scope, as explained at the beginning of this chapter, a list of sources may be headed *Bibliography* or *List of References*. Writings in the sciences often use the heading *Literature Cited*; however, only "literature"—that is, published works—and only works actually cited can be included on such a list, and bibliographic information for unpublished works must be provided within the text itself. Titling the reference list *References Cited* allows the inclusion of unpublished works. Works in press are usually listed under *Literature Cited* heads even though they are not yet published; in lieu of the date, the entry contains the phrase *in press*. Another heading, *Works Cited*, allows the inclusion of the references described below as "special cases."

Annotated bibliographies In an annotated bibliography, entries are followed by a sentence or paragraph of description, in order to lead the reader to the most useful works for further study. These comments may be added to all or just some of the entries. The descriptive part may be run in with the entry or be set off by lines of space, indentation, italics, or smaller type.

Special Cases

Lists of references frequently contain items that do not fit neatly into any of the categories described in the previous sections of this chapter. Some are printed items like government publications, others are nonprint items. These special references are styled, as far as possible, in formats similar to those used for the published and unpublished works described and illustrated in the previous sections. They are arranged and punctuated in a way that corresponds to whatever form has been chosen for the publication's notes, parenthetical references, and bibliography entries.

In the following paragraphs there are several references to enclosing titles in quotation marks or italics. These refer only to the bibliographic documentation used in the humanities and in general-purpose writing.

Nonprint Sources

Many sources in the following categories are often not cited in bibliographies and lists of references. When they are not, however, full documentation should be supplied within the text or in a note.

1. **Personal communications** The name of the person who supplied information in a personal communication is listed first, styled like an author's name. A descriptive word or phrase (like *personal communication* or *telephone interview*) follows, un-

italicized and without quotation marks. The place (if applicable) and date of the communication are also given. This type of source is rarely included in a list of references. In scientific publications a form is often found as a parenthetical reference.

(J. Scott, pers. comm. 1993).

2. **Speeches** Lectures and other addresses are listed with the speaker's name first, then the title of the speech in quotation marks (or a descriptive term if the speech has no title), the name of the meeting or sponsoring organization or the occasion, then the place and date.

> Jones, William. "The Future of Western Art." Thursday Evening Club. Cushman, Mass.: 26 Jan. 1981.

3. **Television and radio programs** The title of the program is usually listed first and is italicized. If the program is an episode of a multipart series, the episode title is placed in quotation marks and the name of the series follows without italics. If the reference is to a particular performer, director, or other person, that person's name may be listed before the title. Following the title are the names of the network, the local station and city (in a bibliography entry these two are separated by a comma, not a period), and the date of the broadcast. Depending on its relevance, additional information may be given after the title, such as the names of the performers, the composer, or the director.

> Burns, Ken. *Baseball*. PBS. WGBY–TV, Springfield, Mass. 28 Sept. 1994.

4. **Sound recordings, films, and videotapes** Sound recordings, films and film scripts, and videotapes are usually documented according to their titles.

If the name of a particular writer, composer, or performer is stressed in the text, and especially if the source is a recording, that person's name may be listed first. The italicized title is usually followed by whatever names are needed to identify the work, such as writers, performers, conductors, and others. Some programs may need to be further identified by a descriptive term like *filmstrip*, *slide program*, or *videocassette*. The director's name follows, preceded by the abbreviation *dir*. Finally, the name of the distributor, the year, the catalog number, and other information is added as needed to complete the identification. The following example illustrates a bibliography entry for a recording.

> Mozart, Wolfgang Amadeus. *Symphony No. 34 in C major (K.338)*. Cond. Ivan Fischer. Budapest Festival Orchestra. Compact disc. Hungaroton, HCD 12982, 1988.

5. Works of art   References to works of art include the artist's name, an italicized title, the name of the museum or collection, and the city.

> Monet, Claude. *Field of Poppies near Giverny*. Museum of Fine Arts, Boston.

6. Computer software   References to computer software contain the following elements: the name of the program's writer, if known; the title of the program, which is italicized; the descriptive term (such as *computer software*); the name and location of the distributor; and the year of publication. Additional information, such as the machines or the operating systems the software is designed for, may be added at the end.

> *World Atlas*. CD-ROM. Novato, Calif.: The Software Toolworks, 1990.

7. **Microforms** Materials in microform are documented in whatever styling is appropriate for their contents—periodical articles, unpublished reports, etc. To the end of the note or the bibliography entry is added a descriptive term (*microfilm, microfiche, ultrafiche,* etc.) and the name and location of the commercial service that supplied the form. However, regular published material that has been microfilmed and preserved in a library is cited as if the actual works had been handled, and there is no mention of the microform process.

> "Marine Mammals; Permit Modification: Naval Facilities Engineering Commission (P8D)." *Federal Register* 55.1:90. Washington: CIS, 1990. Microfiche.

8. **Material from an information service** Sources from an information service are documented like books, articles, reports, and other printed materials. At the end of the note or bibliography entry is added the name of the service, its location, and any identification numbers for the material.

> Bean, John P. *A Causal Model of Faculty Research Productivity.* Arlington, Va.: ERIC, 1982. ED 216 661.

Government Publications

9. If a publication by a government agency has a named author, that name may appear first. Most government publications, however, are authored by an agency. The name of the government (for example, United States, Montana, or Chicago) often comes first, then the name of the department if applicable, then the name of the agency responsible for the publication. These names are not abbreviated when they precede the title of the work.

Next comes the title, italicized like a book title and further identified as needed by series or publication numbers or by whatever format the agency uses to identify the work. Most U.S. government publications are published by the Government Printing Office, which is usually referred to in notes and bibliographies as *GPO*. References to congressional documents usually omit the GPO publication data because it is understood. Standardized abbreviations are often used in these references, but names may also be spelled out, especially in writings for the general public.

> United States. Department of Labor. Employment and Training Administration. *Dictionary of Occupational Titles*. Rev. 4th ed. Washington: GPO, 1991.

10. Congressional documents are often attributed first to the "U.S. Congress" in notes and bibliography entries but not in parenthetical references. The name of the appropriate house follows (the short forms *House* and *Senate* are used), and then the name of the committee, if applicable. The document title is listed next, followed by the number and session of Congress. The date is listed next, then the number or other description of the document.

> U.S. Congress. Senate. Subcommittee on Administrative Law and Government Relations of the Committee on the Judiciary. *Hearings on Post-Employment Restrictions for Federal Officers and Employees*. 101st Cong., 1st sess. 27 Apr. 1989. H.R. 2267.

The *Congressional Record* needs to be identified only by date and page number.

> *Congressional Record*. 29 June 1993: S8269–70.

11. Bills in Congress are identified in a special way. *H.R.* is the conventional abbreviation for the House of Representatives, and *S.* for the Senate. Thus, bills are referred to as "H.R. 93" or "S. 120." In citations to congressional reports, however, the House is abbreviated *H.* (as in "H. Rept. 1303"). In each case, the number and session of Congress follow the document title, as shown in the example under paragraph 10 above.

12. **Laws and constitutions** References to laws and constitutions are documented in notes and bibliography entries unless full information is provided in the text. These citations are not italicized. In legal writing many standard abbreviations are used, but in most writing for a general audience the abbreviations are limited to those which can be readily understood by the public. Roman numerals are traditionally used to denote certain sections of constitutions, as shown in the first two examples below.

> U.S. Constitution, Amendment XIII.
> Indiana Constitution, Art. III, sec. 2, cl. 4.
> Trade Agreements Act, Public Law 96–39, sec. 32, 96th Cong., 1st sess., July 26, 1979.
> 90 Stat. 1113 (1976).

The last reference above is an example of the abbreviated form typical of legal citations. The volume number comes *before* the name of the multivolume work; thus, the reference points to a statute found in volume 90 of the *U.S. Statutes at Large* beginning on page 1113. Inclusive numbers are not used in legal references. The examples below illustrate a reference to a federal statute found in volume 28, section 17, of the *U.S. Code,* together with its supplement.

28 U.S.C. sec. 17 (1964).

28 U.S.C. sec. 17 (1964), as amended (Supp. II, 1966).

13. Regulations of the federal government also conform to official citation form. Like codified statutes, regulations codified in the *Code of Federal Regulations* or the *Federal Register* are identified first by volume number, then by section or page number and date.

33 C.F.R. sec. 403.2 (1980).

43 Fed. Reg. 54221 (1978).

Court Cases

14. Titles of court cases are italicized within the text, whether they involve two opposing parties (for example, *Surner* v. *Kellogg*) or instead have titles like *In re Watson* or *In the matter of John Watson.* When these cases are listed in a bibliography, however, they are not italicized. The *v.* (for *versus*) within a case title is usually set in lowercase roman in printed matter. A citation to a court case gives the name of the case, the number, title, and page of the volume in which it is recorded, and the date.

A Minor v. *State,* 85 Nev. 323, 454 P. 2d 895 (1969).

The example above refers the reader to two sources in one reference: volume 85 of *Nevada Reports* on page 323, and also volume 454 of the second series of the *Pacific Reporter,* on page 895. Frequently the name of the court that decided the case is listed before the date.

Literary Works

15. Since literary works are printed in so many different editions, each paginated differently, docu-

mentation of poems, stories, plays, and novels frequently refers to the divisions of the work (chapter, book, part, act, scene, or line) rather than page numbers. Page numbers are referred to in prose works if the edition used is clearly identified; but in poetry and verse plays where each line has a number, documentation refers to lines rather than to pages.

Numerals alone, without accompanying terms like *chapter, verse, act, scene,* or *line,* are often used in footnotes and endnotes and especially in parenthetical references, since they take up little space. Numerals are used wherever they can be easily understood without accompanying words or abbreviations. Frequently two numerals are used together, one that indicates a large division of the work and another that indicates a smaller division (for example, "4.122" for book 4, line 122). The two numerals are separated by a period or sometimes a comma. Capital and lowercase Roman numerals may be used for the act and scene of a play, but the Arabic form is also found.

> *Hamlet* III.ii [for *act 3, scene 2*]
>   *or*
> *Hamlet* 3.2

When a single numeral is used in a reference, it usually requires an identifying word or abbreviation. The abbreviations for *line* and *lines* (*l.* and *ll.*) should be used with great care, since they are easily confused with the numbers 1 and 11.

> (*Hamlet,* Act 3)
> (*The Waste Land,* part 4)

The Bible

16. Biblical references are not usually listed in a bibliography unless a particular version or edition is specified in the text. A text reference includes the name of the book, which is not italicized and is often abbreviated, followed by Arabic numerals representing chapter and verse. Chapter and verse numerals are traditionally separated by a colon, but a period is a common alternative. For a book with two or more parts, an Arabic numeral precedes the name of the book. Page numbers are never used to refer to biblical material.

2 Chron. 2:18
Ruth 3.1–18

Index

A, an, 137, 200
Abbreviations, 132–149
  a or an with, 137, 200
  acronyms, 135
  in addresses, 139–140, 142–143
  with ampersand, 2–3, 139
  with apostrophe, 3, 4, 5
  at beginning of sentences, 138
  of Bible books, 138–139,
    319–320
  capitalization of, 68–69, 134–135
  in compound words, 134,
    135–137
  and contractions, 140
  in dates, 140
  division of, 141
  in documentation of sources,
    315–316, 319–320
    bibliographies, 302–303, 304,
      308
    footnotes and endnotes, 278,
      281–282, 284
    journal titles, 305–306
    Latin terms, 287–288
    parenthetical references, 293,
      294
  full forms of, when to use,
    141–142
  hyphen with, 41–42, 137
  inflected forms of, 4, 41–42,
    135–136
  of Latin words and phrases,
    95–96, 144, 287–288
  in legal citations, 317
  within parentheses, 43, 141–142
  with period, 47, 133–134
  of phrases, 133–134, 135, 139
  plural forms, 99, 135–137
  possessive forms, 111, 135–137
  of proper nouns and adjectives,
    68–69, 134
  punctuation of, 133–134
  purpose of, 132–133
  with slash, 62
  of units of measurement, 136,
    149, 177
  variation in styling of, 132–133
Above, use of, 250
Absolute adjectives, 179–180
Absolute phrases, 231
Abstractions, capitalization of, 69,
  94
Academic degrees. See Degrees,
  academic
Acknowledgment of sources. See
  Documentation of sources
Acronyms, 135
Act, of play, 318–319
A.D., 137–138, 165–166
Adapt and adopt, use of, 250
Addresses, street
  abbreviations in, 139–140, 142,
    146
  with comma, 25–27
  numbers in, 161–162
  punctuation of, 25–27
Adjective clauses, 233–234
Adjectives, 179–185
  absolute, 179–180
  and adverbs, 180, 184, 185, 186,
    187, 229
  agreement with nouns, 180
  comparison of, 180–182
  compound, 118–124
  in compound words, 115–117
  coordinate, 182
  demonstrative, 182
  descriptive, 182–183
  double comparisons, 183
  indefinite, 183
  infinitives used as, 223–224, 232
  interrogative, 183
  noncoordinate, 182
  nouns used as, 118, 120–121,
    184, 201
  plural forms, 182
  position in sentence, 118–119,
    184, 201–202

Merriam-Webster's Rhyming Dictionary

Looking for a word to rhyme with *wailer* for that great new song you're writing? *Merriam-Webster's Rhyming Dictionary* makes it easy. Just look up the spelling of the rhyming sound—*ailer*—to find a list of possibilities.

Ideal for copywriters, songwriters, poets, editors, and crossword puzzle enthusiasts.

Following is an example from
Merriam-Webster's Rhyming Dictionary:

headword is the most common spelling of the rhyming sound

pronunciation

rhyming words arranged alphabetically and by number of syllables

cross-reference to aid use

ailed \āld\ mailed, nailed, sailed, scaled, tailed, veiled, detailed, engrailed, hobnailed, pigtailed, ring-tailed, unveiled, ponytailed, swallow-tailed—*also pasts of verbs listed at* AIL

ailer \ā-lər\ alar, bailer, bailor, baler, hailer, jailer, mailer, malar, nailer, sailer, sailor, scalar, scaler, tailer, tailor, Taylor, trailer, wailer, waler, whaler, blackmailer, curtailer, derailleur, detailer, entailer, inhaler, loud-haler, retailer, wassailer, wholesaler, semitrailer—*also comparatives of adjectives listed at* AIL

ailey \ā-lē\ *see* AILY

341

Merriam-Webster's Vocabulary Builder

Informative and entertaining discussions of English words derived from 200 Greek and Latin roots form the framework for gaining a greater command of the language right now—and for continuing lifelong vocabulary acquisition.

For adult readers and learners as well as high-school and college students, especially those preparing for standardized tests.

Following is an example from *Merriam-Webster's Vocabulary Builder* including one of the quizzes used throughout the book:

PUNG/PUNC comes from the Latin verb *pungere*, meaning "to prick or stab," and the noun *punctum*, meaning "point." A period is a form of *punctuation* that is literally a point. A *punctured* tire, pricked by a sharp point, can make it hard to be *punctual*—that is, to arrive "on the dot" or at a precise point in time.

compunction \kəm-'pəŋk-shən\ (1) Anxiety caused by guilt. (2) A slight misgiving or scruple.

• Speeding is something many people seem to do without compunction.

To feel compunction is to feel the sharp sting or prick of conscience. The word *compunction* is most often used in describing people who don't feel it. Hardened criminals have no compunctions about committing their crimes. Ruthless businessmen steal clients and contracts from other ruthless businessmen without compunction.

expunge \ik-'spənj\ To remove, erase, or destroy.

• After years of good behavior, all mention of his juvenile criminal career was expunged from his record.

Expunge comes directly from the Latin *expungere*, which means "to

342

mark for deletion with dots." In English, the material expunged is no longer marked with dots but is erased or removed completely. It is easier to expunge something written down than it is to expunge a memory.

punctilious \pəŋk-'ti-lē-əs\ Marked by exact agreement or conformity to the details of codes or conventions.

• A good proofreader has to be punctilious about matters of spelling and punctuation.

A *punctilio* is a small point—a minor detail of conduct in a ceremony or in the observance of a code. A person who pays close attention to such minor details is punctilious. *Punctiliousness* can be valuable in the right circumstances, but you don't want to become so concerned about small points that you fail to pay attention to the large ones.

pungent \pən-jənt\ (1) Having a sharp, cutting quality. (2) Sharp or harsh to the sense of taste or smell.

• We could smell the pungent aroma of the spicy Indian food before we even entered the restaurant.

Someone with a pungent wit has a sharp sense of humor. Many people enjoy the aroma and flavor of pungent food, even if it does make their eyes water. The *pungency* of a cheap cigar can have the same effect, but it's more likely to clear a room than to draw a crowd.

Quizzes

A. Choose the closest definition:

1. expunge   a. mop up   b. partially restore   c. remove completely   d. hesitate slightly
2. pungent   a. sharp   b. rotten   c. round   d. funny
3. punctilious   a. pointed   b. careful   c. prompt   d. unusual
4. compunction   a. desire   b. bravery   c. scruple
     d. conviction

B. Indicate whether the following pairs of words have the same or different meanings:

1. pungent / smoky   same__ / different__
2. expunge / erase   same__ / different__
3. compunction / threat   same__ / different__
4. punctilious / absurd   same__ / different__

Answers: A. 1. c.; 2. a.; 3. b.; 4. c.   **B.** 1. different; 2. same; 3. different; 4. different